Praise for

MEANINGFUL WORK

"A timely, clear, and actionable book about the science and practice of making work more worthwhile."

—Adam Grant, #1 *New York Times*–bestselling author of *Think Again*

"*Meaningful Work* is a remarkable guide to more passion, meaning, and greater contribution to the world! If you want to challenge yourself to do more for others, start here!"

—Tom Rath, author of *StrengthsFinder 2.0*

"*Meaningful Work* is a powerful exploration of how leaders can truly unlock the potential within their teams by creating environments rooted in purpose, well-being, and growth. Adams and Myles masterfully blend compelling, real-world stories with the latest insights from positive psychology to offer a roadmap for transforming organizational culture. This book is a must-read for leaders who want to move beyond traditional management and foster workplaces where employees feel valued, inspired, and driven to achieve their best."

—Dr. Marshall Goldsmith, *New York Times*–bestselling author of *What Got You Here Won't Get You There*

"Happy employees feel needed and have a job that matters. As a leader, you have to make this possible. But how? The answers are in this wonderful new book. Read *Meaningful Work* today and watch the morale in your company improve."

—Arthur C. Brooks, #1 *New York Times*–bestselling author of *Build the Life You Want*

"Every leader today should know the 3 Cs of meaningful work. A must-read for anyone who wants to create a workplace that thrives."

—Dan Heath, #1 *New York Times*–bestselling coauthor of *Switch*

"*Meaningful Work* brilliantly captures the essence of what every modern leader needs to understand: that fostering purpose and passion in the workplace isn't just a nice-to-have—it's critical to unlocking extraordinary performance. With deep research and actionable insights, this book provides a roadmap for leaders who want to ignite the full potential of their teams. A must-read for anyone committed to creating more fulfilling, high-impact work environments."

—Chip Conley, *New York Times*–bestselling author of *Peak*

"This book is a must-read for anyone who wants their work to be meaningfully connected to their values and purpose. The authors make a convincing case that every job can and should be meaningful, and they teach you how to live the life you want to live in the most effective and connected way."

—Scott Barry Kaufman, author of *Rise Above*

"Adams and Myles offer practical tools for leaders to create environments where employees feel valued, connected, and challenged. They show that meaningful work ignites passion and drives extraordinary performance. By fostering community, contribution, and growth, leaders can transform not just their organizations but society itself. This book provides a powerful roadmap for creating workplaces where people and profits thrive together. This is not just about improving performance—it's about elevating humanity through business, one employee and one company at a time."

—Raj Sisodia, coauthor of *Conscious Capitalism*

"People thrive when their work is meaningful, and they feel cared for and part of the shared purpose. *Meaningful Work* is an inspiring and practical guidebook for anyone looking to improve their leadership and the lives of those in their span of care!"

—Bob Chapman, CEO, Barry-Wehmiller, and author of *Everybody Matters*

"This book is an essential companion for any professional seeking to reimagine a future workplace and workforce that is driven by purpose. Adams and Myles have tapped into something profound, reminding us that meaning at work matters more than anything else, not only because it unleashes each of our deepest motivations, but also drives long-term impact for an organization. With plenty of useful examples and tools, *Meaningful Work* gives us a comprehensive roadmap to take action (as well as a feeling of hope and inspiration to transform how we work)."

—Tina Mylon, chief talent and diversity officer, Schneider Electric

"*Meaningful Work* is a valuable guide to create a corporate culture where community and purpose converge. With poignant examples and relevant anecdotes, it details how, both personally and professionally, individuals and organizations can thrive when their work aligns with a deeper sense of meaning. With practical insight, it explores how business and community are interdependent, showing that when companies invest in the well-being of their people and the greater good, they not only enhance their bottom line but also contribute to a more fulfilling and sustainable future for all. I recommend *Meaningful Work* for anyone seeking ways to add purpose to their work life. With wisdom and practical insight, it illustrates how to inspire your team and infuse purpose into your corporate culture."

—Kenneth Cole

"What work means to people has gone through dramatic evolution over the last decade, from being a source of income to a source of identity, purpose, and fulfillment. This book is a remarkable resource, offering practical methods to define meaningful work, enabling its thoughtful integration into the employee experience, and measuring the powerful return on meaning." —Deep Mahajan, VP, talent management, Juniper Networks

MEANINGFUL
WORK

MEANINGFUL
WORK

*How to Ignite
Passion and Performance
in Every Employee*

WES ADAMS AND TAMARA MYLES

PUBLICAFFAIRS
New York

PublicAffairs
Hachette Book Group
1290 Avenue of the Americas, New York, NY 10104
www.publicaffairsbooks.com
@Public_Affairs

Printed in the United States of America

First Edition: April 2025

Published by PublicAffairs, an imprint of Hachette Book Group, Inc. The PublicAffairs
name and logo is a registered trademark of the Hachette Book Group.

The Hachette Speakers Bureau provides a wide range of authors for speaking events.
To find out more, go to hachettespeakersbureau.com or
email HachetteSpeakers@hbgusa.com.

PublicAffairs books may be purchased in bulk for business, educational, or
promotional use. For more information, please contact your local bookseller or the
Hachette Book Group Special Markets Department at special.markets@hbgusa.com.

The publisher is not responsible for websites (or their content) that are
not owned by the publisher.

Print book interior design by Bart Dawson.

Library of Congress Cataloging-in-Publication Data

Names: Adams, Wes (Founder of SV Consulting Group), author. | Myles, Tamara
Schwambach Kano, author.
Title: Meaningful work : how to ignite passion and performance in every
employee / Wes Adams and Tamara Myles.
Description: First edition. | New York : PublicAffairs, 2025. | Includes
bibliographical references and index.
Identifiers: LCCN 2024046468 | ISBN 9781541704534 (hardcover) | ISBN
9781541704541 (ebook)
Subjects: LCSH: Work—Psychological aspects. | Job satisfaction. | Employee morale.
Classification: LCC BF481 .A328 2025 | DDC 158.7—dc23/eng/20241210
LC record available at https://lccn.loc.gov/2024046468

ISBNs: 9781541704534 (hardcover), 9781541704541 (ebook)

LSC-C

Printing 1, 2025

From Tamara:
To Bella, Eddie, and Vivi,
May you always find meaning in every endeavor.
This book is for you, with the hope that you will
lead with purpose and inspire others to
create a more meaningful world.

From Wes:
To Mom,
Who planted and nurtured the seeds of meaning that
grew into this book and so much more.

CONTENTS

CONTENTS

PART IV
CREATING MEANING THROUGH CHALLENGE

INTRODUCTION

As Matt Fishman locked eyes with the 110-pound rottweiler growling at him, he fought back a wave of panic. The massive animal was standing a few feet from him with curled lips, revealing strikingly sharp canines. Matt knew that jaw could easily snap his forearm. The dog bent his legs and threatened to lunge.

Time seemed to stop as Matt reflected on the series of events that brought him to this moment. *How had things gotten so out of control that his job had put him in actual, physical peril?*

He and a friend from business school had purchased a successful dog daycare business in Atlanta a few years earlier. The company had a few locations that were already profitable, and the market was ripe for expansion. Dog ownership was on the rise. Busy professionals needed a safe, reliable, and caring place for their dogs to play while they were working. In fact, Matt himself was a customer of Barking Hound Village (BHV) before he bought it. He loved dogs, and the business's financial projections were very promising. His plan was to open new locations and branch out into additional services like grooming and training to capitalize on the demand. Matt threw himself into the business, and at first, things seemed to be going smoothly. He soon found, however, that the day-to-day operation required much more than he had expected. Behind the tidy financials and promising expansion plans lurked a big problem.

When we first met Matt, employee turnover at BHV was incredibly high—close to 200 percent each year across the company. The customer base was growing, but there wasn't enough support to keep up. New team members often failed to show up for their shifts. They regularly quit without notice. The revolving door of employees meant that the dog daycare locations were always short staffed. People were often asked to do much more than they could reasonably handle. This was demoralizing for the team, and it put the care and safety of the dogs at risk. To keep the quality of care high, store managers, and sometimes even the owners, had to pick up floor shifts. That's how Matt found himself face-to-face with a massive rottweiler named Mr. Mondo.

Mr. Mondo had always been a gentle dog. He was actually a staff favorite. But today, yet another employee had failed to show up. With no one else available, Matt had stepped in to cover the shift. In the confusion, Mr. Mondo hadn't gotten his lunch. On top of missing his meal, he'd also been put in the yard with Axel, a standard poodle known for stirring up trouble. A staff member who was regularly on the floor would have known not to put the two together. Axel had antagonized Mr. Mondo relentlessly. Harassed and hungry, Mr. Mondo snapped.

As he stared down the rottweiler, Matt realized he was looking into the face of another challenge. Like Mr. Mondo, the once amicable culture of the company had turned toxic. Growls of dissatisfaction, canine and human, had set all of BHV's daycare locations on edge. Even the most committed employees were burned out. Things had reached a breaking point. Matt began to doubt the business model, the expansion plans, and his own ability to lead. He knew something had to change, and that's when we got his call.

We work with leaders to cultivate high-performing teams and thriving organizations. Our clients are at the helm of Fortune 500s as well as scaling businesses like Barking Hound Village. You'll meet some of them in this book, and their challenges will likely sound familiar to you—increased competition for talent, dramatic changes in the expectations of employees, and the demands of managing teams that span generations and geographies.

Our approach to helping them, however, may not be what you expect.

We're a part of a newer, growing movement to reimagine the way we work for the next generation. We believe that work can give us more than a paycheck. Work can provide us with community. Work can be a way for us to contribute to something bigger than ourselves. Work can challenge us to learn and grow.

We've spent years studying the leaders of this new movement to build a playbook that can transform organizations, and we want to share that playbook with you.

Our journey together began in grad school. We both came to the University of Pennsylvania to study positive psychology under the field's legendary founder, Martin Seligman. Most of us are familiar with the important work of traditional psychology, which focuses primarily on helping people navigate mental health challenges such as depression, anxiety, or posttraumatic stress. Addressing these issues is critical to our well-being, but these challenges are only half of the human equation.

Navigating adversity and solving problems is like pulling weeds in a garden. Removing them keeps the plants from being choked off, but more is needed for them to thrive. If you want your garden to flourish, you must also cultivate the conditions your plants need to prosper. The soil must be rich in nutrients. The plants must have enough, but not too much, exposure to sunlight. They must have the appropriate space to grow.

The field of positive psychology focuses on the factors that lead to a flourishing, meaningful life. It is the study of the mindsets, behaviors, and structures that bring out the best in each of us. It is the science of the soil, sun, and space needed for our gardens to thrive. Simply put, positive psychology is the pursuit of human potential.

Since its formal introduction as a field in 1998, the seeds of positive psychology have spread rapidly through our culture. Use of terms like *well-being, resilience, growth mindset, flow,* and *grit,* which would have garnered blank stares just a few decades ago, is prolific on our social media feeds.

The focus on well being, resilience, and personal development has only accelerated in recent years. From Shawn Achor's case for positive emotion in *The Happiness Advantage*, to Carol Dweck's reframing of personal growth in *Mindset*, to Angela Duckworth's exploration of grit as a driving force for achievement, the idea that excellence requires us to focus on what's good has permeated culture, society, and business. In recent years, these are no longer things we look for solely in our personal lives. We have come to expect them, and even demand them, at work.

When applied in a work setting, positive psychology focuses on the elements that lead to high performance and well-being for individuals, teams, and entire organizations. In the same way that gardens don't thrive simply by pulling weeds, organizations don't thrive simply by fixing what's wrong. It isn't enough for our work to "not suck." To realize our full potential, we have to feel a sense of belonging to our organizational community. We have to understand how our day-to-day contributions matter to others. We have to be challenged to learn and grow.

Great leaders cultivate the conditions their people need to thrive. They know that none of us dream of mediocrity. What we really want, what we hope for, and what we all deserve is the opportunity to do meaningful work—work that builds community, work that gives us a sense of contribution to something bigger, and work that challenges us to learn and grow.

Our shared belief that work could be a place where people thrive brought us both to positive psychology and to Penn. On the first day of the program, about a dozen of our classmates decided to have dinner together at a popular Chinese restaurant near campus. We ended up seated next to each other at a huge booth in the corner of the room. As our group passed bamboo steamers of soup dumplings around the table on a lazy Susan, we each took turns sharing our stories.

Over twenty years, Wes had helped launch and grow dozens of ventures, including a hospitality business nominated for multiple James

Beard Awards, a social impact organization recognized as one of *Fast Company*'s Most Innovative Companies, and a groundbreaking LGBTQ rights campaign for the United Nations that changed global policy. His proudest accomplishments, however, had been helping others expand their capabilities and reach their full potential. After working for leaders who lit him up and leaders who burned him out, he learned that the difference between them typically wasn't their character. Many of them just hadn't had the experience or exposure to tools that they needed to help others thrive. They had never known anything but pulling weeds. What brought Wes to the table that night was a hope that the science of positive psychology could help create a leadership playbook that would help each person move closer to their full potential.

Tamara wanted to discover what lies beyond productivity. Over fifteen years, she had built a successful consulting business helping leaders design systems to increase productivity. She was the first to apply Maslow's hierarchy of needs to the realm of productivity with her groundbreaking model—the Peak Productivity Pyramid—which helps individuals overcome barriers that other productivity models didn't. Her book, *The Secret to Peak Productivity*, had been translated into multiple languages and was sold globally. Tamara was traveling the world speaking and consulting with organizations such as Unilever, Best Buy, and Microsoft, but ultimately, she realized that productivity wasn't enough. It was a stepping-stone to a much more powerful source of motivation and peak performance—meaningful work. She recognized that a virtuous cycle was in place—productivity creates space for meaningful work, and meaning unleashes productivity. And in the process, people become happier and organizations more successful. Tamara wanted to understand the science behind this cycle and the pivotal role of leaders in creating it. What brought Tamara to the table that night was her unwavering belief that leaders hold the key to unlock this transformative potential at scale.

Although we had very different backgrounds, we shared a common vision. By the time the red bean cakes were served, we had become friends. Throughout the first few months of grad school, we shared many more meals. We also devoured decades of research from positive psychology, as well as organizational psychology, neuroscience, business management, and leadership methods. We mined our own work experiences for insights, debated the merits of various leadership styles, and traded research articles in an effort to home in on the key ingredients of thriving organizations. As the first semester drew to a close, our proverbial North Star emerged from below the horizon.

One key ingredient came up again and again. Although often hidden, it's the driving factor for nearly every thriving employee and high-performing team: **meaning**.

Take a moment now to think about a time at work that was particularly meaningful to you. It doesn't have to be a heroic accomplishment that won you a big award, although it could be. It could also be a brief interaction you had with a customer that stuck with you. It could be a moment when you clicked with a colleague and realized you would be friends. It could be the time your mentor pushed you to take on a project you didn't yet think you could do. Whatever that specific moment is for you, sit with it for a minute. Where were you when it happened? What were you feeling at the time? How did it change you?

Chances are that reflecting on this moment is powerful for you. It simultaneously gives significance to your work and motivates you to take on what's next. As you'll soon learn, meaning is what really powers high performance and well-being at work. It is the sun, soil, and space that make our gardens grow. Throughout this book, we'll unpack decades of research showing that meaning at work leads to higher individual performance, resilience, and overall well-being. We'll talk about how meaningful work increases organizational adaptability, improves client outcomes, and results in greater profitability. One study estimates an annual gain of nearly $10,000 for each employee who finds their work meaningful. The return on meaning is measurable, and it is compelling.

Even more compelling are the data that show that this return holds across generations. All of us, from boomers to Gen Z, want meaningful work, and we all define it similarly. Remote workers value meaning just as much as those who come to an office. People of all races, genders, and sexual orientations respond the same way when work is meaningful. Meaning drives us, and meaning-driven leaders inspire us to do our best work.

Once we recognized that meaning is the most effective strategy to attract, inspire, and retain high-performing teams, we set to work on developing a playbook for leaders to create it. What we found surprised us.

There was an enormous gap in the research. The existing studies on meaningful work focused mostly on how employees can create more meaning for themselves. Bestselling books such as *What Color Is Your Parachute: Your Guide to a Lifetime of Meaningful Work and Career Success* and more recently *The Search: Finding Meaningful Work in a Post-Career World* take an individual approach to finding meaning. However, almost no resources were available for leaders.

Leaders who wanted to build a more meaningful workplace for their teams lacked a road map. Even those who already recognized the value of meaning struggled with the tools to help their people find it.

Tom Rath, the bestselling author of *StrengthsFinder 2.0*, summarized it best when he told us, "Many leaders know that meaning at work is important. That's not the issue. The issue is that they don't know how to get there."

We've made it our mission to bridge that gap. Over the past several years we've studied meaning-driven leaders and partnered with dozens of high-performing organizations to study meaning at work and how leaders can cultivate it. In partnership with researchers at the University of Pennsylvania and Colorado State University, we conducted the first rigorous, empirical studies that measure the impact leaders have on meaning at work. And that impact is staggering.

Nearly 50 percent of an employee's experience of meaning at work is tied to what their leaders do—or fail to do. This impact represents an enormous responsibility and an incredible opportunity. When our leaders set a bad example, micromanage us, or foster competition over collaboration, we don't feel our work is meaningful. On the other hand, leaders who build community, help people understand how their contributions matter, and challenge them with opportunities to learn and grow, foster meaning for everyone on their teams. Regardless of a person's industry or job, leaders with the right set of skills can tap into the power of meaning to unlock each employee's full potential.

Our research looked closely at leaders who excel at creating meaning at work. We included people across industries, demographics, and work arrangements to identify the unique traits, behaviors, and strategies they employ. We conducted empirical studies to test if the practices we uncovered really do make work meaningful for employees. We confirmed that when leaders build community, highlight employee contributions, and challenge team members to grow, work becomes more meaningful.

With this research under our belt, we have developed an evidence-based framework for meaning-driven leadership. Drawing from the experiences of thousands of people from twenty-five industries, we identified specific leadership practices and organizational structures that make work more meaningful. We've seen leaders from all types of organizations apply these practices to create more meaning at work. When their teams find more meaning, they begin to operate at their highest potential and deliver extraordinary results.

We identified three pillars of meaningful work—**community, contribution,** and **challenge**—what we call the Three C's. They are the elements of our jobs that tell us that we matter, that our work matters, and that we are growing into better versions of ourselves. When they are present, we thrive. When they are missing, we languish.

One of these pillars was missing at Barking Hound Village.

Before we started working with Matt's leadership team, we interviewed employees across the company to learn the cause of the high turnover. We found that the main issue driving it was a lack of meaningful **challenge.** Employees received little development after their initial onboarding. Dog daycare managers, the only senior role at the company, were often hired from the outside. This meant that employees didn't have a clear path to grow. They were stuck in their existing jobs, doing the same tasks over and over again, until they burned out. Without the opportunity to develop within the company, employees had to go elsewhere to advance—which they did in droves.

Fortunately, the showdown between Matt and Mr. Mondo had a happy ending. Matt was able to calm the dog and avoid an altercation. The Barking Hound Village story has a happy ending too. We worked with Matt and his senior team to redesign the company's employee experience from recruiting to exit. From their first day, employees now have a choice of three development paths—becoming an expert dog handler, becoming a store manager, or becoming part of the team that trains new puppies. We'll share more on this later.

As of this writing, turnover is down by nearly half. Employees report higher job satisfaction and are even referring their friends to join the company. The daycares are running smoothly, and the dogs are happy. Mr. Mondo never misses lunch, doesn't have to deal with Axel, and remains one of the staff's favorite dogs.

As for Matt, he no longer spends his days picking up shifts or putting out fires. He and his business partner have opened a successful new location. They've expanded into grooming and dog hiking services. The transformation has helped his team thrive and, in turn, allowed him to pursue bigger goals. Matt's work, and the work of his team, is now much more meaningful.

Matt's crisis isn't unique. So many of the leaders we work with—from large companies like Microsoft to small businesses like Barking Hound Village—struggle to guide their employees successfully in an increasingly uncertain world. Sometimes this struggle shows up as a conflict around flexibility or hybrid work. Sometimes generational or cultural differences get in the way. Often, there is a misalignment between what managers *think* employees want and what employees *actually* want. Leaders come to us with many names for their struggles—disengagement, quiet quitting, burnout, and turnover. We find it is all rooted in the same issue: a lack of meaning.

We'll start by outlining our research on the role that leaders play in creating meaning. Next, we explore the specific leadership practices that increase community, contribution, and challenge—the three sources of meaning at work. Finally, we share what we believe meaning-driven organizations could, and should, look like in the rapidly approaching, increasingly dynamic future.

Throughout the book, we share real-world examples of meaning-driven leadership. Many of these stories highlight leaders that participated in our original research, a list of which is in the Appendix. Others are examples that illustrate the leadership practices we discovered, and we have included them to bring these practices to life more clearly for you.

In many chapters, we've also included practical tools that you can use to make work meaningful for your team. You can find a library of them, along with other resources, on our website at www.makeworkmeaningful.com.

This book is not a manifesto that makes the case for *why* meaningful work matters. That's already been proven. In fact, as you'll see, the call for meaning at work has never been louder. Community, contribution, and challenge have taken center stage in the cultural conversation. What we offer here is a comprehensive playbook for leaders to leverage the power of meaning to cultivate high performance and well-being. This book, the culmination of years of research and practical business application, is a guide for you to become a master gardener. Instead of just pulling weeds, we share the secrets to cultivating a company that thrives.

We believe that every job can and should be meaningful with the help of a great leader—and we want to show you how.

PART I

EVERY JOB CAN AND SHOULD BE MEANINGFUL

1

THE POWER OF MEANINGFUL WORK

Never have we expected so much from work. We want from work today what we used to get from religion and community—belonging, purpose, meaning.

—ESTHER PEREL

Picture a gigantic warehouse the size of several football fields packed with endless stacks of blinking servers that look virtually identical. Imagine a more mundane version of the Department of Mysteries from *Harry Potter*, and you'll begin to get a sense of the labyrinth-like scale. This particular warehouse is a Microsoft data center, part of what we commonly refer to as "the cloud." Data centers like this support the applications that power our social media, deliver Netflix to our TVs, and deposit paychecks into our bank accounts.

The centers can be quite cold—the temperature stays low to keep the servers from overheating. Because servers have to be protected from physical as well as digital attacks, data centers are typically located in remote areas, far from busy urban centers. This can mean long commutes for employees. Data center work can be repetitive and mundane. Day after day, new servers need to be set up, while the existing ones need to be perfectly maintained. To protect the confidentiality of Microsoft's clients, the staff doesn't even know who the servers are for or what they are processing—and this is a key point. This necessary anonymity obscures something very important—the ability of employees to see exactly how their work helps others.

During some of the most difficult days of the pandemic, Microsoft asked us to work with their Cloud Operations and Innovation (CO+I) data centers to try to improve employee engagement and morale. When COVID-19 hit, the staff was designated essential and expected to go to work as usual, greatly amplifying the uncertainty and anxiety that most of us experienced from the safety of our homes.

Keisha,* who worked in a logistics role in a center outside Toronto, was one of those struggling. A native of the Caribbean, Keisha was far away from her family and support network. She had recently joined the data center and had been thrilled to have the opportunity to grow within the company. Microsoft had excellent development programs, and her data center was full of people she admired.

Six months into the pandemic, however, Keisha's excitement and hope for the future had crumbled. She worried every day about being exposed to COVID and the risks to her health. The daily news headlines were demoralizing, and she had a tough time seeing why her work even mattered given everything going on in the world. Surely there were far more important things than making sure wires were plugged in and cooling fans were running?

Keisha wasn't the only one who felt that way during that challenging time. Many of her team members were struggling to understand

---

* Name changed to protect anonymity.

the meaning in their work. We taught Keisha's managers how to take the team through a series of exercises to help them identify what made work meaningful for them. Each team member shared a story of a time at work when they felt inspired and identified what made that moment special. Sometimes it was when someone excelled in their role or developed a new skill. Sometimes it was an authentic connection with a coworker. Often it was when someone knew they had made a positive difference in someone else's life—a colleague, a customer, or a business partner.

As team members went through this exercise, Keisha had a flash of insight. Despite not knowing which Microsoft clients she supported, she knew that the servers she helped set up and maintain were providing critical infrastructure for millions of people. She recognized that, during those extended lockdowns, video calls had become social lifelines. The volume of emails and virtual meetings had skyrocketed as businesses tried to stay afloat. Kids and teens relied on applications running on Keisha's servers to continue their education remotely. Doctors, nurses, and scientists, desperate to get ahead of the virus's spread, were sharing resources and real-time data that passed through her data center. Patients in hospitals around the world were being monitored and treated via cloud-based tools on the servers she had helped acquire and maintain.

At that moment, plugging in wires and keeping cooling fans running was literally saving lives.

As Keisha shared this realization with the team, her demeanor transformed. Months of stress and doubt melted away. Understanding how her work benefited others unleashed a sense of contribution that she didn't realize she had been missing.

Keisha grabbed a sticky note and wrote down the ways in which her work was helping people: "We're having a positive global impact by keeping services and the cloud running for health care, schools, and for maintaining positive well-being for people through Microsoft services." She fixed it to her monitor. When she left our workshop that day, Keisha was beaming.

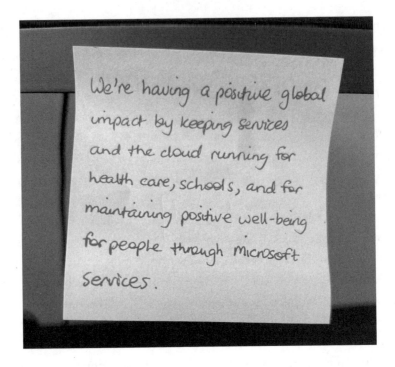

After we finished, leaders continued on with exercises to help employees find and identify meaning in their work. Several months later, we caught up with Keisha and her team. The note was still on her monitor. Since our workshop, she had had days when she considered dropping everything to take a flight back home to be with her family, and days when she felt lonely or disconnected from the outside world. During those challenging moments, the note on her monitor helped her to pause, connect with her team, and be grateful to know that there is "a life's purpose in our work."

By recognizing the larger impact of her day-to-day work, Keisha found new meaning in her job. The isolated and cold atmosphere of the data center was infused with a deep sense of meaning. As she walked the rows of servers, Keisha could now see beyond the black boxes and the piles of spaghetti-like wires to the people she was connecting. She could see the faces of elementary school children focused on their teachers, the grateful smiles of loved ones on video calls, and the relief of nurses discharging a recovered patient.

Meaningful work is the difference between connecting wires and connecting people. It is the essence that transforms everyday drudgery into work that makes us feel connected, fulfilled, and engaged.

Over the past few years, we have asked hundreds of leaders, and the thousands of employees they lead, a simple question: "How do you want to *feel* at work?" Some of the most common answers we get are that they want to feel fulfilled, connected, motivated, valued, appreciated, respected, and in control. People want to feel a sense of belonging to their work community, to understand how their efforts contribute to the lives of others, and to be challenged to grow beyond their comfort zone. Whether or not they use the term *meaningful work*, they have all felt the call to do something that matters with the third of their waking lives that is dedicated to work. Before the pandemic, the idea that work can and should be meaningful had been quietly brewing beneath the surface for decades. Now it has become an urgent demand.

In the drive to increase productivity, retention, and innovation, many leaders have forgotten where those things come from. They don't come from elaborate loyalty programs, targeted incentives, unlimited vacation, or providing ping-pong tables and free snacks at work. They come from finding meaning in our work. When work is meaningful—when it builds community, gives us a sense of contribution to something bigger, and challenges us to learn and grow—both individuals and organizations thrive.

Only by shifting from means-based to meaning-based leadership can leaders unlock the full potential of their employees. If leaders fail to make this shift, their people will inevitably seek out organizations that have already embraced a meaning-driven approach.

I COULDN'T BE MYSELF

Rushmie Nofsinger is a seasoned corporate affairs executive in the biotech industry and mother of three young daughters. She is one of the millions who recently left a job in search of more meaning. As the vice president of communications at a global pharmaceuticals company, Rushmie was responsible for leading a team of twenty professionals and shaping the company's response to social justice and DEI issues. This was supposed to be a challenging role where Rushmie could use her strengths to make an impact on issues that really matter to her. Over time, however, it became clear that she wouldn't have a lot of room to grow.

Rushmie's leader was set in her ways and resistant to Rushmie's innovative ideas. "Anyone can write a message or a press release; that's not where I can add the most value," she told us. Rushmie quickly learned that she couldn't use her unique strengths—creativity and strategic thinking—to propose new ideas because she was constantly shut down. She didn't feel she could be herself at work. Not only was Rushmie not being challenged, but she was also lacking a sense of contribution and community. Despite the fact that the very purpose of this organization is to develop medicines that improve and save patients' lives, Rushmie didn't feel connected to that purpose or to the people she worked with.

Gradually, Rushmie realized that there was a disconnect between the organization's stated values and her day-to-day experiences within the company. She felt emotionally detached and lonely at work. Rushmie sought guidance from a career coach, engaging in discussions about personal identity and work priorities. These conversations gave her the opportunity to dive deeper into her values and aspirations. Ultimately, Rushmie realized that despite a high salary, great benefits, and excellent perks, her job wasn't fulfilling in a meaningful way. She decided to leave the organization. Rushmie wanted to feel connected to her colleagues, to be valued and appreciated for her strengths, and to feel like what she is doing every day contributes to the organization's greater purpose.

Now Rushmie is working with a leader who truly believes in her and pushes her to grow. She took a role at a start-up biotech company in Cambridge, Massachusetts. Just a few months in, Rushmie was given the chance to expand her role and lead the organization's investor relations strategy. On paper, she actually didn't meet all the requirements for this new role, but her boss told her, "You're 70 percent of the way there, and I can teach you the rest." This leap of faith from a manager is a rarity—but also a gift. Leaders like this make work meaningful.

Rushmie's relationship with her job has transformed. She is excited to come in every day. She's motivated to work hard, to contribute innovative ideas, and to keep learning. At the end of the day, like so many of us, she wants to know that her career means something. The value of finding meaning at work spills over into her personal life as well. She finds she is happier with her girls and husband when she comes home at the end of the day. For Rushmie, that is priceless.

The positive effects of finding meaning at work extend beyond the individual, impacting the organization and touching families and communities. That is the power of meaningful work.

A WIN-WIN STRATEGY

Decades of research show that when employees like Rushmie experience meaningful work, they are happier, are more engaged, and stay with their companies longer. When that happens, organizations become more innovative, adaptable, and profitable. Employees who report high levels of meaning at work are 64 percent more fulfilled, 4.5 times more engaged, and 69 percent less likely to quit. Additionally, research shows that work well-being has the strongest impact on overall well-being. Well-being at work isn't just about the total number of hours worked, but also whether we spend those hours working on something that matters to us. We want a collective sense of belonging and, like Rushmie, to be valued by our organizations and managers. In a recent study, nine out of ten workers stated that meaning at work is so important that they would take a more meaningful job elsewhere, even if it paid less. These workers were willing to give up almost a quarter of their lifetime earnings for work that is more meaningful.

The positive outcomes of meaningful work extend far beyond the performance of an employee. The same study found that for every ten thousand employees who feel that their work is meaningful, there are $82 million in productivity gains per year. Seminal research by Wharton professor and bestselling author Adam Grant found that when people experience the impact of their work, they are 142 percent more productive, and organizational revenue increases by 172 percent. Meaning not only makes us happier—it also drives results. It is truly a win-win strategy.

In late 2022, the US surgeon general, Dr. Vivek Murthy, released a new framework for mental health and well-being in the workplace. In the accompanying report, Dr. Murthy called on leaders to design workplaces that "become engines of wellbeing, showing workers that they matter, that their work matters" and included meaningful work as a pathway to getting there. We couldn't agree more. While fair pay and decent work are foundational, we also want to feel genuinely appreciated and valued by our organizations and managers. As we saw in Rushmie's situation, she quit a job where she didn't have these needs met. Organizations who want to succeed in the future of work must answer this call for meaning or continue to risk losing high-performers like her.

MEANINGFUL WORK IS GOOD BUSINESS

Marriott, the global hospitality company, leaned on their meaningful work culture to navigate the disruption of the pandemic. It is well documented that COVID-19 had an outsized impact on the hospitality industry, extending beyond hotels to many businesses in local communities. In the spring of 2020, a few months into the pandemic, we interviewed Debbie Marriott Harrison, global officer of Marriott culture and granddaughter of the company's founders. Debbie and other leaders were navigating one of the worst crises in Marriott's history and had to make difficult decisions, including furloughing employees. At the beginning of the pandemic, they had to shut down two thousand hotels and furlough about 80 percent of their associates across the globe. Debbie described it as "just awful."

Marriott leaned on their five core values—put people first, pursue excellence, embrace change, act with integrity, and serve our world—to meet the challenging time. As we'll see, acting in line with your stated values is the foundation of meaningful work. Marriott made efforts to assist associates in finding alternative employment, continued to pay for their health care benefits, and repurposed hotels to support pandemic response efforts. The then CEO of Marriott, Arne Sorenson, offered furloughed employees a chance to leave and accept a severance package. But a very small percentage decided to look for another job. Debbie feels that is because "our associates really feel that it's more than just a job coming to work here; that it is meaningful to work at Marriott. They told us 'We will wait it out.'"

In April 2021, Marriott was named one of the 2021 Fortune 100 Best Companies to Work For by Great Place To Work for a record twenty-fourth year in a row, the only hospitality company with this distinction. According to Fortune, the 2021 list honored the "most heroic companies supporting their people and communities in the U.S. during this historically challenging year." Taking care of people is good for business.

A simple yet powerful motto from the founders, J. Willard and Alice S. Marriott, still drives the company's leadership today: "Take care of associates and they will take care of the customers"—and the customers will come back again and again. During the pandemic, they lived up to their values by supporting their struggling workforce. Debbie told us that when the pandemic ended people were anxious to get back to work, reestablish their relationships, and forge new ones. "The glue that holds our Marriott culture together is having strong and caring relationships with our associates and guests." A sales coordinator from Florida shared her experience at the organization: "Marriott teaches us, from the first day on the job, that the people they care most about taking care of are their employees because by doing that, we will then take care of their guests. Overall, they truly believe in that goal. This is the first company I have ever worked for that actually shows appreciation for their employees and made me feel valued." In the pandemic, many companies let their values go by the wayside, but not Marriott.

Marriott's long history of success is built on their commitment to putting their people first. The company continually invests in creating meaningful work opportunities for their associates with a focus on development, recognition, compensation, career advancement, and skills training. As a pioneer in the hospitality industry, Marriott was also one of the first companies to introduce a global well-being program more than two decades ago, focused on nurturing the physical, mental, and financial health of associates worldwide.

RECLAIMING MEANINGFUL WORK

Before we teach you the strategies to increase meaning at work, it's important that we define it and dispel some misconceptions. You might find yourself talking about your organization's purpose as a way employees can find meaning. Purpose is extremely important. Although often used interchangeably, meaningful work isn't just about purpose. For at least two decades, many organizations have focused on purpose—on clarifying why they exist and what goals they are striving for other than simply making money. But we have found a key distinction: while purpose contributes to meaningful work, purpose alone is not enough to make work meaningful. Meaning also comes from a sense of belonging to a community and from the challenge of growing and mastering new skills.

We have worked with nonprofit organizations where people feel connected to the purpose and yet don't experience meaning at work. Sometimes it's because they don't feel like they belong or don't have close relationships at work. Often it's because they feel stuck in their career, without challenging opportunities to grow and develop. Their work is purposeful but not meaningful. In addition to helping people understand their contribution to the organization's purpose, leaders must also build belonging and help people learn and grow.

With this in mind, we define meaningful work as **work that provides community, helps us contribute to something that matters, and challenges us to learn and grow.**

Many people believe meaningful work is reserved only for those in helping professions, nonprofits, or social impact. This is not the case. While it's true that some jobs have built-in elements that make them seem more meaningful, we have found that any job can and, we believe, should be meaningful.

In 2001, a pioneering study was conducted to understand how individuals in seemingly low-status and low-skilled occupations find meaning in their work. The researchers selected hospital janitors because their work, although essential, is often undervalued and overlooked. They asked the cleaners questions about their day-to-day tasks, their relationships at work, and how significant they believed their work to be. Perhaps you wouldn't expect these cleaners to find their work meaningful in comparison to high-status and high-skill occupations like doctor or nurse. The researchers discovered, however, that many of them strongly felt the importance of their contribution to the healing of the patients. They had brief interactions with patients, visitors, and colleagues that made them feel energized and appreciated. These janitors viewed their work as deeply meaningful, describing themselves as "healers" and their hospital as a "house of hope."

Research has since looked at a wide range of industries—from manufacturing to hospitality, education, and technology—and found that meaningful work is less about the type of work you do and more about your understanding of how that work matters. We can see this clearly in this chapter's story about Keisha in the data center.

Another common misconception about meaningful work is that it is the same as happiness. Leaders have spent billions on programs to try to keep employees happy and engaged. Taking their cue from Silicon Valley start-up culture, many installed ping-pong tables and gave away free snacks. Formerly bare office kitchens became stocked with nitro cold brew, kombucha, or craft beer. Happy hour outings on the company credit card were commonplace, along with team trips to escape rooms and karaoke bars. The theory was that fun places to work would attract and retain better talent.

Snacks, games, and team-building trips are all fine, but the happiness they create is fleeting at best. Katie Burke, former chief people officer at HubSpot, a leading inbound marketing and sales software platform known for its extraordinary culture, told us, "I can make people really happy by just building a circus at work and telling them to come in every day. But we believe that our job is to make HubSpot the best place to do your best work. And so, to me, the work itself is a meaningful part of that."

Extrinsic motivators—the proverbial carrots—aren't great tools for increasing and sustaining engagement. According to recent research, even financial rewards such as higher salaries, commissions, and bonuses can backfire and *decrease* engagement by turning meaningful work into work that feels transactional. Only when leaders shift their focus from meaningless perks to meaningful work can they truly foster a culture of sustained engagement.

Our research shows that leaders have an outsized impact on whether employees experience work as meaningful. Leaders who build community, help people understand how their contributions matter, and challenge them with opportunities to learn and grow, foster meaning for everyone on their teams. In the next chapter we'll take a closer look at how leaders make work meaningful.

2

HOW LEADERS MAKE WORK MEANINGFUL

There is a big difference between understanding the value of the people inside an organization and actually making decisions that consider their needs.

—BOB CHAPMAN

Early in our multiyear journey studying standout leaders and the things they do to help their teams find meaning in their work, we found ourselves on a call with Katie Burke, whom you briefly met in the previous chapter. It was a call that opened our eyes to the profound impact leaders have on making work meaningful.

HubSpot has ranked at the top of Glassdoor's Best Places to Work list for nearly a decade, including a year at the number-one spot. A growing tech company that makes marketing and sales software, Hub-Spot perhaps seems an unlikely place for people to find their life's calling. However, it is exactly that—and that's no accident.

Katie, along with the rest of the senior leadership at HubSpot, is highly engaged in the design and execution of the company culture. That culture revolves around the idea that every person should be doing work that matters. This idea is codified in their now-famous Culture Code, which set the benchmark for building a values-driven company when it was first released in 2013. The document is publicly available and has been viewed over five million times. It offers an inside look at what HubSpot believes in and how it operates. Some highlights include "Employees who work at HubSpot have HEART: Humble, Empathetic, Adaptable, Remarkable, Transparent" and "We'd rather be failing frequently than never trying."

We were eager to press Katie for the magic formula that she and her colleagues had discovered to fuel such a dedicated team. What she ended up telling us confirmed what we had long suspected—it is up to *leaders* to design the environments where individuals can experience meaning at work.

We first met with Katie in May of 2020, just two months into the global COVID-19 pandemic. Even in those early days of lockdown, when the better part of the world was in full-on crisis mode, Katie exuded calmness. She met us with an intent, magnetic focus. Over Zoom from her home outside Boston, she told us about HubSpot's internal response to the pandemic.

Less than a week in, while most companies were trying to figure out how to navigate video calls and file sharing, Katie and her team had quickly pivoted to support the HubSpotters who needed the most help. Realizing that parents of small children were struggling, they hired musicians to keep their kids entertained over Zoom to give parents a short break. They set up a virtual fireside chat with a sober author to discuss "navigating sobriety through the pandemic" to support HubSpotters in recovery who had suddenly become separated from their networks. Realizing that many of their employees were taking advantage of the company's free books program to purchase antiracism texts given the national reckoning with systemic racism and social injustice, Katie's team found Black-owned bookstores in every market and asked HubSpotters to support them.

Even during a time of crisis, leaders at HubSpot didn't just focus on pulling the proverbial weeds—managing burnout, reducing uncertainty, and clearing roadblocks to productivity. Of course, they did those things. But what set them apart is that they focused as strongly on nourishing the soil—supporting their employees and showing them that they truly care. As we dug deeper into Katie's approach, we worked to piece together the day-to-day actions she took to cultivate more meaning at work. She told us about efforts to create a sense of belonging, to show each HubSpotter how their work positively impacts others, and to challenge team members to learn and grow.

We wanted to know why she thought it was important for leaders to cultivate meaning at work. "Meaningful work has of course economic value, but I also believe that it has great personal value," Katie told us. "People are happier with their family and friends when they're fulfilled at work. We think about our impact as certainly helping *customers* grow better [HubSpot's mission] but also as helping our *employees and their families* grow better."

Those three sentences struck a chord. The sentiment is simple, but underlying it is a shift in mindset that holds incredible promise. Katie takes for granted the economic value of meaningful work, emphasizing instead the human value—the factor from which all these outcomes grow. Instead of leading downstream—focusing on outcomes like engagement, productivity, and retention—Katie leads with upstream strategies—focusing on creating the conditions for these outcomes to occur. And make no mistake, HubSpot's outcomes are remarkable.

The company is in the top 5 percent of similar sized organizations in its ability to retain quality employees. Not only that, 83 percent of employees would not leave HubSpot if they were offered a job for more money, while 86 percent are excited to go to work each day. Additionally, the company's revenue has grown at an average rate of 40 percent every year since 2014, the year after they implemented their Culture Code.

This mindset shift has positioned HubSpot as a leader in its field and a place where high performers thrive. We want to share what we learned from Katie and the other leaders we've studied to help you make that shift.

UPSTREAM LEADERSHIP

Imagine that you and a friend are enjoying a picnic by the river on a beautiful, sunny day. Suddenly, you hear a child screaming for help, floundering in the river. You both jump into the water, grab the child, and swim back to shore. Before you can catch your breath, you hear another child crying for help, so you jump back in and rescue them as well. Then a third child comes into sight—and another and another. With both of you near exhaustion at this point, your friend abandons the rescue effort and starts running up the riverbank. You call out to ask why. The reply: "I'm going upstream to stop these kids from falling in the water!"

This classic parable is a metaphor for the way we lead today. By staying in reactive mode, downstream leadership may save some employees from drowning, but it never addresses the root causes of burnout and turnover. Upstream leadership, on the other hand, takes a proactive approach to achieving excellence. Its focus isn't on solving problems after they occur. It's on creating the conditions for people to do their best work. It's about nourishing the soil, not just pulling the weeds. This kind of leadership requires asking fundamental questions like, How do we create a workplace that inspires people to be their best selves? To perform at their full potential? To understand how their work makes a difference? This approach is the key not only to preventing your people from falling in the river in the first place, but also to helping them do their best work. It is a simple yet powerful shift.

Meaning-driven leadership is the upstream strategy that leads to innovation, creativity, performance, retention, and engagement. Many leaders try to solve one employee crisis at a time. They deal with issues like faltering productivity, low engagement, chronic burnout, quiet quitting, and high turnover as individual problems to be solved. Only a few, like Katie, look upstream for a systemic solution that will not only prevent future problems, but will also unlock the full potential of every employee. The future of work demands that leaders make this shift.

Katie told us that HubSpot intentionally trains its managers on these upstream leadership skills. She feels that we typically don't teach enough about people management in college or graduate school. As a result, most new managers have to wing it, and bad management habits get passed down from generation to generation of leaders. To combat this, HubSpot retrains all of its leaders rather than assuming that, just because someone was promoted to a management role, they know how to lead others thoughtfully. When people ask Katie, "How do I fix my Glassdoor score?" or "How do I get someone to write a good LinkedIn review?," she tells them that they are asking the wrong questions. To have happy employees and get good reviews, leaders need to interrogate how they are enabling people to build strong relationships with each other, to find significance in their tasks, and to reach their full potential.

DESIGNING FOR MEANING

Human nature is shaped by human design. This means that leaders need to design for meaningful work. The idea of intentional business design is not new. Grocery stores are cleverly designed to influence our behavior in subtle yet powerful ways.

The strategic placement of milk and eggs at the back of the store compels us to navigate through aisles filled with enticing products, increasing the chances of additional purchases. Produce is placed near the entrance, allowing us to select healthy foods early, which makes us feel virtuous, and then reward ourselves with less healthy items we might not have considered. The arrangement of items on shelves is meticulously orchestrated to capture our attention. Eye-catching displays, carefully crafted product packaging, and attractive signage all play a role in grabbing our interest and encouraging impulse buying. At the root of grocery store design is a drive to increase sales. In the same way, leaders can design workplaces to increase meaning.

Prior to our research, most of the studies on meaningful work were focused on the behavior of the employee. While it is important to learn how individuals can increase their own sense of meaning at work, it is not enough. Expecting individuals to construct their own meaning, rather than creating an environment that fosters meaning, is like asking someone to build a house without providing them with the necessary tools and materials. Just as a house requires proper tools, materials, and a blueprint to be constructed successfully, meaning at work requires leaders who design workplaces around community, contribution, and challenge and give individuals the tools to build them.

THE THREE C'S OF MEANINGFUL WORK

Devon Still is a former NFL defensive lineman and cherished member of our positive psychology community. During his second year in the NFL with the Cincinnati Bengals, Devon's life took an unexpected turn. Faced with daunting challenges, he experienced firsthand the strength of community and unwavering support. "Sometimes life hits you hard when you are least expecting it, and you have to find a way to get back in the game," he told us.

In late 2013, Devon dislocated his elbow in a game against the Detroit Lions. Five weeks later, he blew out his back in a game against the Pittsburgh Steelers and had to have a season-ending surgery. One week after that, Devon almost died from multiple blood clots in his lungs. The worst news came five months later. In June of 2014, his then four-year-old daughter Leah was diagnosed with neuroblastoma, a rare form of pediatric cancer.

Through these trials, Devon's leaders rallied behind him. Recognizing the importance of standing by one of their own, the Bengals released Devon from the team, but immediately re-signed him to the practice squad to help Devon pay for Leah's cancer treatment. As part of the practice squad, Devon did not have to travel with the team and could stay home to support his daughter. This act of compassion allowed Devon to be there for Leah's demanding treatment while still being a part of the team he loved. Their support extended beyond the field as they joined forces to raise awareness for pediatric cancer research and the Cincinnati Children's Hospital by selling Devon Still jerseys. They helped to rally the greater Cincinnati community around Devon. In just a few months, jersey sale donations neared $1 million.

More than a decade later, Leah is cancer-free. Devon now travels the world as an inspirational speaker and podcast host. His powerful story illustrates the immeasurable power of **community**, the first C of meaning at work.

Meaning-driven leaders help employees thrive by encouraging social connections like the ones that tied Devon to his team. Belonging to a group that shares values, promotes authentic relationships, and supports us as individuals with full lives is the foundation for building community. Positive psychology studies have found that social connection isn't just a major driver of our well-being—our well-being also has a positive effect on our relationships. It is a virtuous cycle. The late Ed Diener, a leading empirical scientist on happiness, found that in every country, close relationships lead to happiness and that the happiest people in the world have strong, supportive relationships.

Dedicating time to promote positive social interactions at work can be a powerful way to build community. Feeling connected and believing that others care about us are basic and universal psychological needs. It is no surprise that Chris Peterson, a founding father of positive psychology, summarized the entire field in three words: *other people matter*.

Like the leaders of the Cincinnati Bengals, organizational leaders who want to create meaning at work must start by prioritizing relationships and building community.

The second C of meaning at work is **contribution**. Meaning-driven leaders help people understand how their work adds value. When people are able to see the positive impact their efforts have on others, or how their day-to-day tasks ladder up to the larger goals of the organization, work becomes more meaningful. Contribution is about seeing the impact of the tasks we perform each day—and understanding how those tasks benefit something larger than ourselves.

Meaning-driven leaders clarify the impact that people have on the team, the organization, its customers, or a greater purpose. A sense of contribution comes from seeing progress toward shared goals—from *advancing* our organization's purpose. When we believe that we are part of something bigger, we worry less about ourselves and find our jobs more fulfilling. Research from positive psychology shows that people who have a strong connection to purpose are happier with their lives, are more motivated and engaged, and have better psychological and physiological well-being.

Zach Mercurio, our research partner and a professor at Colorado State University's Center for Meaning and Purpose, teaches a simple yet powerful practice to highlight people's contributions. Zach prompts leaders to regularly tell people, *If it wasn't for you . . .* and then describe the unique contribution they made. He emphasizes that these five words make people feel indispensable and needed. Take a moment now to imagine someone saying these words to you. How would it feel? It is inspiring when you understand how your work makes a difference to others. Research finds that employees who are regularly thanked by their manager are twice as likely to stay than employees who aren't. A simple thank-you can be that meaningful.

The final C of meaning at work is **challenge**. Meaning-driven leaders help employees reach their full potential. Tom,* a successful

---

* Name changed to protect anonymity.

finance executive in Boston, experienced a transformative leadership moment under the guidance of Bill, his CEO. Early in his tenure with the organization, Tom pitched the idea of selling one of the company's subsidiaries at an executive meeting, expecting that he would be involved in the financial and operational aspects of the deal. However, Bill saw it as an opportunity for Tom's development and handed him full control of the sale. Tom wasn't sure he was ready but embraced the opportunity he was given. "I thought, *Well, if Bill believes that I can do it, I am going to prove him right!*"

Tom started putting all the pieces in place. He interviewed investment bankers, built a compelling case for the board, and garnered their support. Then, he formed a fifty-person internal working group, set a vision, and challenged his own team to rise to the occasion. After six months, Tom's team successfully closed the deal. This experience, marked by the trust placed in him, a shared sense of ownership, and valuable learning opportunities, remains a career highlight for Tom and was transformational for his company and its employees.

Robert Quinn, a professor at the University of Michigan and cofounder at the Center for Positive Organizations, likens this idea of challenge to the leader having one hand on your back, pushing you to be the best possible version of yourself. The other hand is under your arm, supporting you to navigate the trickiest terrain. Pushing and supporting simultaneously—the two work together. That is exactly what Bill did for Tom.

One of the most enduring human needs is the desire for personal growth and development. We consistently seek opportunities to learn, improve, and expand our skills. When leaders believe in us and provide challenging opportunities, we stretch our capabilities and feel that our work supports our personal growth. Accomplishing difficult goals gives us confidence in our abilities and builds self-efficacy over time. Research in positive psychology shows that self-efficacy, a person's belief in their ability to achieve a desired outcome based on their actions, is one of the most powerful determinants of success. Self-efficacy is simply the belief that "I can do this." It plays an important role in mental health, in physical health, and in perseverance in the face of challenges. Strong beliefs in our ability to achieve desired outcomes influence not only the quality of goals we set but also our thoughts, emotions, and actions in pursuit of these goals. Like muscles, humans need challenges and stressors to learn, adapt, and grow. Leaders who see our strengths, support us, and give us challenging opportunities make work meaningful by empowering us to reach our full potential.

Each of the Three C's—community, contribution, and challenge—makes work meaningful in a different way. Each one is a necessary component of meaningful work but is not sufficient on its own. We found that when all three are present at a high level, they create a powerful multiplier effect. If just one of these factors is missing, however, the other two may fail to foster a sense of meaning. No matter how much a single factor adds to an employee's sense of meaning, lack of investment by leaders in the other two factors can bring it crashing down. After all, if you multiply something by zero, the result is always zero. Meaningful work lives at the powerful intersection of the Three C's. To truly make work meaningful, it is necessary for leaders to invest in all three domains.

PUTTING ON YOUR OXYGEN MASK FIRST

You might be wondering how you can create meaning at work for your employees if you yourself are not experiencing work as meaningful. You can, and should, attend to both. Below, we offer some questions that can serve as a starting point for your reflection about your own sense of meaning at work.

That said, you don't need to wait until you find your own work meaningful to start creating meaning for others. In fact, research finds, again and again, that one of the best ways to make yourself happy is to make other people happy. When leaders increase meaning at work for their teams, their own sense of meaning often also increases.

Start by examining the Three C's in your own work and reflect on how you can increase each one:

- **Community:** Do you feel a sense of belonging and inclusion with your team or department? Why or why not? What efforts do you make to build relationships and connections with your colleagues? One leader we work with starts her meetings with a brief show-and-tell activity. Each week, a different team member brings something meaningful to them—a photo, an object, a song—and spends a few minutes telling the story of the item. This has sparked many connections within the team, as people get to know a more personal side of one another and realize they share common interests. Are there opportunities for collaboration, teamwork, and shared goals within your work environment? Are you capitalizing on opportunities for socializing, team-building activities, or community events?

- **Contribution:** When is the last time you got to experience the impact of your work? Recently, one of the leaders we work with participated in a fundraising walk dedicated to curing a disease that his company is actively developing drugs to fight. Spending a few hours with children affected by the disease renewed his sense of purpose. You can also feel a sense of contribution when someone expresses gratitude or appreciation. When was the last time someone thanked you for the impact you had on their day or their career? Saving some of these messages to go back to when you need to boost your sense of contribution can be helpful. If you don't feel a sense of fulfillment and purpose in your current contributions, what changes or adjustments could you make to enhance this sense of meaning?

- **Challenge:** In what ways do you feel you are actively learning and expanding your skills in your role? Are there any specific tasks, projects, or assignments that have provided you with a sense of challenge and growth? Do you feel that your current role allows you to stretch and develop your abilities? One of our friends, who works in client services at an advertising agency, recently asked her manager if she could work with a new client in an entirely different industry—one that she was curious to learn more about. Her proactive initiative allowed her to expand her expertise and develop new skills. What are some areas for professional growth or skill development that you would like to explore further? Are there opportunities for training, mentorship, or professional development programs that you can access?

Taking time to reflect on your own experience of meaning at work is important and will help you become even more intentional about making work meaningful for your team. During our interview with Katie Burke, we asked her what makes work meaningful for her personally. She told us that for her meaning is all about incremental wins on the path to creating a meaningful culture. "I see meaningful work as not just hitting an end goal because, candidly, this work is never going to be done. But when you feel like you're not just making a difference to the company, but also making a difference to the lives of the people you touch, that feels meaningful to me."

3

ALIGNMENT

THE FOUNDATION OF
MEANING AT WORK

As a leader, you don't have a choice in being a role model.
The only choice is whether to be a good or bad one.

—JOHN AMAECHI

At X, the secretive "moonshot factory" inside Google's parent company, Alphabet, innovation isn't just a buzzword. It's a way of being.

X has an ambitious goal: "10x impact on some of the world's most intractable problems, not just 10% improvement." To achieve that mandate, the leaders at X have articulated a clear set of operating principles to create "a culture with the values and practices that can resist the pull toward the comfortable and conventional, and make radical, purpose-driven creativity the path of least resistance." Those values—which include pushing for the audacious, using a counterintuitive approach, experimentation, balancing optimism with intellectual honesty, and taking the long-term view—aren't just words on the wall.

Just ask Astro Teller, X's CEO, better known as the Captain of Moonshots. As the leader of the company, Astro's focus is to make sure those values live in the organization every day. To reward people for successfully following X's values of experimentation and intellectual honesty, he's designed a very successful incentive program. He gives team members a healthy financial bonus—not when they succeed but when they fail.

Once a new project has made it through the initial approval stage, which is designed to find fatal flaws before the team commits resources to it, it becomes a team's mission to bring the project's big idea to life. One of these teams might spend millions of dollars and several years trying to get the project off the ground. The more investment they make in a project, the harder it gets for the team to walk away. After giving so much time and energy to realizing a big idea, letting it go isn't easy. But from a business perspective, the sooner a team realizes that an idea won't work, the sooner their energy and company resources can be redirected to another idea that might.

"If there's an Achilles' heel in one of our projects, we want to know it now, up front, not way down the road," Astro said in his TED Talk. "You cannot yell at people and force them to fail fast. People resist. They worry. 'What will happen to me if I fail? Will people laugh at me? Will I be fired?'"

As the company's leader, Astro made a point to be the team's most vocal supporter when they call it quits. He continued, "We work hard at X to make it safe to fail. Teams kill their ideas as soon as the evidence is on the table because they are *rewarded* for it. They get applause from their peers. Hugs and high fives from their manager, me in particular." X kills an estimated one hundred projects a year, and the team celebrates every time they put one down. "They get promoted for it," Astro said. "We have bonused every single person on teams that ended their projects."

Astro Teller understands that it's not enough to talk about experimentation and intellectual honesty—these values have to be lived in every part of the organization. Values keep the team at X laser focused only on big ideas that have real potential. Over the past dozen years, X has developed industry-changing technologies including self-driving cars (Waymo), contact lenses for diabetics that measure blood glucose (Verily), atmospheric balloons that provide internet to people in remote areas (Loon), autonomous delivery drones (Wing), and even a way to store electricity in salt (Malta). X is also responsible for Google Brain, the deep learning software that powers Google Search. It's likely that some of the things you use every day are the end product of a crazy idea that originated at X.

While X's mission and the values that drive it are unique, the commitment that Astro shows to them is not. Across all of the organizations we've studied and the meaning-driven leaders we've interviewed, every single one made it a priority to bring their company's values to life every day. As we dug deeper into the factors that create meaning, we found that alignment between values and action isn't just a contributor to meaningful work—it is a core requirement for it.

Chris Peterson, one of the founders of positive psychology whom you met earlier in the book, wrote, "Values are beliefs held by individuals and shared by groups about desirable ends...they guide how we select actions and evaluate others and ourselves." Values are the rules of the road that tell us how we should behave as we journey toward our goals. In organizations, values are our shared understanding of what is most important to the team. They provide both guides and guardrails for our behavior and our operation.

Our research found that alignment—the consistency between organizational values and observable behavior—is a requirement for meaning. We also found that a misalignment of values—when leaders say one thing but do another—is the quickest way to destroy meaning at work. While alignment of words and deeds allows the roots of trust and confidence to take hold, misalignment poisons the soil of an organization. Alignment provides fertile ground for meaningful work to grow.

VALUES IN ACTION

Values guide employees' behavior while also forming the basis of an organization's culture. They communicate to the group which behaviors are rewarded and which are punished. The more clearly these guides and guardrails are defined, the better the ability of leaders to foster meaning at work.

Whether you are defining your values for the first time or revisiting existing ones, it's not enough to list them on your website or post them on your wall. Words like *integrity* and *teamwork* sound great. Who wouldn't want those things at work? In practice, however, these words can mean very different things to different people. To be clearly understood, values must be translated into practical behaviors.

Perhaps your team has already done the work to clearly outline the valued behaviors within your organization. If so, we applaud you! If, like many of us, you haven't fully explored these behaviors, we suggest that you try the **Values in Action** exercise below before moving on to the next section.

VALUES IN ACTION EXERCISE

Start by selecting one of your organization's values. If your organization has not yet defined a set of values, think about what you believe as a group. What makes someone successful in your organization? What advice would you give a new employee about working there? Some common values are integrity, accountability, and teamwork. You can also take a look at the list of organizational values on our website www .makeworkmeaningful.com. Pick one value that applies to your organization and use that for this exercise.

Once you've chosen a value, you can begin to define what that value looks like in action. Start by creating two columns on a blank page. On the left side, write down as many examples as you can of behavior you've seen at your organization that's aligned with the value. On the right side, list behaviors you've seen that are not aligned with the value.

We've included an example below of what that might look like for the value of integrity:

Aligned	Misaligned
• Speaking up when you've made a mistake	• Lying to a client about your ability to do a piece of work
• Giving accurate estimates of when a project will be delivered	• Passing off someone else's work as your own
• Giving honest feedback to your colleagues	• Keeping quiet when you see a problem

After you've made these two lists, review the aligned behaviors. Can you think of a specific story of a time when you saw someone in your organization exhibit one of these behaviors? What was the context? What did that person do exactly? What was the outcome and how was it connected to the value?

On another page, write down the full story of this experience. This alignment story will serve as a tool to help to bring the value to life for your colleagues.

Pinterest, the image-sharing platform, went through a process to revisit its values in early 2022 as the social media industry faced some existential questions about its role in society. "When I met the folks at Pinterest, what really lit me up was this idea of being a better place on the internet," said Christine Deputy, the company's chief people officer at the time. "I have two teenage kids. We've learned about some of the negative impacts that social media can have on teenagers. There was a real commitment to design the platform to be a better place."

When Christine came on board, her team engaged the entire organization to redefine its values with a new future in mind. Pinterest surveyed the full company to understand what it believed the real values of the organization to be. Employees were asked what they were seeing from leaders and also what they thought the values *should* be. Through that process, they were able to identify a common narrative of what people wanted the company to become: to take more risks, to be more ambitious and bolder. In the end, Pinterest kept two of its original values and changed three to meet the new moment they were in. Their five values are put Pinners (what the company calls its employees) first, aim for extraordinary, create belonging, act as one, and win or learn. The executive team took a hands-on role in crafting the language of the updated values. Then, leaders asked all of the employees to help define the behaviors associated with them.

They created a "Life at Pinterest" board with each of the values. They invited employees to add "pins" with thoughts on how those values should be brought to life in day-to-day work. More than three thousand employees took part in translating the new values into practical behaviors. For example, some of the behaviors associated with "put Pinners first" were practices like inviting everyone to share their views in meetings and including more people in decision-making processes around which new products get built. "We really wanted people to share their own examples of what these values look like— and what these values don't look like," said Christine. Now a central place exists for people to revisit, add to, and pull examples from. For the team at Pinterest, this has been a successful way to maintain alignment.

By making values-aligned behaviors explicit, Pinterest set clear expectations for employees at all levels. Once values have been translated into actionable behaviors, people look to leaders to demonstrate alignment. Our research revealed two ways that leaders create and maintain alignment: by **visibly modeling values** in their day-to-day behavior and by **designing values-driven systems**.

VISIBLY MODELING VALUES

When we spoke to Rob Waldron about the importance of being a role model, he shared a story we didn't expect. Rob is the CEO of Curriculum Associates, makers of academic software i-Ready, which is used by a third of US grade school students. He has guided the company successfully through many ups and downs as the education sector has faced disruption after disruption in recent years. Rob credits his success to the company's strong values alignment. Those values include "Low Ego" and "We Say It Like It Is." When he thinks about modeling company values, however, his most memorable lesson isn't from work—it's from his wedding.

"I was married on the rainiest day in the history of the state of Rhode Island in a tent on a cliff walk," Rob laughed as he told us. "The tent was shaking, and it was flooded everywhere." More than two hundred people had flown in from all over the world for what was meant to be a beautiful wedding on the shore. Months of planning and preparation had gone into making it a perfect day. But things didn't go the way that Rob and his then fiancée Jennifer had hoped. After months of planning and anticipation, it looked like their big day was ruined. A torrential downpour had soaked the venue and gave no indication of letting up. Rob and Jennifer were devastated—until their wedding planner pulled them aside. He told the couple that rain couldn't ruin the day. Only one person could do that—the bride.

The wedding planner shared the most important piece of wisdom he had. He said to Jennifer, "If you think the rain is funny and you love it and laugh, the guests will think it's funny. If you are uptight and worry and apologize to the guests, then they're going to feel bad. People are looking to you to set the tone. Everyone follows the bride." As the "leader" of the wedding, Jennifer took the advice to heart and decided she would embrace the rain. Her dress got covered in mud as she danced the night away. People slipped on the slick grass and the wedding party was soaked to the bone. It was a total mess—and it was one of the best days of the Waldrons' lives.

As the leader of an organization, Rob knows that people look to him for cues on how to behave. Whether he's making a routine decision or facing an unexpected crisis, he knows that if he demonstrates the organization's values in action, his team will follow. When faced with a tough choice, he leans into the company values by reminding himself that people always "follow the bride."

Research on social learning, the process of learning by observing others, shows that the actions of leaders strongly influence a group's understanding of appropriate behavior. This is especially the case when it comes to values alignment in organizations. As Rob and many other leaders have taught us, values must be more than just words on the wall. True values are expressed in the actions that leaders of the community take every day. They can be gleaned from each email, heard in the language of meetings, and seen in the decisions, big and small, that leaders make. To learn an organization's true values, we focus far less on a leader's talk and much more on their walk. For work to be meaningful, their words and deeds must be in alignment.

Integrity is a core value at Curriculum Associates. At a recent six-hundred-person annual meeting, Rob was leading a discussion with a board member and a private equity investor. The board member was a forty-five-year-old man and the investor was a woman in her early thirties. Rob spent most of the session talking to the board member and didn't give the investor as much airtime. Afterward, one of his employees shared with Rob that she felt he had missed an opportunity. She said that he had a woman in private equity, which is too rare, sitting up on the stage, but he didn't give her a chance to talk. At first, Rob was defensive—the board member was a partner in the business and had much more business experience. But by Rob's account, he realized his initial reaction came from the "white suburban executive male" part of his brain. When he thought about it, he realized his employee was right.

At Curriculum Associates, part of demonstrating integrity is owning up to your mistakes. Rob recognized that this was an opportunity to model that behavior for the team. That night, he wrote an email to the whole company saying he had made a mistake and missed an opportunity. He received 150 emails back from people thanking him for acknowledging his mistake and living up to the company's values.

Alignment between what a leader says and how they behave sets the tone for the rest of the organization. When leaders walk the talk like Rob did, they show us what values look like in action and create an expectation for the rest of the company. Leaders who translate values into concrete behaviors lay the foundation for meaningful work.

Over the last forty years, Kenneth Cole, founder and chair of the eponymous shoe and clothing retailer, has made a name for himself as an activist and advocate. He was one of the first to publicly call for more research and care during the early days of the HIV/AIDS epidemic. He has campaigned to combat homelessness, helped provide critical services in Haiti following the earthquake, and most recently focused his efforts on reducing the stigma around mental health issues. He founded the Mental Health Coalition to bring together a cross section of businesses, nonprofits, and service providers to destigmatize mental health challenges and empower access to vital resources.

"One in four people today struggles with mental health issues," Kenneth told us. "We say it's actually four in four—if it isn't you, it's somebody you love, somebody in the family, the community, the workplace. Everybody knows somebody who's struggling."

Through the coalition, Kenneth works with leading technology companies to track and quantify the impact that mental health resources have on individuals and on businesses. In typical Kenneth Cole style, he talks about the importance of supporting mental health at every opportunity. For Kenneth, it's not just a marketing campaign—it's something he models in his own company. Care and compassion are core values within the organization.

Ingrid Yan, a longtime employee, appreciates that Kenneth doesn't just talk about the importance of mental health—he demonstrates care and compassion every day. He openly discusses his own mental health journey and regularly sends out emails with mental health tips. He has also developed programming to support employees' mental health ranging from group meditations in the office to interactive conversations with experts like Deepak Chopra.

"Kenneth lives our values," shared Jed Berger, president of Kenneth Cole Productions. "A lot of people have been here for a long time because he is an activist who walks his talk, and he cares about humans."

Before joining the company, Jed was a highly successful retail executive who had his pick of places to work. When the opportunity at Kenneth Cole presented itself, he leapt at the chance to work for a values-aligned leader. As he took over the role of president, he knew it was his responsibility to model the company's values in the same way Kenneth did.

From day one, Jed set an example for the team. On his very first day, he told his story at a town hall meeting. He said that mental health and work-life balance were important to him. He shared that he has a son with special needs. He has Down syndrome and is autistic, and routine is incredibly important for him. Jed told his team that he planned to drop his son off at the bus in the morning, and he would be there when he gets home at night. He shared that being there for his family was important to his own mental health and well-being. He made it clear that he would support everyone's efforts to prioritize what was important to their own mental health.

Jed's example quickly rippled throughout the organization. Sharing his story created the space for employees to share their own stories without fear of stigma. As someone who had battled severe depression, Ingrid knew that mental health challenges could be isolating. It was something she didn't normally share with people at work. Kenneth's and Jed's efforts to destigmatize the conversation allowed her to share her own journey as well. She feels comfortable speaking openly about how she takes medication and makes it a point to reach out to employees who she can tell are struggling. With them, she'll share that she sees a therapist and offer to talk about her experiences.

Modeling doesn't have to be about big moments. As a leader, every interaction with your team is an opportunity to live your values. The way you greet people in the morning, the language you use to give feedback on a project, and the questions you ask in an email all add up to reveal the things you truly value. Each day, people look to those small behaviors for alignment.

As Jed shared his story, Kenneth took note. He and Jed talk constantly, but Kenneth has never once called him during the times when he's picking up or dropping off his son. Jed sees this as a small but powerful example of modeling the value of supporting mental health.

MODELING IN THE MODERN WORLD

In today's work environment, hybrid and remote structures can make it more difficult for employees to consistently observe their leaders. For those leading in these environments, alignment won't always be obvious. Many decisions may go unobserved. The small, day-to-day actions of leaders are harder to see through a flood of emails, Slacks, and Zoom meetings. When we are separated by this digital distance, it's often unclear how the limited behaviors that are seen connect to an organization's values. Bridging this distance requires more intentional communication from leaders. The values that drive your actions, the reasons you choose to pursue one path over another, must be shared more explicitly.

In his role as CEO of A–B Partners, Andre Banks invests a considerable amount of time communicating his decisions to the team. A–B, a mission-driven creative agency, is a fully remote company with nearly one hundred employees. While many businesses of its size have struggled to keep high-performing talent in recent years, A–B has thrived. Andre believes this success is partly due to the efforts he's made to model values at the top.

He and his leadership team work hard to create an environment in which people feel there is accountability to the company values. To demonstrate alignment with his remote team, Andre intentionally explains the reasons behind his decisions in order to help employees understand how each one aligns with A–B's values. When payroll shifted from once a month to twice a month, Andre made sure that the motivation for the change was communicated thoroughly. He sent multiple Slack messages, discussed it in a full team meeting, and created space for a Q and A. He made sure everyone understood how paying people more frequently better aligned with the organization's value of equity.

We call this practice of communicating alignment "spotlighting." Like a lighting technician at the back of a theater, Andre shines a spotlight on the key players (the company's values) in the story. By highlighting those key players for his audience (the team), he shows them how his actions stay aligned with expectations.

At a recent retreat of the senior team, a big decision was made to acquire an analytics company to expand A–B's work. By bringing new expertise and capabilities into the organization, Andre saw an opportunity to better serve clients and live up to the company's value of being bold. To connect this big move to company values, Andre created a series of video drops to share with the staff on Slack. In these brief explainer videos, he focused on making the connection between the new acquisition and the reasons behind it.

Andre feels strongly that alignment isn't about telling people *what* he decided to do; it's about telling them *why*. "It's about bringing them into the decision-making process and helping them understand how this initiative connects to the things we all care about—the values that brought people here in the first place," he told us. The explainer videos were a hit and gave Andre an effective new tool to model remotely. Video drops have become a regular part of Andre's efforts to visibly walk the talk for his team.

Spotlighting your decisions helps bridge the digital distance between leaders and employees by communicating alignment. We encourage you to take a minute and think through an opportunity to spotlight one of your own decisions.

SPOT-LIGHTING EXERCISE

Think of a decision you have to make this week that impacts others on your team. You may be introducing a new policy, making a strategic business choice, or simply implementing a change to the weekly team meeting. Use the SPOT-lighting model to connect the decision to your team's values. Then share this information explicitly with your team in an email, a video, or a meeting.

Situation

Outline the situation you're facing. What's the context of this decision? Who are the parties that will be affected? What's at stake? Who else has been involved in the decision-making process?

For Andre, the opportunity arose to acquire an analytics company that A–B had already partnered with. A–B was doing a great deal of campaigning work for its clients and needed the data to deliver at a high level. The chance to bring those capabilities in-house would allow A–B to leverage market insights to develop more targeted campaigns.

Priorities

Be clear about how you've prioritized the factors that have gone into this decision. Which values are guiding you? What makes the decision more difficult? What might have gotten in the way of living all of the organization's values?

In the real world, values sometimes compete with each other. For example, your organization may have values of "Employees First" and "Customer Excellence." In a situation where you are under pressure to deliver something to your client quickly, you may have to prioritize staying late to get the work done at the expense of employee well-being. Or, you might decide that employees really do come first and push back on the client for more time to deliver an excellent result while protecting employee well-being. Either way, it's important to make it clear how and why you prioritized one value over another.

A–B values bold moves. While a sustainable long-term operation is critical to success, employees at A–B are encouraged to take big swings when they see an opportunity for impact. Although it was a financial risk to acquire the business and figure out how to integrate the new capabilities—something A–B hadn't done before—it was a bold move. When Andre announced the decision to the team, he focused on the ways that this move could level up the business and build more value for its clients. He made it clear that it was the A–B thing to do.

Outcomes

When you share the decision with the team, tell them what you expect to accomplish. How will you measure and report back on the results? What's your vision for where this decision will take you?

Andre believes that this acquisition will take the company to a new level. The added capabilities will allow them to work with a broader range of clients and provide more value to their existing ones. It also means the current employees will have exposure to new practices and have the opportunity to learn new skills. A year from now, this decision should bring the team closer to delivering on its mission.

Talkback

After a theater performance, directors and actors sometimes stay to take questions from the audience, a tradition known as a talkback. After spotlighting a decision, end by giving the team an opportunity to ask questions and share feedback. They will likely have ideas and concerns that you haven't anticipated. Creating the space for discussion gives them ownership of the decision and ensures that you can communicate alignment more fully.

After sharing the decision to acquire the analytics company, Andre set up a town hall so that employees could ask questions and share feedback. Through this process, he learned that some of the designers were concerned that their creative ideas would be stifled by a new data-dominant process. Andre was able to assuage concerns that might have gone unvoiced and further clarify his vision in a way that rallied his team to the cause.

Spotlighting is a powerful way to communicate alignment when everyone isn't in the same room. It is an investment that pays long-term dividends, but it takes considerable time and energy to do. It would be impossible for a leader to spotlight every decision every day—and exhausting to try. To be clear, we're not advocating for this. We do, however, encourage leaders to make spotlighting a regular practice. Modeling is a critical part of building alignment. In a remote or hybrid environment, leaders have to work harder to do it well. And while digital distance has made modeling more difficult, the expectation for leaders to do it has never been higher.

Leaders are more accountable to their teams than ever before. Seasoned workers have come to expect more transparency from their employers, and newer generations outright demand it. A recent survey revealed that 40 percent of Gen Z respondents had refused to do a task because it wasn't clear to them how it aligned with their organization's values. While that may seem audacious, this cohort is willing to put their money where their mouth is. More than a third of Gen Z workers reported turning down a job because they didn't believe the company leaders walked their talk.

Andre has noticed a significant shift in expectations at A–B, where a large percentage of the team are Gen Z. But despite trends of high turnover within this age group, A–B has a higher retention rate among Gen Z employees than any other cohort. In this respect, Andre's modeling efforts have paid off. He acknowledges that meeting the expectations of Gen Z employees involves a mindset shift for many leaders. He feels that "younger people are skeptical of leadership. They've seen that a lot of leaders are full of shit, and they want to work for people who are not. They have a higher expectation for alignment than we did in the past. Some of my colleagues struggle with this. It really shocks them that they have to be so communicative, that they have to be transparent, that they have to be accountable to junior employees."

For Gen Z employees that work at A–B, this accountability drives their commitment to the organization. Kahlil Shepard is one of those who came to the organization largely because of its values. For him, working at A–B is about more than a paycheck. "My generation is looking for candidness. Why are leaders making this decision? Why do they believe that it is important? How do they go beyond just an email to the staff to have a dialogue with us about it?" Kahlil was part of several conversations with Andre about the acquisition, which helped him understand why it mattered in that moment, how it aligned with A–B's values, and how it connected to his personal goals. Andre's spotlighting efforts highlight for Kahlil the reasons he chose to work at A–B and are why he continues to be highly engaged.

We remember some similar experiences resonating with us earlier in our own careers. When Wes first started working for the social-impact agency Purpose, the company was a young start-up with less than twenty people. Jeremy Heimans, the cofounder and CEO, strongly valued transparency and lived that value boldly. Each month, Jeremy would hold a full company meeting and review the financials of the organization—good or bad. As an early stage company, revenue was not always consistent, and the possibility of failure always loomed close. Jeremy didn't put on a brave face and talk things up to try to keep morale high—something Wes experienced at other companies. Instead, Jeremy made the company books, as well as the reasoning behind his financial decisions, public for everyone in the organization to see.

Wes had come from organizations that were compartmentalized and only shared that kind of information with people who needed to know. He had never had his boss get up in front of the team to explain his decisions or share the struggle happening behind the scenes. Jeremy believed that, to work as an amazing team, it was important that everyone have an unobstructed view of the company. He stuck to this belief even when the view wasn't pretty and when he couldn't be confident that his decisions would pay off. Because Jeremy walked the talk, he earned the trust and dedication of his team. Wes also knew, because

Jeremy modeled it, that he could be transparent about his own performance, even if he had stumbled.

That alignment helped build a tightly knit community driven to tackle some of the world's biggest problems. Purpose, now a part of Capgemini Group, has grown exponentially since then. The company has played a significant role in fighting the climate crisis, advancing equality for LGBTQ people, and securing better opportunities for women and girls around the world, among many other issues. The sailing wasn't always smooth, but the confidence that Jeremy built by modeling transparency allowed him to navigate rough waters by keeping the team aligned.

Whether you are a CEO of a large organization or the manager of a single person, team members of every generation will watch your behavior closely. Consistently demonstrating alignment is critical to fostering meaning. As you may recognize from your own experience, alignment matters most in situations where it's also the most difficult to maintain—in moments of crisis.

ALIGNMENT IN CRISIS

Like many other organizations during the financial crisis of 2008, Barry-Wehmiller's business took a major hit. The company, a provider of manufacturing technology, saw equipment orders drop by more than 35 percent. It was clear that drastic measures would be needed to survive. The company's CEO, Bob Chapman, reluctantly began exploring layoffs to compensate for the dramatic reduction in revenue.

Barry-Wehmiller was originally founded in 1885 and was no stranger to weathering crisis. This time, however, things were different. Beginning in 2002, Bob and his leadership team had made an intentional decision to focus the organization on a new set of values— what they called the "Guiding Principles of Leadership." By the time they faced the financial crisis, they had spent years building alignment around the idea that the company "measures success by the way we touch the lives of people." Those people included the company's employees, most of whom had been there for many years.

Bob felt this was truly a moment that walking the talk mattered. Instead of making cuts to the staff, he leaned into the organization's values and asked the question, "What would a caring family do when faced with a crisis?"

Bob and his leadership team worked to figure out a way to avoid letting go of valued team members and putting those people in difficult financial positions themselves. Instead of some of the team experiencing a devastating job loss, they decided that it would be most aligned with their values to have everyone share the burden. Bob started by taking a pay cut himself—from $875,000 to $10,500. He put bonuses and 401(k) matches on hold. The leadership asked all its associates to take an unpaid four-week furlough to distribute the impact equally. Many associates voluntarily took double furloughs so that others who had the most need didn't have to take one. Those nearing retirement were given an opportunity to take a generous package to leave early.

Through these and other initiatives, Bob saved enough money to keep from having to let team members go. Perhaps more importantly, he demonstrated his commitment to the values that he had championed so strongly during better times. Employees learned that the Guiding Principles of Leadership were more than words on the wall. Bob's efforts built trust and confidence that Barry-Wehmiller was a community of values and that they would stick together through thick and thin.

The company successfully navigated the crisis and managed to quickly turn things around. The year 2010 was a record financial year for the organization. Bob's team invested those profits in repaying the 401(k) matches that had been suspended, further demonstrating his investment in the team. Of the Guiding Principles, Bob said, "It has become our moral compass. Since its adoption, our Guiding Principles have steered us to make sweeping changes in how we approach safety and layoffs (especially during the economic downturn of 2008–2009) as well as a multitude of decisions—big and small—every single day."

ALIGNMENT

When your values and your behavior are aligned, they are meaningful signposts for the road ahead. On the other hand, if you don't walk your talk, employees see organizational values as just empty words on the wall. Trust erodes and cynicism takes root. Meaning is quickly destroyed. This is true even in organizations that we would assume are inherently meaningful places to work, such as hospitals, schools, or nonprofits.

THE COSTS OF MISALIGNMENT

In late November of 1960, English lawyer Peter Benenson was reading the day's paper while riding the London Underground to work. He was outraged to find that a couple of students in Portugal had been sentenced to prison for publicly toasting to freedom—something the authoritarian government of the time didn't appreciate. Benenson's rage grew as he investigated other cases of people jailed for their political beliefs. He wrote an article for the *Observer* in 1961 highlighting a number of these individuals, whom he dubbed "Prisoners of Conscience," and the human rights violations perpetrated upon them. The article became the basis for a campaign to release those prisoners under the banner of an "Appeal for Amnesty." The campaign resonated, and his article was reprinted in media around the world, spawning a global movement. Benenson and his colleagues saw they had struck a chord and moved to formalize their efforts to fight against human rights abuses by creating the organization Amnesty International.

Since then, Amnesty's purview has expanded to protect against a wide range of human rights abuses, including ending torture; protecting the rights of women, children, minorities, and Indigenous peoples; safeguarding the rights of refugees; and ending the death penalty. For its efforts, Amnesty was awarded the Nobel Peace Prize in 1977. Amnesty lobbied for the establishment of the United Nations High Commission on Human Rights as well as the International Criminal Court. It is credited with helping to bring human rights issues into the popular zeitgeist. As an organization founded on principles of human rights with a grand purpose of fighting against discrimination and abuse, you might expect Amnesty to be a group of eager idealists and a bastion of alignment. You'd be very wrong.

In early 2019, an independently commissioned investigation into Amnesty International was launched following the suicide of two employees. The extensive report labeled the organization's culture toxic and found that harassment and bullying of employees by management was commonplace. More than a third of the hundreds of employees surveyed felt bullied or badly treated, and according to reporting by the BBC, there were "multiple accounts of discrimination on the basis of race and gender, and in which women, staff of color, and LGBT employees were allegedly targeted or treated unfairly." More than 60 percent of the staff didn't believe that their well-being was a priority for the organization's leadership. Amnesty International, one of the most well-known and longest-standing organizations working to advance human rights and dignity around the world, had leaders who were doing just the opposite within its own walls. The scathing report found many contributors to the toxic culture, which by many accounts had started to become a problem as early as the 1990s. The organization's values of universal human rights and mutual respect were not reflected in the actions of Amnesty's leaders.

This misalignment wreaked havoc at the organization and destroyed the meaning that should have come from working at a mission-driven organization. Employees signed up to work at an organization that promoted dignity for all, but their leaders weren't walking the talk.

Since the report came out, Amnesty has made a number of changes to try to realign its internal culture around its core values. As of this writing, it seems that progress has been made, but the road will be long and regaining confidence will be slow. In the face of a major misalignment that erodes trust and stifles meaning, it can be difficult to fully recover. The most important reason to walk your talk is that, when you don't, nothing else matters.

ALIGNMENT

There is also a second way that leaders demonstrate alignment with values. In addition to keeping their own behavior aligned, leaders must also align the policies, procedures, and processes of the organization around its values.

VALUES-DRIVEN SYSTEMS

We've already seen how Astro Teller walks his talk at X. His commitment to alignment shows in his behavior, and it also shows in the way he has designed the company's incentives. X's value of intellectual honesty is built into the business through his policy of rewarding failure. Just as leaders must communicate alignment by modeling values, they must also reinforce alignment by designing values into day-to-day operations. A misalignment between values and behavior can be detrimental. The same is true of a misalignment between values and policy.

When we take on a new consulting client, one of the first things we do is audit the company's policies for alignment. When we think of company policy, we often think of rules that are meant to ensure compliance with laws, to promote consistent processes across a large group, and to police individual behaviors. In addition to creating guardrails for operations, however, policy also serves to codify an organization's values. The formal rules guide us toward behaviors that are rewarded and away from those that are punished.

Policies and practices that are misaligned with values quickly erode trust. They send the message that values aren't a priority and destroy meaning on the job. Claudia Saran, former vice chair of culture at the accounting firm KPMG, shared what can happen when an individual's key performance indicators (KPIs) aren't clearly aligned with the organization's values: "People in a staffing role are measured on the efficiency and the expediency with which they staff people. In one of these roles, I could just callously and coldly bark out orders and assign people to different projects, and I would look good from a KPI standpoint because I've staffed X number of people a day and gotten them all billable. But my week is a week of carnage because those people feel that they had no say and don't feel good about their assignments. They don't feel informed or involved in any way and I've failed to live up to KPMG's value of working together." The senior team at KPMG works hard to avoid these types of policy misalignments.

Incentives expert Uri Gneezy has explored the unintended consequences that policies can have on alignment. One of his studies looks at the surprising impact of a program intended to reduce lateness. A school in Tel Aviv was struggling with parents showing up late to pick up their kids. The parents' lateness meant teachers also had to stay late, which was not popular with the teachers. It also conflicted with a core value the school was trying to teach—respect for others' time. In an effort to curb the behavior, the school instituted a two-dollar fine each time a parent was late to pick up their kids. Administrators believed that the largely symbolic fine would communicate that lateness was not acceptable without causing parents to get upset. Unfortunately, the policy had the opposite effect they had intended.

Instead of reducing lateness, the minor fine actually increased it. By assigning a dollar value to the behavior, lateness became a financial transaction instead of a values-based decision. Busy parents realized that by being late, they were essentially paying two dollars for a half hour of babysitting—a great deal! Even after the school eliminated the fines, the damage had been done. Respect for others' time had been devalued, and lateness continued to be an issue. The sense of alignment had eroded and couldn't be easily rebuilt.

Misalignments are especially destructive to meaning when they exist in performance reviews, financial rewards, and formal recognition programs. These policies, which focus on incentivizing specific behaviors, are usually designed to increase revenue in the short term. Leaders often develop them without fully considering the broader impacts they might have on the team. Incentives often reward certain outcomes, such as staff utilization, at the expense of behaviors and outcomes that have no financial value assigned to them. Measures of collaboration, risk-taking, and care for coworkers are rarely included in bonus calculations. These poorly designed financial incentives can decrease meaning at work.

At Barking Hound Village, the dog daycare business we discussed earlier, one of the core values is "It takes a village." This value captures the idea that all roles are required to properly take care of the dogs in the daycare's charge, and that the team is at its best when everyone works together. When we first started working with Barking Hound Village, store managers received a bonus based on their store's profitability. The intention was to incentivize managers to be more efficient and share in the financial upside of the business. However, the design of the bonus also had the unintended effect of making it personally costly to managers when the store was fully staffed. By understaffing their store—having eight people work a shift instead of ten, for example—managers could reduce costs and increase profitability, thereby putting more money in their own pockets. People who worked these shifts weren't able to give the dogs the care they needed and felt unsupported as a result. The bonus actually encouraged behavior that was misaligned with values and detrimental to the business long term. We redesigned the bonus to include measures of employee and customer satisfaction, which helped clear a roadblock to alignment.

Like the bonus at Barking Hound Village or the fine for lateness at the Tel Aviv school, misaligned incentives can unintentionally lead to meaning-destroying transactions. To avoid this, it is critical to carefully align values and policy. Meaning-driven leaders design pay, perks, and processes to maintain alignment with values.

At Kenneth Cole, leaders have made changes to their time-off policies to better support their value of mental health. In addition to giving people mental health days to take as needed, they created a Wellness Week. During this week, everyone is off from work at the same time. "When it's a mandated, company-wide week off, nobody gets called about work. I don't have to feel guilty about not checking my emails, and I can take a real break to recharge," shared Ingrid. As the benefits of collective time off become clearer, this is becoming common practice at a number of organizations.

Some organizations, like Zappos, the online shoe retailer, and BetterUp, a provider of executive coaching services, incorporate values into their performance reviews to demonstrate their focus on alignment. Others proactively provide specific training on values during the employee onboarding process. More on these practices later in the book.

Policies, just like the small, day-to-day behaviors of leaders, are opportunities to communicate alignment. These policies don't just communicate the rules; they also reveal the true priorities of the organization.

Like living organisms, organizations thrive by adapting to a changing environment. As organizations grow in size and scope, their operations must evolve to keep pace. What worked for a company of one hundred will not be sufficient to support a company of one thousand or ten thousand. In addition to updating their structures as they scale, organizations must also revisit their values. To maintain alignment over time, meaning-driven leaders create the space for iteration and individual expression of core values.

ALIGNMENT AND ACCOUNTABILITY

Earlier, we saw how leaders at Pinterest engaged the whole organization in an intentional process of redefining values. This culture of collective ownership is a critical part of maintaining alignment in the long term. Our research found that broad engagement in the process of alignment sends the message that everyone is committed to core values and working toward common goals. Experiences of meaningful work are increased when there is a sense of shared ownership and responsibility.

HubSpot's Katie Burke, whom you met in Chapter 2, thinks about cultural alignment as a family recipe that is passed down from generation to generation. She wants her team to keep the core elements of it, but if someone discovers a better way of doing things or a way to spice it up that makes it better, she believes they should make a change. As the company has expanded, Katie has had to give up the idea that every team would operate according to top-down cultural guidelines.

When HubSpot opened a new office in Dublin, Ireland, the company felt a responsibility to protect the culture it had worked so hard to build in Cambridge, Massachusetts. It quickly became clear, however, that differences were an inevitable and even valuable part of growth. The Dublin office showed that making the culture the same should never be the goal—instead the company framed international offices as *adding* to their culture and adopted this mindset for additional office openings in new markets. This idea of collective ownership of culture isn't unique to HubSpot.

Deep Mahajan, vice president of Talent Management at Juniper Networks, calls this sort of values evolution the "software of alignment." While company policies make up the "hardware," the "software" is found in meeting rooms, emails, and Teams channels. Leaders at Juniper encourage employees to openly discuss the company's values and agree on how they should be prioritized and enacted in specific situations. They are given the space to live those values in the way that feels most authentic to them. In Deep's view, the more people are empowered, the more they are engaged.

Whether you call it software, a family recipe, or something else, this shared ownership of values is linked to an increased sense of meaning. An active conversation around values builds employees' investment in the organization and their own commitment to the organization's goals.

Regardless of which values your organization prioritizes, alignment with those values lays the necessary foundation for meaningful work. Our research found that high alignment is a prerequisite for building meaningful work, while low alignment quickly erodes it. Alignment is a necessary, but not sufficient, component of meaning at work and must exist for the rest of the practices we'll share to be effective.

Leaders can build on the foundation of alignment to create meaning through each of the Three C's—community, contribution, and challenge. We now invite you to take the Meaning-Driven Leadership

Self-Assessment. You can access it on our website at www.makework meaningful.com or in the Appendix. The assessment, which we developed through our research, will evaluate your current use of the leadership practices and organizational structures that foster each of the Three C's. In the next section, we'll explore community, contribution, and challenge in more detail and show you how to build them more effectively in your own organization.

PART II

CREATING MEANING THROUGH COMMUNITY

The Harvard Study of Adult Development is the longest-running study on human well-being ever conducted. Since 1938, researchers have followed the lives of more than seven hundred participants and their spouses and, eventually, fifteen hundred of their children to find out what factors most impact a person's physical and mental health. Every two years, participants have answered detailed surveys about every aspect of their lives. Questions cover physical and mental fitness, social engagement, career, and most other aspects of life. The research team, which has evolved over the years as the original scientists retired and handed the reins to the next generation, has collected the richest set of data ever on the factors that contribute to well-being and success. This treasure trove of information has revealed the most critical component of human thriving—community.

Humans are social animals. We developed over millennia to survive and thrive as members of a group. It should be no surprise, then, that one of the main sources of meaning in life and at work comes from the quality of our relationships with others. The Harvard study found that authentic relationships with others don't just predict health and happiness. They also predict job satisfaction, professional achievement, and financial success. Participants who had deeper relationships experienced more meaningful work and lived more meaningful lives.

Unfortunately, traditional sources of community have steadily eroded over the past several decades. In his book *Bowling Alone*, sociologist Robert Putnam traces the decline of social and civic organizations in the United States. Memberships in Rotary Clubs, Boy and Girl Scouts, and local bowling leagues have fallen consistently since the 1980s. In their place, we have turned increasingly to our workplaces to find connection with others. This increase in demand for community at work comes at a time when we are physically more separate than ever. The pandemic taught us that productivity can be maintained, and even increased, when we work remotely. Without intentional effort, however, our sense of connection to our colleagues can quickly fade. We need the guidance and facilitation of leaders to ensure that our day-to-day interactions don't become mere transactions.

The first of the Three C's, community, comes from our sense that we belong to a group with shared values and that members of our group value us for who we really are. Leaders foster community by cultivating connection, facilitating authentic engagement, prioritizing values in the hiring process, and building belonging during the onboarding process.

First, we'll explore how leaders enrich the soil of community by cultivating connections across their organizations.

4

CULTIVATE CONNECTION

Success is not just about how creative or smart or driven you are, but how well you are able to connect with, contribute to, and benefit from the ecosystem of people around you.

—SHAWN ACHOR

Suzanne Simard grew up in the lush rainforests of British Columbia, where her family's roots were deeply embedded in the world of logging. Generations of her family, including her great-grandfather, grandfather, and father, were dedicated horse loggers. They crafted their own tools and boats to transport logs across the lakes and built houseboats to serve as their homes during their logging expeditions.

When Suzanne was just six years old, the entire family was jolted awake by the sound of howling echoing from the dense forest nearby.

They soon discovered that their spirited beagle, Jigs, had fallen into the outhouse pit. The family swiftly rallied to the scene wielding shovels and pickaxes to free the trapped canine. As she watched the men start to dig through the dirt beside the pit to rescue Jigs, Suzanne was captivated. She watched as they unearthed layers of soil, each with distinct colors, textures, and signs of life. First a thick layer of moss, followed by a white layer, a red layer, a yellow layer, and an intricate white and brown root system emerged from the ground. The experience left Suzanne mesmerized by the masterpiece that was the soil beneath their feet. After much digging, the family managed to extract Jigs from the ground. He was promptly treated to a cleansing dip in the lake, and while Jigs's ordeal was over, Suzanne's fascination with the intricate world of soil and the hidden wonders of the forest floor was just beginning.

At the age of twenty, Suzanne started working for a clear-cutting logging company, as one of the first women to secure a summer job in the forest industry. Her job involved planting trees in areas that had been recently clear-cut, aiming to restore the forest. While doing this work, Suzanne noticed a significant difference between the trees she planted and those that grew naturally from fallen seeds. The planted trees often struggled with yellowing leaves and poor growth while the naturally growing ones thrived. Curious about this difference, she began investigating the root systems of these trees. What she discovered was a revelation—the naturally regenerated trees had extensive root networks, while the planted ones were bare.

Suzanne's curiosity led her to graduate school to study how trees compete for water and nutrients. Commercial loggers believed that replacing diverse forests with a single type of tree would help the newly planted trees thrive, since they would not have to compete with other species for food and nutrients. However, these new plantings were increasingly susceptible to disease and stress. Suzanne believed the reason was hidden in the soil. Interested in how different species interact underground, Suzanne decided to investigate root and fungal links between the Douglas fir and paper birch species for her doctoral thesis.

In her groundbreaking work, Suzanne discovered that fungal threads, called mycorrhizal networks, serve as vital conduits, enabling the exchange of carbon, water, nutrients, alarm signals, and hormones among trees, even those of different species. Through meticulous experimentation and analysis, Suzanne demonstrated that the mycorrhizal networks play a pivotal role in supporting the growth and resilience of forests. Prior to her study, research had established that the mycorrhizal fungi could link trees together. However, Suzanne was the first to show that carbon was moving back and forth through these networks. Her paper was published on the cover of the influential scientific journal *Nature* in 1997, with the title "The Wood-Wide Web," a term that soon spread through the pages of science writing.

Popular culture readily embraced Suzanne's discovery. The Tree of Souls in James Cameron's movie *Avatar* is based on her research, and she was the inspiration for the character Patricia Westford in Richard Powers's 2019 Pulitzer Prize–winning novel *The Overstory*. She is now a professor of forest ecology at the University of British Columbia and in 2021 published a memoir, *Finding the Mother Tree*, which describes her enduring mission to prove that "the forest is more than just a collection of trees." Reflecting on why popular culture latched on to this idea, Suzanne told PBS, "We are social creatures; we understand how relationships work. We are affected by our community [and] we affect our community. That a forest would have those qualities as well really resonates with us. That [a forest] is more than just a bunch of trees… that it's a whole social community. We get that as people."

SUPERORGANIZATIONS

Suzanne's research demonstrated that, in healthy forests, trees operate less like individuals competing for resources and more like communal beings, sharing resources to increase their collective resilience. These forests are so interconnected and codependent that scientists have referred to them as superorganisms. Like these healthy forests, high-performing "superorganizations" also leverage the power of connection and cooperation to thrive. In these superorganizations, positive relationships are the connective tissue that strengthens collaboration, fosters innovation, and weaves a vibrant network of mutual support.

By intentionally building community, leaders in superorganizations create connected teams that trust, respect, and care for each other. In short, they build belonging. We experience belonging at work when we feel connected and included rather than isolated and ignored. This leads to powerful benefits for individuals and organizations. In the book *Belonging*, Stanford professor Geoffrey Cohen describes how experiences of belonging can raise our sense of well-being, improve our performance, lessen our defensiveness, and make us more compassionate. He states, "a sense of belonging is not a byproduct of success, but a condition for it."

We found that leaders can intentionally foster belonging at work in two ways: by cultivating connections and enabling authenticity. This chapter will focus on cultivating connections, and in the next chapter, we will learn how leaders enable authenticity.

We crave connection at work. Seventy percent of workers say friendship at work is the most important element to a happy work life, and 58 percent say they would turn down a higher-paying job if it meant not getting along with coworkers. Research shows that for each friend you make at work, you are 5 percent less likely to quit. In contrast, those who don't have a friend at work are 176 percent more likely to be looking for a new job.

Unfortunately, many of us are like the planted trees in the new-growth forests Suzanne studied—disconnected and languishing. More than half of today's workforce is experiencing the opposite of belonging—a deep sense of loneliness. One recent study found that more than half of US workers don't look forward to working because of their coworkers, while 43 percent don't feel any sense of connection inside their organizations.

Loneliness is the gap we experience between the social interactions we have and the ones we wish for. We can be surrounded by people at work and still feel alone. Maybe you have felt like there was no one you could talk to when you ran into a problem. Or perhaps you find yourself eating lunch alone at your desk every single day. This feeling of loneliness can have dangerous consequences for our lives.

In a landmark study, Brigham Young University researcher Julianne Holt-Lunstad and her colleagues found that loneliness increases the risk for early mortality by the same rate as smoking fifteen cigarettes a day. Loneliness increases blood pressure and cholesterol, activates physical and psychological stress responses, and suppresses the immune system. This makes sense from an evolutionary perspective. Thousands of years ago, if we suddenly found ourselves alone in the savannah, our chances of being able to survive greatly diminished. Not only were we less likely to defend ourselves from an attack, but we also had less access to necessary resources. Collaboration with others increased our ability to survive. Even though we no longer face the same threats to our survival, we continue to hunger for social connection.

Loneliness affects not only our health but also how we perform in the workplace. More than one in three working adults feel a general sense of emptiness or disconnection from others at work. The situation is even more grim for remote workers, who are less likely to report feeling that their relationships with others are meaningful. A study by the Wharton School found that the lonelier people are at work, the worse they perform. Even a single incident where someone feels excluded can lead to an instant decline in their performance.

The cost of loneliness is significant for organizations, including lower productivity, lower quality of work, and higher turnover. Researchers asked nearly six thousand American workers to complete a survey to measure loneliness and its impact on work, and they discovered that lonely workers are more likely to miss work due to stress. In the United States alone, missed workdays attributed to loneliness cost organizations an estimated $154 billion annually.

It doesn't have to be this way.

THE POWER OF CONNECTION

Supportive relationships at work are a source of growth, well-being, and meaning. Leaders who facilitate frequent positive interactions with others, strengthen the connective tissue of their superorganizations. Over time, this social connective tissue becomes a conduit—like the mycorrhizal network—enabling greater collaboration, innovation, and adaptability.

The level of connection individuals experience at work significantly drives performance. That is because relationships with others shape the context of a job. Highly connected employees are 92 percent more likely to grow professionally and 34 percent more likely to reach goals. When researchers ask the question, "Do you have a best friend at work?" they find that those who answer yes are seven times more likely to be engaged.

Work relationships don't have to be intense to be valuable. Jane Dutton, a positive organizational psychologist at the University of Michigan, found that brief moments of positive connection in the workplace can have a considerable positive effect on our experience at work. Along with her colleague Emily Heaphy, Jane coined the phrase "high-quality connections" to describe moments of positive connection that make us feel seen and energized. That brief exchange you have with a colleague about your plans for the weekend? It matters more than you think. Jane has found that these micromoments of connection—as little as forty seconds—can enhance the capacity for cooperation and coordination across teams. They can increase resilience and authenticity, strengthen an individual's attachment to their organization, support ongoing learning and development, and facilitate a shared sense of purpose.

Because most adults spend about one-third of their time at work, much of it interacting with others, their highest-quality connections are often with colleagues. Research has determined the number of work friends you need to not feel lonely at work—one. All we need is a single individual whom we feel connected to and can share positive experiences with. That's all it takes.

Meaning-driven leaders are intentional about cultivating connection to increase feelings of belonging. We've found two powerful ways in which leaders can increase the quality of connections at work: **building trust** and **designing shared experiences.**

Building Trust

Erica Elam grew up in Nashville, Tennessee, as the oldest of four children. A self-proclaimed control freak, Erica was a straight-A student, top of her class, and president of numerous clubs. "I really had the oldest daughter syndrome, where I was trying to be perfect all the time," she reflects. During her senior year, at a friend's birthday party, Erica was invited to play an improv game. She was scared, nervous, shy, and, as she describes herself, "very awkward and nerdy." But she decided to give it a shot. That moment was transformative for Erica. She got to be a different kind of person in that game. One who wasn't scared, who could go with the flow, think quickly, and be playful. It was a surprising experience for her and planted a seed that would bloom later in her life.

After high school, Erica moved to Georgia to attend college as an English major. She wanted to be a writer but quickly realized that she didn't like the solitude of writing. She craved being with a group of people, collaborating and creating together. She wasn't planning on studying theater, but when she found the drama department, she loved it. After graduation, Erica moved to Chicago and started working as a casting intern for the Goodman Theatre. One fateful night, Erica and her friends attended a show at The Second City, the renowned and influential improv comedy theater. Erica was stunned—she didn't know that anything like that existed.

After that night, Erica started taking improv classes, which would transform her. Improv became a kind of "life gym" for Erica, a place where she could practice trusting herself and others. She realized that she was really good at thinking on her feet and that she could pivot, trust other people, listen, and react appropriately.

Erica is now on the faculty at The Second City and teaches improv techniques at many top business schools, including Princeton, Dartmouth, and Stanford. She also facilitates corporate trainings for organizations such as Google, Facebook, Budweiser, and Hershey's to build trust and improve communication and creativity. She believes that trust is the foundation for a successful improv experience because in improv, no one knows exactly what's coming next. Everyone risks not knowing together, and to navigate that successfully, everyone must trust the people that they are taking that risk with.

A core tenet of improv is the "yes, and" philosophy, which encourages performers to accept and build on each other's ideas. This philosophy is about listening and adding value. The *yes* is about awareness, acceptance, and being in the moment. The *and* is about making a contribution so you can build something together. Improvisors have to be brave and vulnerable to contribute, and they can't do that without trusting that they will be well received and supported.

Just as trust is crucial for a successful improv performance, it is also the foundation for effective communication and collaboration at work, where we constantly navigate uncertainty and change. Imagine you and a colleague are working together on a project with a tight deadline. In a trusting relationship, you freely share insights, collaborate seamlessly, and succeed together. If trust is absent, however, you might hold back your knowledge, worried that your colleague might somehow use it against you or, worse, take credit for your ideas.

In a recent study exploring the experiences of eighteen million workers around the world, researchers found that the biggest differentiator of great places to work was the presence of trust. In high-trust organizations, 90 percent of employees report having a meaningful work experience. A different study found that in high-trust organizations, employees are 260 percent more motivated to work and are 50 percent less likely to look for another job. Only when trust exists can true collaboration and community thrive. So how can you build trust?

Roger Mayer, professor of leadership at North Carolina State University, identified three components of trust: integrity, competence, and benevolence. Think of someone you trust. What is it about this person that makes you trust them? It is likely that they act with integrity, are competent in specific domains, and consistently demonstrate benevolence through their goodwill and actions. By understanding the different pieces that make up trust, we can more easily work on improving it.

The first element of trust is integrity. At its core, integrity is about doing the right thing. It is about being dependable, being fair in your interactions with others, and honoring your commitments. You can demonstrate integrity by ensuring that your actions align with your words. This component is particularly important for leaders, as we saw in Chapter 3 on alignment. When there is a misalignment, you can show integrity by being transparent about it and providing clear, honest explanations. You also demonstrate integrity by keeping your promises and meeting deadlines. As the saying goes, "Do what you say you will do, by when you say you will do it." When you keep your word and deliver on your commitments, people learn that they can trust you.

The second element of trust is competence, your ability to perform your job well. This includes your qualifications, skills, knowledge, and proficiency in executing tasks and achieving goals. Competence is domain specific, which means that someone can be highly skilled in one area, for example finance, while having little ability or training in another area like computer programming. Evidence of your competence, such as diplomas, awards, and word of mouth, builds early trust. Although much of competence comes from this early trust, it has to be maintained and reinforced over time. Consistently demonstrating competence establishes your credibility. You can do this by being prepared and delivering high-quality results in your work. You can also seek opportunities to learn and stay active in your field of expertise. And while it may sound counterintuitive, asking for help is a great way to demonstrate competence. Admitting what you don't know is a sign of a secure leader, which builds credibility over time. By asking for help instead of just telling people to do things, you can also harness the human drive to cooperate with others. Don't forget to acknowledge and express sincere appreciation for the help received. As you will learn later, this is critical to making work meaningful.

The final element of trust is benevolence. Benevolence at work is about showing genuine care and helping others succeed. When we are benevolent, people believe in our good intentions, and that we are dedicated to the success of the team. In improv, this is a critical part of building trust. Erica shared, "The great thing about improv is that team interest is self-interest. If someone goes down in flames, everybody fails together." This drives true motivation to support each other—making other people look good also makes you look good. One of the best ways to show benevolence at work is to offer help. Research shows that when we help someone succeed, the strength of our connection increases. Start by looking for opportunities to be helpful and show your team you care. Perhaps you read a recent article related to a project someone on your team is working on. You could send them the article with a nice note. You could also demonstrate benevolence by making yourself available, addressing concerns, being transparent, and hearing different perspectives. Additionally, you could find opportunities to mentor others and help them develop their skills and knowledge. Finally, you can show that you care by asking people what is going on in their lives outside work and remembering what they said in follow-up conversations. Connection before direction helps build trust. Benevolence creates a culture where supporting each other is second nature.

It is important to note that these components exist within a continuum. Trust is not all or nothing. It is possible for someone to be high in integrity and benevolence but low in competence, for example, and still be trustworthy. By understanding what makes up trust, you can more easily evaluate it and improve it.

In superorganizations, trust strengthens connection over time, just like the nutrients that feed the fungal threads in Suzanne's forests.

When leaders are intentional about building a high-trust organization, community flourishes.

Elevating Trust in Your Organization

Mark DiMassimo is the founder and creative chief of DiMassimo Goldstein (DiGo), a global marketing, design, and advertising agency headquartered in New York City. Growing up in New Jersey, Mark was steeped in a culture of invention. His grandparents lived on Thomas Edison's old property, and every time he visited, they would make a pilgrimage to where Edison invented the light bulb.

His family were all bitten by the innovation bug—his father created the speed dial feature for phones and his uncle George was an engineer who worked for Bell Labs and Ford. It was an environment where the stories of inventors and their achievements were in the air before Mark was even conscious of what he was absorbing. After college, Mark put his innovative nature to work at different advertising agencies in New York City, starting in account management, and then moving on to the creative department.

The desire to innovate persisted, and Mark knew he wanted to start his own agency, one with a different approach to branding. He didn't want to do it, however, until he loved working for another boss. Mark realized that to be a great leader, even a competent leader, he first had to be a good follower. Mark found that leader in Richard Kirshenbaum, cofounder of the agency Kirshenbaum Bond Senecal & Partners, where Mark was the creative director. "I liked having Richard as a boss. We saw eye to eye, and he really trusted me. I had a lot of autonomy. But I also really trusted him." Reflecting on the impact of Richard's leadership, Mark adds, "Richard taught me that trust is the bedrock of not just building stronger relationships but also producing better work."

In 1996, armed with $8,000 and a vision, Mark started his own advertising agency. His first client? His car service driver, Nikolay, who had recently started a chocolate company with his wife, Alexandra. It was a great opportunity to brand something from the beginning.

Mark always knew that trust would be at the center of his leadership approach. Clients were putting so much trust in this brand-new agency, and he really wanted to deserve that trust. Mark knew that to keep earning his clients' trust, he needed to first cultivate trust within his team. To build a culture of trust, Mark didn't just role-model the behaviors he learned from Richard, he elevated them. "Keeping my word wasn't just a priority; it was nonnegotiable. If I committed to something, you could bet that it would get done. And if things shifted, I would let you know."

Mark's commitment to trust went beyond personal integrity to creating a culture of reliability and shared responsibility. One of the ways the agency built a culture of trust was by hiring and cultivating what Mark calls "high-responsibility employees," people who do not need to be motivated by their supervisor. They may need help getting unstuck, or they may need help figuring out how to get some obstacles out of their way. But they take responsibility for their own level of inspiration, and they speak up when they need help.

This deliberate approach to trust building has contributed to DiGo's enduring success and ability to continually innovate and adapt. A few years ago, the agency adopted a "Work Freedom" policy to try out remote work. Four years into the new approach, Mark reflected, "Without a culture of trust, I don't think this transition would have worked. We not only trust each other, but we trust that everyone wants to do their best work, and we trust that we can ask for help when we need to."

The transition hasn't always been smooth. Mark shared that one employee, whom we will call John, was constantly adding unnecessary stress to the workflow as projects moved into his domain. Without the same level of oversight he had when they were together in the office, John was having a hard time trusting his colleagues. His constant micromanaging created bottlenecks for the rest of the team, who were becoming increasingly frustrated.

The culture of trust at DiGo, where team members are committed to each other's success, meant that John's teammates were empowered to give him candid feedback. Mark recounted an impactful conversation where a colleague addressed the issue directly, providing several specific examples when his micromanagement disrupted the workflow and created unnecessary stress. They continued, "You don't have to control every aspect of the project; you can trust us. We will speak up if we have questions or need help."

By providing candid feedback and offering support, team members showed John that they were invested in his growth and the team's collective success. This open communication fosters a sense of trust and mutual respect, ultimately strengthening their relationships and enabling them to work more effectively together. Although it was a difficult conversation, John not only accepted the feedback but embraced the opportunity for growth. He is now thriving at DiGo and contributing positively to the continued success of the team.

In their fully remote environment, Mark is vigilant about monitoring nonverbal cues and focusing on benevolence. "I will say, 'You seemed uncomfortable in that meeting. You seemed worried about that. I felt like maybe you didn't get your questions answered. I'm here for that now.'" Mark believes that now, more than ever, trust is about caring for people and helping everyone prioritize community and connection: "We have learned that nothing works unless everybody feels that creating, defending, and building connection is part of their job. Every single person needs to feel that." At DiGo, they do.

Trust at work—like in improv—is the oil that keeps the gears turning smoothly. It's essential for everything to run effectively. When people truly trust each other—when they have confidence in each other's integrity, competence, and benevolence—it strengthens their connection and boosts their performance as a team. Erica, the improv coach, shared, "In improv, the act of creating something together builds belonging in such a powerful way. We have to trust that we are all there to create the best scene that we can. We are all in it together." At work, we are building things together as a team every day. Every project, every collaboration, every interaction is an opportunity to build trust and lay the groundwork for stronger connections.

The second part of cultivating connections is **designing shared experiences.** Like trust, these shared experiences hold the potential to amplify collaboration and cohesion among your teams, strengthening a sense of community and increasing meaning.

Designing Shared Experiences

In the "Office Olympics" episode of the classic television series *The Office*, the employees of Dunder Mifflin's Scranton branch find themselves with some unexpected free time when a meeting gets canceled. Looking to alleviate their boredom, Jim and Pam decide to host their version of the Olympics right there in the office. With the help of the team, they invent a series of improvised games using office supplies and different parts of the office. Some of the memorable games include "Flonkerton," where employees race clumsily with reams of paper as makeshift skis, and "How Many M&Ms Can You Fit in Your Mouth?" The entire office gets involved, as they all embrace the opportunity to compete and have some fun together. "Office Olympics" is a fan-favorite episode that captures the essence of the show's unique blend of humor and heart.

While *The Office* isn't quite the work model we're advocating, there is something to be learned from this episode. What makes it special is how the games bring the characters together in a lighthearted and playful manner. They collaborate, compete, and cheer one another on, fostering a sense of camaraderie that goes beyond their usual work roles. Shared experiences, like the "Office Olympics," create a feeling of belonging, where everyone is part of something fun and meaningful. More than that, they create lasting memories that become part of the office culture, help break down barriers, and strengthen bonds.

Dedicating time to promote positive social interactions at work can be a powerful way to build belonging. Shared experiences provide the opportunity for teams to collaborate, have fun, and achieve together. Research finds that positive shared experiences are critical to forming and maintaining strong relationships. When we do things together, whether it's solving a challenging problem, celebrating a collective achievement, playing games, or simply enjoying each other's company, we create bonds that extend beyond the confines of our professional roles.

Not all shared experiences are created equally, however. We found that meaning-driven leaders intentionally create a range of experiences that foster authentic social interactions. From the traditional happy hour and Zoom coffees to volunteering together, to collectively tackling challenging business problems, each type of experience serves a distinct purpose. Whether it's fostering camaraderie during a relaxed chat or strengthening collaboration through problem-solving, the combination of these diverse experiences contributes to a more connected team.

A Portfolio Approach

Augusto Giacoman is a partner at Strategy&, a global strategy consulting business in the PwC network. A graduate of the United States Military Academy at West Point, Augusto spent almost six years in the army before going to business school then transitioning to a leadership role in consulting. In the military, leadership is a core capability. Everything is built around leadership—according to Augusto it's the coin of the realm in the army. When he got to consulting, however, Augusto found that many senior people simply weren't great leaders. They weren't great at setting a vision or building a connected team who was motivated to reach that vision.

This contrast prompted Augusto to start thinking about how to get everyone on his team to become more connected. He started thinking about the different types of team events he had been a part of at work. From team dinners to learning opportunities and even an improv workshop at The Second City, different experiences drove different levels of bonding.

The more Augusto thought about it, the more he realized that the improv workshop was more powerful than a happy hour because more difficulty was involved. Drawing from his army experience as well, he theorized that there's a relationship between purpose and difficulty that can really drive connection. The more difficult a shared experience is, the more purpose it has, the more it can help bring people together. His hypothesis is that when we do difficult things together, it builds up our collective emotional intelligence. You learn how people work and they learn how you work. You get through the forming and storming stages of team building faster and build stronger norming and performing. Of course, if you push the difficulty too far, it creates unnecessary stress, and it's not going to be effective. There is a difficulty threshold.

In addition to the improv workshop, a bike-building event stands out to Augusto as one of the most deeply meaningful and impactful bonding experiences he had at work. His team of five was given all the parts to a bike and told to assemble the bike together—with no instructions. At the end of the day, the bikes got donated to disadvantaged kids. Figuring out how to put together bikes with no instructions was pretty difficult, but they managed to work together to get it done. Then, they got the emotional reward of giving the bike away.

Augusto's purpose-difficulty framework can help you craft a comprehensive portfolio of shared experiences that span the continuum of purpose and difficulty. The goal is to have an approach that feels authentic to your organization and team. Much like a well-managed investment portfolio, diversity within your shared experiences is crucial. There is a need for both low-risk, low-return opportunities—casual connections that are easygoing in purpose and difficulty like happy hours and Zoom chats—and high-reward, strategic experiences such as Augusto's improv workshop. Consider the casual connections as the blue-chip stocks in your portfolio—reliable, easily accessible, and forming the foundation. On the other hand, the deeper, more challenging experiences act as the high-yield investments, offering substantial returns in terms of team cohesion and connection.

Let's take a closer look at some of the more unique shared experiences that leaders of superorganizations have designed to cultivate connection and build belonging.

LOWER-DIFFICULTY, LOWER-PURPOSE EXPERIENCES

On the lower end of the purpose-difficulty continuum are casual connections, a great opportunity for people who don't know each other well to become acquainted and form friendships. These activities are what most organizations are already doing to increase belonging. They include experiences such as sharing meals and happy hours. While they can be a great first step and important to the mix, these types of experiences are not enough to forge deep bonds. In addition, most are designed as add-ons to employees' already busy workdays. This can exclude entire populations, such as parents of young children who need to leave right after the workday is over, or those who don't drink alcohol.

One way to design more inclusive casual connections is to incorporate them into the workday. Successful shared experiences have to have an intentional design. Priya Parker, author of the book *The Art of Gathering*, suggests that one of the most common mistakes we make when we gather is lack of structure. Creating structure allows people to ease into the experience and make connections rather than having to fend for themselves. The key is to find the right balance between organized elements and spontaneous interactions to create a dynamic and engaging gathering. Here are some examples:

Synchronized Breaks

In a typical workday, most of us take breaks to recharge, refill our coffee, or chat with colleagues. To turn this existing practice into a more meaningful opportunity to connect, you can synchronize these daily breaks. MIT professor Alex Pentland and his team conducted a study of communication patterns at a call center of a large US bank. They were interested in looking at the impact of social connection on overall productivity levels and to test strategies to increase the strength of these connections. They studied employees from four teams of roughly twenty people each. Originally, each employee on a team had a separate fifteen-minute break during the day. The breaks were separate so call loads did not have to be shifted significantly to other teams. Unfortunately, this break structure made it difficult for cohesive relationships to develop, since people had limited opportunities for shared interactions.

To create more of these opportunities, the researchers changed the break structure of two of the four teams so that all the employees on a team were given a break at the same time. After giving this change three months to stabilize, they returned to the call center and measured the behavior of the employees again. The results were astonishing. Employees on synchronized breaks yielded the company $15 million in productivity gains, and employee satisfaction increased by up to 10 percent.

Synchronized breaks don't have to be lengthy to be meaningful. Even a short ten- to twenty-five-minute break can be sufficient to promote connection and camaraderie. The key is to create a dedicated time for breaks, allowing team members to step away from their desks, recharge, and connect on a more personal level.

In Sweden, where employees experience some of the lowest levels of stress globally, they have embraced synchronized breaks as a key to building community. *Fika*, a Swedish word that means "coffee break" or "to have coffee," is deeply ingrained in Swedish culture and is practiced in both workplaces and social settings. This cherished custom involves taking a break, usually involving coffee and a snack, to socialize and connect with others. While it originated in Sweden, the concept of fika has gained popularity in other parts of the world, with many organizations and individuals embracing it as a way to build stronger connections.

Quartz, the global news organization, decided to give fika a try for one week. The initiative, led by reporter Lila MacLellan, started with a team of six employees who committed to taking their breaks at the same time each day. On the first day, Lila reported that she sat alone in the breakroom with a book while a colleague who was working from home messaged to say that she was taking a break as well. Eventually, another member of the team wandered over. They started off talking about work, but once the awkwardness wore off, they moved on to more personal topics. The second fika day was more festive, with a plate of snacks and more colleagues in attendance. By the end of the week, they fell into a groove. The self-consciousness wore away, and they all felt they were just "fika-ing." She reported that "conversation flowed and we acquired real facts about each other. . . . Because of fika, we learned that one of our podmates was going to have surgery, and another was planning a relocation to Los Angeles."

Synchronized breaks can transform what might have been individual coffee breaks into shared moments of connection. As the Quartz team experienced, the initial moments may feel a bit awkward, but with time, it becomes a natural and valued part of the day. The key is consistency and creating a welcoming environment where team members feel encouraged to participate.

Home Base Teams

Much of today's workforce is distributed, and individuals are often rotated to different projects with different teams. These factors can make it hard for people to cultivate strong connections over time. Even for teams who work together regularly, it is often difficult to build relationships with others across the broader organization. A great solution is to create "home base" teams, particularly for those employees who crave deeper connections to their colleagues. Much like a home base in middle school or a homeroom in high school, these groups of people stay together over extended periods of time. They don't necessarily work on the same projects but come together—virtually or in person—to connect and support each other.

Dropbox, the cloud-based file storage and collaboration platform that has a virtual first model, created what it calls "Dropbox Neighborhoods," communities of people who are in close locations. These neighborhoods—the company's version of a home base—are run by a local community manager who groups people together on Slack to arrange everything from events to volunteer days and informal meetups. "Neighbors" are also encouraged to share fun updates and local resources like the best restaurants in town. The hope is that this creates a localized sense of belonging for all employees.

HIGHER-PURPOSE, HIGHER-DIFFICULTY EXPERIENCES

Experiences on the higher end of the purpose-difficulty continuum help teams deepen their connections through more substantial and challenging interactions. They can be instrumental in fostering lasting relationships and a sense of belonging among team members. Recall Augusto's improv workshop and bike-building event. These interactions go beyond casual acquaintanceship and require participants to collaborate, problem-solve, take risks, and support one another. These types of activities happen less frequently but are much more meaningful.

You can get creative by asking for input from your team on types of activities they would be interested in and having some fun with them. In our research, the most common experience on this end of the continuum was opportunities to volunteer together.

Volunteer Opportunities

Offering colleagues the opportunity to volunteer together can significantly strengthen their connection. Many studies have shown that volunteer programs increase engagement, productivity, and retention. Research has also shown that individuals who volunteer together often report higher levels of well-being. Martin Seligman, founder of positive psychology, told us that "doing a kindness for others produces the single most reliable increase in well-being of any exercise we've tested."

When positive emotions are simultaneously experienced by two or more individuals—what researchers call positivity resonance—it builds social bonds of trust and commitment over time. These shared positive emotions, such as the joy of attending a concert or the fulfillment from volunteering together, are associated with higher levels of mental health and lower levels of loneliness and depression. Incorporating volunteer opportunities into the workplace not only strengthens connections among colleagues but also contributes to individual well-being, fosters a sense of belonging, and increases meaning at work.

We have seen successful volunteer programs of all shapes and sizes. Some organizations, like Patagonia, give employees paid time off to volunteer for the cause they choose. Others, like Zappos, have an in-house charity group charged with creating opportunities for employees to volunteer together. While all corporate volunteer programs can help employees feel more engaged, more structured opportunities are better for cultivating connection through a meaningful shared experience.

Bombas, the apparel company best known for their high-quality socks and buy-one-donate-one model, has an internal Giving Team charged with creating different monthly opportunities for "Hive members" (as employees are known) to volunteer and connect. Bombas was founded with a mission to help those experiencing homelessness. Since socks are the most requested items in homeless shelters, they donate a pair for every pair they sell.

The Giving Team creates opportunities for Hive members to cook and serve special meals at a women's residence, cohost monthly birthday parties at local shelters, wrap holiday gifts, and host a monthly pizza night. Perhaps one of their most meaningful volunteer efforts was the "60k Day." In New York City, where Bombas is headquartered, there are sixty thousand people experiencing homelessness in any given night. The Giving Team recruited volunteers from across sixty different organizations—including KIND, LinkedIn, and PayPal—to donate sixty thousand pairs of socks to sixty shelters across the city in one night. The day was all about building community—with each other and with the city—and was a big success.

Whether through smaller and more frequent acts of service or more significant moments, volunteering together cultivates community and increases our sense of meaning at work.

We have plotted some shared experiences on the matrix on the following page to illustrate this portfolio approach. These include a combination of commonly used activities and some unique ones that superorganizations use. Our hope is that these examples inspire you to create your own shared experiences portfolio.

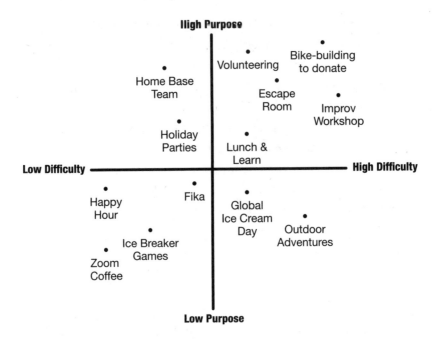

The examples we've discussed highlight how meaning-driven leaders use shared experiences to cultivate connections. These are not meant to be prescriptive, but rather to serve as inspiration as you develop your own portfolio. As organizations navigate the shift toward hybrid and remote environments, the need for cultivating connections has become more evident. It has also become more challenging. In the next example, we'll see how one team is navigating the challenge.

THE CONCIERGE OF CONNECTION

Like many companies, Reddit was forced into remote work during the pandemic. Although it was challenging, leaders at Reddit leaned into their value of continuous improvement to navigate the change. They used the shift to remote work as an opportunity to learn and soon realized that there were many advantages to running and growing the business without centralized offices. They also realized that maintaining a strong sense of community would be more challenging, so they doubled down on cultivating connection.

Reddit's mission is "to bring community, belonging, and empowerment to everyone in the world," and that includes "Snoos" (as employees of Reddit call themselves in a nod to the company's mascot). Reddit still has thirteen offices around the world. The offices are open to anyone anytime they'd like to come in, but no one is required to be there. However, in-person time is still important to the team.

To support Snoos in creating connection-driven experiences that people *want* to show up for, Reddit's senior director of experience, Michelle Lozzi, and her team launched Project Atelier. Project Atelier is Reddit's internal system to track and support in-person gatherings at every level, from a few team members to a full company retreat. Michelle's team acts as a concierge for any manager who is planning to get together with their team. In addition to making sure their team has everything they need to connect with one another when they visit the office, Michelle coordinates happy hours with other local employees, organizes meals with the larger office, and plans cultural activities.

Michelle also ensures that her team lives up to the company's value to "make something people love." Each office has a signature local treat that her team provides anytime people gather in that office. In San Francisco, for example, they have a local bakery that supplies pastries and croissants.

Michelle's team has also designed collectible mugs for each office that employees receive when they visit. "People display these collections behind them on Zoom, and they're really proud. It has been one of our most successful programs," she said. It has been so successful, in fact, that Michelle's team facilitated a five-hundred-person mug exchange where Snoos embraced their local communities and traded mugs from a favorite spot in their town.

To further support community-building gatherings, Michelle and her team also launched the Snoo Community Funds. Any Snoo can submit an application for a grant to bring team members together whether virtually or in person, Michelle's team has never turned down a request to support these employee-led events. "I can't figure out all the ways that we might bring people together or make them happy, so we give them the power to do what *they* want to do." She has helped Snoos in Australia plan kayaking excursions, facilitated a lipstick-making class in New York, and organized outings to see the Cubs play in Chicago.

Michelle and her team have noticed a significant increase in in-person gatherings. Last year, the number of Snoos who reported that they felt they have opportunities to build a meaningful community increased by 10 percent. For Michelle, that is a pretty big deal.

Our research leaves no room for doubt: fostering relationships across the organization is critical to making work meaningful. It is how superorganizations make every individual feel connected. Whether these bonds are nurtured during existing meetings, shared meals, volunteering together, or other shared experiences doesn't matter. What truly matters is that leaders prioritize building belonging to strengthen everyone's sense of community at work. As Jen Fisher, chief well-being officer at Deloitte, stated, "As leaders, we have a responsibility to help people understand that a meaningful career depends on meaningful relationships inside their organization."

OTHER PEOPLE MATTER

We'll repeat the words of Chris Peterson, one of the founders of positive psychology: "Other people matter. . . . Anything that builds relationships between and among people is going to make you happy." As leaders, it is critical that we recognize the pivotal role of positive relationships in making work meaningful.

In any organization or team, you will likely have exceptionally talented individuals. However, what prompts them to collaborate, contribute ideas, and be truly productive is their connection to one another.

The web of relationships that are cultivated through personal connections serves as the invisible threads that create meaning at work.

When leaders build trust and design shared experiences, they foster belonging. In order for these meaningful connections to not only survive but also thrive, it is crucial for leaders to also embrace authenticity. As we're about to see, cultivating connections only works if people can be themselves.

5

EMBRACE AUTHENTICITY

Authenticity is the daily practice of letting go of who we think we're supposed to be and embracing who we are.

—BRENÉ BROWN

On a brisk fall day in September, the two of us arrived in Philadelphia for the start of the Masters of Applied Positive Psychology (MAPP) program at the University of Pennsylvania. As we made our way to Houston Hall, we were feeling nervous and excited for the first day of what we expected to be a transformative experience. In preparation for the week, we had received a welcome packet including short bios of the forty-eight students in our class. Our classmates were a mix of people from around the world ranging in age from early twenties to early sixties with an impressive list of accomplishments. They included the former chief of staff to the managing director of the International Monetary Fund, a special agent with the FBI, and the general counsel for the global fashion house Chanel. The anticipation was palpable as we entered the room and started to meet our classmates.

We were both quietly wondering if we really belonged there. Tamara was a solo entrepreneur, mother of three children, and had immigrated from Brazil in her early twenties. Wes had mostly worked at start-ups and, as a gay man, was apprehensive about the process of coming out that has to happen in every meeting with new people. After a few minutes of mingling, during which we did our best to fit in, we took our seats and the program started. Tamara sat toward the front and Wes a few rows back. The two of us had yet to meet.

Forty-eight faces eagerly stared as Marty Seligman, known as the father of positive psychology, slowly walked to the front of the room with a warm smile on his face. He paused for several moments, looking intently at each of us. After what felt like an eternity, Marty broke the silence by uttering a powerful phrase three times with his deep, baritone voice: "You belong here. You belong here. You belong here." As we sat there nervously wondering exactly that—Did we belong?—hearing these words from a leader was profound. It felt as if Marty could read our minds.

Later, as we met and started to become friends with our classmates, everyone admitted to feeling like impostors. We had all been wondering if we would be accepted into the group. In that transformative moment, it felt as if we collectively exhaled. We could start to let our guards down and focus on why we were truly there. It was a powerful way to kick off what would become one of the most meaningful experiences of our lives—by affirming that we all belonged. Marty and the other leaders at MAPP made good on his words. Throughout the program, they showed us, again and again, that we were welcomed for who we really are.

As we've shared, humans are fundamentally driven by a need to belong. Some of the same alarms that activate in our brains when we are hungry are also activated when we feel lonely or disconnected. Our brains tell us when we're starving for food and starving for connection in the same way. In fact, many of the strongest emotions we experience—both positive and negative—are related to our need to belong. When we feel accepted and included, we experience happiness, joy, and contentment. When we feel rejected or ignored, we can experience anxiety, depression, and loneliness. This need is present and pervasive in all areas of our lives, including at work.

What does it mean to belong at work? In the last chapter, we examined how connections with others build belonging. Strong relationships and the belief that others care about us are important drivers of meaning at work. The strength of those connections depends largely on whether we can show up as our full selves. If we have to hide who we are or what we think in order to be included in the group, our connections lack authenticity. As bestselling author Brené Brown states, "The opposite of belonging is fitting in." We can only experience belonging at work when others see and welcome our whole selves.

The sad truth is that, in many organizations today, most people have a second full-time job—working to maintain a curated version of themselves in order to fit in. These people—and we've both been one of them—edit what they share about themselves and hide their true thoughts about their work for fear of being rejected, judged, or even fired. It's like we are all walking around wearing masks. Not surprisingly, research finds that this second job limits personal and organizational growth, creates silos, thwarts productivity, and hinders collaboration. It takes a tremendous amount of energy and effort to filter every comment, every email, every interaction to try to fit in. It is exhausting to constantly act how we think others want us to be instead of how we really are. When we expend so much energy on maintaining a mask, it is difficult to find meaning at work.

Leaders who welcome people's whole selves and full range of ideas can eliminate this second job and allow individuals to redirect that wasted energy toward more meaningful pursuits. At the start of the MAPP program, Marty invited us to drop the figurative masks we had brought with us so that we could more quickly build community and more effectively connect and collaborate with one another. One of the first things leaders of the program had us do was to share a story about a time when we were at our best. They put us into small groups (which we later found were our working groups for the semester) and had us share our stories. The story could be about a big life event or just a small moment, but we had to highlight one of the core strengths we saw in ourselves.

We often find it hard to share negative events because we don't want to appear vulnerable, but sharing positive events can be difficult too. It can feel awkward to talk about something you're proud of, and it takes some courage to share your strengths. What if you're not seen as humble? What if the strength you highlight isn't one that's valued by the group? What if people think your story is about something trivial and everyone else's is heroic? These thoughts raced through our minds as we started sharing.

Tamara shared about a time when she helped a young mother find her lost toddler at a store in New York City. Wes shared about the day his father passed away unexpectedly, and he was able to step in and take care of things for the rest of his family. After each person shared, the group had a chance to respond. We were encouraged to ask follow-up questions or highlight a strength we noticed in another's story. As we'll discuss later, the way we respond when others share has a significant impact on belonging. By the end of the exercise, we all felt seen and appreciated.

This exercise, the Positive Introduction, accelerated our ability to show up fully and connected us with our cohort partners, whom we would work with on rigorous projects throughout the semester. We facilitate a version of the Positive Introduction when we work with new teams, and it is invariably a powerful exercise that lays the foundation for effective collaboration. When we feel connected and accepted, we can start to share our real thoughts, even when they are different from the group's.

Throughout the MAPP program, classroom leaders continued to invite us to show up fully by sharing our real perspectives and ideas. Professors would make a point to ask questions that welcomed disagreement and highlighted our different views. They invited skepticism to the classroom with questions like, Who disagrees? What is another perspective on this? What did I miss? This enriched the discussions, leveraged the diversity of voices in the room, and deepened our learning.

At work, many of us go along with the perspectives of the loudest voices and hold back on sharing what we really think. Like wearing a mask to fit in, this hinders collaboration and innovation and can be exhausting. We are hired because of our expertise, yet often we feel like we can't share it. This is not only frustrating for us individually, but it also hinders organizational success. Innovation requires diverse perspectives. By welcoming all ideas, organizations gain valuable insights to make better decisions.

When we feel safe to show up fully without a fear of rejection or retaliation, we can bring our most creative, confident, and productive ideas to the discussion. When we feel that we are welcomed and valued, we can drop the mask. This virtuous cycle of authenticity and belonging was present throughout our MAPP experience and endures in us as alumni and instructors in the program. Graduate school remains one of the most meaningful experiences both of us have been a part of. We learned powerful lessons that have helped us both show up more fully at work and teach others how to do the same. When leaders are intentional about enabling authenticity, our sense of community is strengthened, and our work becomes meaningful.

In the extensive research that we have conducted during and since the program, we found that meaning-driven leaders build belonging by **welcoming everyone's full selves** and **welcoming their full range of ideas**.

DROPPING THE MASK

Chad Thomas grew up in the bustling inner-city streets of Newark, New Jersey, as the youngest of three brothers. Although life in the city could be tough, it could also be beautiful. Newark was a close-knit community where people cared for each other, but they were surrounded by poverty, crime, violence, and injustice. Chad shared, "My brothers and I used to joke that we couldn't sleep unless we heard ambulance sirens at least once or twice each night."

As Chad and his brothers approached their teenage years, the stakes got higher. In Newark at that time, once a boy hit twelve or thirteen years old, he became a target for gang recruitment. One summer day, when Chad was just twelve years old, he was leaving a local Chinese restaurant when a well-known drug dealer from the neighborhood pulled him aside. But instead of trying to recruit Chad, he told him that he wished he could have done things differently. He regretted not focusing on school and hoped Chad would use his education to get out of Newark. He emphasized that this wasn't the life he wanted. This encounter was eye-opening for Chad. He remembers being surprised that despite his status in the neighborhood, the drug dealer didn't want that life for himself or anyone else.

Determined to secure a brighter future for their sons, Chad's parents applied for a scholarship program that sent kids from Newark to boarding schools across New England. Chad was awarded a scholarship to the prestigious Taft School in Watertown, Connecticut. Alternating between the different realities at home in Newark and at school at Taft was a big adjustment for Chad. He shared, "The people I grew up with in Newark would tell me I was 'talking white' because I was using subject-verb agreement and that I was losing who I was because of where I was going. My peers at boarding school wouldn't engage me because of where I came from. I was existing between two very different spaces, and I wasn't sure where I belonged."

During Chad's initial years at boarding school, he constantly felt like an outsider. The first two years were particularly brutal for him—he was called racial slurs all the time. It was also the first time he ever struggled academically. The intensity of the coursework was unlike anything Chad had experienced in the Newark public school system. Despite the struggle, Chad drew strength from his brothers' successes at their respective boarding schools. He was determined to keep going, realizing that his future depended on it. No other male that Chad had gone to school with in Newark graduated high school—they dropped out, fell into the legal system, or both. He refused to become another statistic.

At the start of his junior year, Chad took charge of his high school experience. Tired of just getting by, he decided to let go of his anger and embrace who he was, showing up as himself rather than a shell of who he was, even if it resulted in him being treated unkindly. Chad started participating in student government, athletics, and the arts. He ultimately was nominated for class speaker and most improved student. Crucially, once he decided he could be himself, everything changed. He realized that he could still be Chad from Newark, that he didn't have to change to fit in. Everything just clicked.

After high school, Chad attended Boston College, where he majored in developmental psychology and planned to pursue a PhD in counseling. However, Chad's older brother was working on Wall Street, and Chad felt drawn to the allure of financial success. When he received an offer from an investment bank, he decided he "didn't want to be broke anymore." At that time, he believed everything in his world would be fine as long as he made a six-figure income.

Once again, however, Chad found himself in an environment where he couldn't truly be himself. "Being an African American on Wall Street wasn't easy," he explains. "I was told, along with my Black peers, that our voices were too deep and could frighten clients." Despite the good salary, Chad felt disconnected and unfulfilled in his career. He reflects, "I went to work on Wall Street for the money, but it didn't give me purpose. I didn't want to have to spend more of my time covering just to make other people comfortable. I realized that replenishing my checking account every few weeks wasn't going to make me feel whole."

Chad decided that he would not be satisfied with just a steady paycheck. Driven by a desire to align his career with his passions and values, Chad sought out companies that had a positive work environment and cared about making a meaningful impact. His pursuit led him to BetterUp, a digital coaching platform. When he first applied to BetterUp, the company was a start-up and didn't even have a formal application process. Chad sent a cold message to the cofounder, Eddie Medina, and they met for coffee.

From that very first meeting, Chad felt like he could truly be himself. In the interview, Eddie actively sought to learn about who Chad was—his background and schooling, his hopes and dreams. He created an open and welcoming atmosphere where Chad felt comfortable sharing his thoughts and concerns. He showed genuine interest in Chad's values and aspirations, and Eddie shared his own values and the company's mission. Despite this, Chad wasn't immediately sold on the job. He was not interested in working at a company that catered exclusively to those who already have a lot of resources. "I have a deep passion for making sure that all communities get supported," Chad recounts. "I told Eddie that I didn't want to offer coaching only to the top brass in every organization. I didn't want to only serve the 'worried well.'"

Eddie assured Chad that BetterUp's goal was to democratize coaching and to make it accessible to everyone in the world. That felt like a breath of fresh air to Chad. He recalls, "Eddie created the space for me to be direct with him, and he responded positively to my feedback. That was completely different than what I was used to."

Chad joined BetterUp as employee number 47. From the moment he stepped through the doors, Chad knew he had found his professional home. He still remembers the palpable feeling of warmth when he walked into the office. The energy that people had about their mission to "help people pursue their lives with more clarity, purpose, and passion" was evident. Chad had spent his entire career in toxic work environments, but this was something different.

Not only was Chad surrounded by colleagues pursuing a greater purpose, but he was also embraced for who he truly was. From that very first meeting with Eddie, he understood that he could be himself. "I am this kid from Newark who loves positive psychology. I can talk about my faith. I can wear a gold chain at work one day, a suit the next day, or a T-shirt with a hip-hop artist on it, and none of that impacts my perceived value," he explains. Chad didn't have to fit in anymore. Now, he could show up fully and truly belong.

Reflecting on his journey, Chad credits BetterUp's inclusive culture for empowering him to find his voice and unleash his potential. He believes engagement at work is about the energy you get from your job and the immediate impact you see from your efforts. For Chad, BetterUp is a renewable energy source that keeps getting better. He has been able to grow and expand at the organization, and he hasn't compromised himself to do that.

Leaders at BetterUp are intentional about building a workplace where people can bring their whole selves to the table. They go as far as offering employees four paid days each year for what they call Inner Work—a practice dedicated to "looking inward to our authentic selves." They have learned that being able to express your whole self at work improves communication, increases productivity, and supports relationships with coworkers.

Have you ever felt like you couldn't truly be yourself at work? Perhaps, like Chad in his investment banking role when he changed the tenor of his voice, you felt like you had to cover aspects of your identity to blend in. In this context, the term *covering* refers to ways in which people hide or minimize parts of who they are to fit it. This can include age, disability, race, ethnicity, sexual orientation, caregiver status, education, mental health status, and religious affiliation. For example, a mother might avoid discussing her kids in the office to signal more complete commitment to her job. Similarly, a person with a disability might refrain from using accommodations they need to avoid being seen as different.

A recent survey found that a staggering 60 percent of workers regularly engage in covering. This has negative consequences not only for the individuals who cover, but also for the performance of the organization.

Like a second full-time job, behaving in a way that is inconsistent with our genuine feelings is much more draining than authentic behavior and depletes our self-regulation and mental resources.

On the other hand, when leaders create space for people to drop their masks and show up fully, they foster belonging and strengthen connections. Work becomes relational rather than transactional, leading to greater collaboration, innovation, and meaning at work. One tool we've seen meaning-driven leaders use to invite people to share their full selves is a practice we call everyday storytelling.

EVERYDAY STORYTELLING

Storytelling can be a powerful tool to create belonging. Leaders facilitate everyday storytelling by sharing the everyday experiences of their own lives and by actively inviting others to share theirs. When people regularly talk about the things that are happening in their lives outside of work, it sends the message that everyone's experiences are welcomed and valued.

Consider the members of your team. Do you know their favorite foods, how they spend their spare time, or the last book they loved? Leaders who recognize and value employees as multifaceted individuals, acknowledging their roles as parents, spouses, and active community members, increase belonging and make work meaningful.

Everyday storytelling starts with leading by example. Remember, as Rob Waldron shared, people will always "follow the bride," so it's important to start by sharing parts of your whole self. This can be done directly, such as by discussing interests and hobbies outside work, or indirectly, by showcasing personal items and photos in your office or on your Zoom screen. A little vulnerability can go a long way. The appropriate amount may vary by culture, but you can adapt accordingly. Additional ideas for modeling everyday storytelling include the following:

- Sharing stories or anecdotes from your personal life during team meetings or informal gatherings. These could be memorable experiences, lessons learned, or funny incidents that allow your team members to get to know you on a deeper level.
- Sharing your weekend plans whether it includes cheering for your kids on the soccer field, attending religious ceremonies, or pursuing a quirky hobby that not many people know about.
- Joining and actively participating in employee resource groups (ERGs). These groups are powerful for strengthening connections and fostering belonging within organizations. By joining an ERG, you actively engage with colleagues who share common interests, experiences, or backgrounds.
- Using your email signature or virtual backgrounds on video calls to showcase elements of your personality or interests. For example, you could include a quote that inspires you, a picture of a place you love, or a symbol that holds significance to you.
- Embracing transparency if you need to leave work early for personal reasons. A senior leader we work with schedules exercise time on her calendar and occasionally leaves early to attend her daughter's lacrosse games. By openly displaying these activities on her calendar, she has fostered a more open environment within her team, encouraging others to do the same.

These small details can offer glimpses into your whole self and spark connections with others. While it is important for leaders to model everyday storytelling directly and indirectly, it is not enough. Leaders must also explicitly enable individuals to do the same. Everyday work activities, like meetings, present an untapped opportunity to invite others to share their own everyday stories. When this happens, we start to understand our colleagues as whole people.

Dr. Vivek Murthy, surgeon general of the United States and author of *Together: The Healing Power of Human Connection in a Sometimes Lonely World,* is known for his emphasis on well-being, community, and the importance of addressing social and emotional factors in health care and leadership. In October 2019, at the annual conference of MAPP students and alumni at the University of Pennsylvania, Dr. Murthy shared with us a practice he implemented with his own team to create a more inclusive environment where individuals feel comfortable sharing aspects of their personal lives. He calls this practice "Inside Scoop."

As part of their weekly all-hands meeting, one individual has five minutes to show a few photos related to their life and tell the others about them. Participants take turns each week with this show-and-tell. In an interview with the *Washington Post,* Dr. Murthy shared, "We would give an individual the floor for five minutes and they would tell their own story. Some people focused on their family, other people focused on experiences they had before they came to the office, some people focused on what their dreams are for the future. But in that brief five minutes people were able to give a window into their lives that we didn't [normally] see. Of everything we discussed in those weekly staff meetings, those five minutes were the most interesting." Over time, Dr. Murthy observed that people felt more connected as colleagues learned about their personal lives. By dedicating just five minutes to everyday storytelling, the team transitioned from seeing work as transactional to embracing a more relational approach.

When people reveal more of themselves and share something positive in their lives, it not only fosters belonging, but it also helps to generate positive emotions in the room. Barbara Fredrickson, professor at the University of North Carolina at Chapel Hill, is the leading positive psychology researcher studying positive emotions. According to her "broaden and build" theory, positive emotions such as joy, gratitude, and curiosity expand our thinking and prompt us to explore new possibilities and ideas. This enables us to build lasting personal resources, such as resilience and coping skills, contributing to improved well-being and personal growth.

For example, feeling gratitude leads us to acknowledge that others have helped us and to thank them. This strengthens relationships and fosters a sense of reciprocity. Feeling hope leads us to plan for the future, set goals, and maintain optimism. This fosters resilience by providing a sense of purpose and direction, even in challenging circumstances. These examples highlight how positive emotions drive actions, enabling us to develop essential resources such as cognitive agility, emotional resilience, and motivational drive.

By providing opportunities for individuals to share and connect on a personal level, meetings can help people feel seen and heard, experience positive emotions, and strengthen connections. You can create these opportunities in team meetings or one-on-ones, in person, or virtually. What really matters is demonstrating genuine interest in people's lives outside work.

Everyday storytelling is a powerful way to share aspects of your whole self and encourage others to do the same. Once someone shares something personal, however, the way you respond can significantly impact your efforts to enable authenticity. Your response can either make people feel seen and strengthen your connection, or it can inadvertently signal dismissal and discourage further sharing.

WAS THAT OK?

On a sunny day in May 2013 in Cambridge, Massachusetts, Oprah Winfrey delivered an inspiring commencement speech to the graduating class of Harvard University. In an especially poignant segment of her address, Oprah revealed the most important lesson that she learned in twenty-five years of talking to people every day: "What we want, the common denominator that I found in every single interview, is we want to be validated. We want to be understood."

Oprah went on to share that she had conducted over 35,000 interviews in her career, and that once the camera shuts off, everyone always turns to her and asks the same question: "Was that okay?" She continued, "I heard it from President Bush, I heard it from President Obama. I've heard it from heroes and from housewives. I've heard it from victims and perpetrators of crimes. I even heard it from Beyonce in all of her Beyonceness. She finishes performing, hands me the microphone and says, 'Was that okay?'" Oprah closed her speech by emphasizing that every single one of us, in our interactions, wants to know one thing: "Did you hear me? Do you see me? Did what I say mean anything to you?"

In this part of her speech, Oprah insightfully observed a fundamental human need—to be accepted and valued for who we truly are. When we share our everyday stories, we're all silently asking, Was that OK?

In a seminal paper titled "Will You Be There for Me When Things Go Right?" Shelly Gable and colleagues found that small moments of connection around positive experiences can significantly strengthen relationships. The researchers found that there are four ways in which we typically respond when someone shares good news with us, but only one builds trust and belonging. Being genuinely engaged when people share moments of celebration, success, and positive news can help turn a good relationship into an excellent one. This is important because positive events occur three times more frequently than negative ones. And at work, people are more likely to share good things.

Imagine you are catching up about the weekend with a woman who works on your team. She excitedly shares an everyday story, telling you about her son's wrestling tournament and his first-place win. You are busy, don't really care about wrestling, and have never met her son. How do you respond? Perhaps you say something like, "Congratulations! Good for him!" While nice, that response likely doesn't make her feel seen. It does not show that what she said was OK or that it meant anything to you.

The following table illustrates the four different styles of responding to good news that Gable and colleagues found in their study and what each one might sound like in the example above.

		WEAKENS RELATIONSHIPS		STRENGTHENS RELATIONSHIPS
STYLE	Nod and Neglect	Pivot and Prevail	Critique and Crush	Engage and Elevate
RESEARCH TERM	Passive Constructive	Passive Destructive	Active Destructive	Active Constructive
BEHAVIORS	Distracted and disengaged; focused on something else	Changes the conversation; one-ups the news	Focuses on the negative; points out concerns	Genuinely engaged; enthusiastically supportive
WHAT IT SOUNDS LIKE	That's great. Congratulations! (looks at phone or email, half listening)	Wow, that's nice! My daughter also won her ski race last weekend. Did you know she is ranked nationally? We are so proud of how hard she has been working. Just the other day . . .	Wrestling can be so dangerous! I just read an article about how it is the number-one sport for injuries. Don't you worry about concussions?	That's amazing, congratulations! You must be so proud. How many matches did he have? How was his final match?

The impact of these responses on strengthening—or inadvertently weakening—relationships is surprisingly powerful. In the initial stages of our MAPP program mentioned earlier, when we shared our strength stories, experiencing the Engage and Elevate responses from our classmates played a pivotal role in forging strong relationships. Unfortunately, we also thought of many times in our lives when the people who are most important to us—our family members, friends, and colleagues—shared something positive, and we were disengaged or disinterested.

It is hard to be genuinely engaged when we have multiple demands on our time and attention. When we teach this skill, we often hear responses like, "I don't have the time to respond this way." The great news is that Engage and Elevate doesn't take long—it can be done in less than a minute. Our professors jokingly called this the "minute to win it" skill. Yes, we are all busy, but we all crave connection and belonging. By taking just a brief moment to actively engage when someone shares a positive experience, we not only contribute to their sense of feeling seen and validated, we also strengthen overall community and increase meaning at work.

Responding in the Engage and Elevate style involves actively engaging when someone shares something positive with you. These positive experiences can range from significant events, like being promoted, winning an award, or booking a dream vacation, to smaller moments, such as enjoying a delicious meal, watching a beautiful sunrise, or finding some spare change in a pocket. What matters is that when someone shares these moments with you, they are seeking to capitalize on that positive experience and hoping to feel seen and validated. You can do that by asking open-ended questions, making eye contact, expressing positive emotion, and minimizing distractions.

Although responding this way sounds simple, it can be difficult. Chris Peterson, whom you met earlier, devised a simple intervention to help us practice Engage and Elevate responses. He calls it the "but-free" day. Chris describes, "When someone relates good news, respond without using the word *but*... or any of its close cousins like however, whereas, yet, then again, and on the other hand."

Practicing the Engage and Elevate response style doesn't require much time, yet its impact is profound. Even in our busy lives, a brief moment of genuine engagement speaks volumes—it says, "You matter."

This encourages future sharing, reinforcing that people's whole selves are welcome. Over time, this helps people quit their second full-time jobs and frees up their energy to contribute more effectively.

EVERYONE WANTS TO HAVE A VOICE

Recall ecology researcher Suzanne Simard's findings: forests with only one tree species struggle, while diverse forests thrive as different trees share resources, boosting their collective strength. Just as diverse forests flourish, diverse teams fuel innovation, creativity, and problem-solving. The second practice for enabling authenticity is to welcome people's full range of ideas.

Only when people are comfortable being themselves can they bring their real and diverse perspectives to the table. After all, you can't expect someone who doesn't feel included to share what they really think. But to fully realize the potential of diverse teams, you need a key ingredient—psychological safety.

Psychological safety is the belief that you can freely contribute ideas, ask questions, and share concerns without worrying that you will be rejected, embarrassed, or punished. It creates a culture where people feel comfortable expressing their true perspectives. You know you have psychological safety when constructive disagreements are welcomed, diverse viewpoints are respected, and people feel able—even obligated—to be candid. Much like nutrients that feed the mycorrhizal network, psychological safety enables the exchange of ideas, fosters open communication, and cultivates an environment where individuals feel empowered to take risks.

During BetterUp's first-ever company retreat, cofounders Alexi Robichaux and Eddie Medina emphasized the importance of diversity. Chad, who was a fairly new employee at the time, seized the opportunity to raise a critical point: "Saying we need to do better with diversity is like saying we need to get along. It's not measurable; therefore it's meaningless." Chad told the team that they must be specific with their goals; otherwise they would risk blending in with every other tech company—they would hit a 10 percent diversity mark and be done.

After Chad's remarks, there was a brief silence followed by some nervous applause, as everyone anxiously awaited the cofounders' response. To Chad's surprise and satisfaction, Alexi and Eddie embraced his perspective, expressing appreciation for his challenge and soliciting his input on next steps. Chad recalls, "Here's the cool thing. They said I was right, and they actually believed it." Once the session ended, the cofounders invited Chad to help them set some concrete goals. Chad recounts, "They were really vulnerable. They said, 'We've never run a company before, so we're not going to pretend like we know everything that we're doing. We would love your help thinking about what this actually means.'"

Chad helped the founders focus not only on diversifying talent within the organization, but also on fostering spaces for difficult conversations around diversity and inclusion. They created forums for bold conversations and then focused on "putting their money where their mouth is." For BetterUp, this meant investing in nonprofits dedicated to supporting underrepresented minorities. "We help underrepresented teenagers in inner cities all throughout the country," Chad elaborates. "We prepare them for success in STEM fields, providing career coaching and guidance. And what I like about BetterUp is that this is not performative. We don't promote this work on our website. We just do it because it's the right thing to do."

Six years after joining BetterUp, Chad remains unreserved in challenging established beliefs within the organization and welcomes being challenged himself. "Everyone wants to have a voice and contribute. We hire people for their amazing experience and expertise. Why would we want to shut them down?"

When others make us feel like our ideas and perspectives matter, our sense of belonging increases and work becomes more meaningful. Conversely, in an environment where our ideas and perspectives aren't recognized, we tend to withdraw, withholding the expertise we were specifically hired to contribute. This not only hinders our personal growth but also deprives the collective team of the valuable insights and skills we bring to the table.

Research has found that in the most effective teams, what really matters is not who's on the team but how well the team welcomes different ideas. Psychological safety fosters open communication and builds trust. It allows individuals to take risks and innovate because they know that their contributions will be valued, even if they don't always succeed. Unfortunately, most workplaces today are not fostering a climate of psychological safety, and their performance suffers accordingly. A recent survey found that only 26 percent of leaders display the behaviors that create psychological safety.

This is an untapped opportunity for leaders to make work more meaningful. A question we often get asked is, "Where do I start?" Psychological safety is created (or destroyed) in everyday group interactions, so we once again recommend starting in your next meeting.

Begin by clearly stating that everyone, regardless of position or status, is expected to contribute and challenge assumptions when appropriate. Explicitly affirm that differences in perspectives are valuable. You can say something like, "We are likely to have different ideas about how to best move this project forward. This will help us better understand all the issues involved and make an informed decision." Early in our work with one of our clients, we created a group norm that "no one speaks twice until everyone speaks once" when we were discussing the organization's new values and the expected behaviors around them. This helped everyone understand that their ideas were needed. It allowed those who need more time to think the space to be thoughtful and contribute, and kept those that tended to talk the most from dominating the conversation. It also encouraged individuals who felt skeptical to speak up and raise concerns.

Next, actively invite participation and solicit concerns. Research finds that teams perform three times better in environments when there are differing viewpoints about how to get something done. Just like inviting people to share their authentic identities, you have to explicitly invite them to share their authentic ideas by asking questions like, Who disagrees? What do you think? What are our blind spots? These questions signal to the group that different perspectives are welcomed. During graduate school, our professors explicitly invited our voices to the classroom by asking questions like these. This not only made us feel like our perspectives mattered, it also enriched everyone's learning.

Finally, be humble about what you don't know and emphasize that there is always room for learning. At BetterUp, Alexi and Eddie institutionalized a high-impact behavior they call "work to learn." At the start of new projects, BetterUp leaders ask the team, "What are we trying to learn?" The goal is to destigmatize failure and reinforce continuous learning. When a leader says, "I don't know," they model vulnerability, demonstrate a willingness to learn, and make others more comfortable asking questions.

It's important to highlight that working in a psychologically safe environment does not mean that people always agree with one another, and it is also not about "being nice" or lack of accountability at work. Rather, psychological safety enables candor and empowers individuals to share their authentic ideas and engage in constructive disagreement for the betterment of the team and the organization.

Psychological safety is about acknowledging that it is OK to be uncomfortable. After all, it will rarely feel comfortable to disagree with your boss, voice concerns about a project's direction, or challenge the status quo in a brainstorming session. Instead, psychological safety encourages individuals to embrace discomfort as a natural part of growth, collaboration, and innovation. It is like the discomfort we experience during a rigorous workout—the temporary discomfort signifies strength building and improvement. Similarly, in a psychologically safe environment, the temporary discomfort of addressing mistakes or challenging ideas can lead to enhanced team dynamics, a stronger sense of belonging, and increased meaning at work.

When you explicitly invite participation and solicit concerns, people will likely share thoughts and opinions you disagree with. Your response when that happens can make or break your efforts to increase psychological safety.

THE POWER TO CHOOSE YOUR RESPONSE

Responding productively when people raise concerns, disagree, or challenge our assumptions can be tough. It is natural to get defensive when someone points out our blind spots. However, you are the "bride" and everyone, not just the person who raised a concern, is watching your response. If you truly want to build a community where individuals share their authentic ideas, you have to model responding productively. This creates a ripple effect that extends beyond just the meeting. Each productive response is like a brick in a wall of community, but even a single unproductive response is like a wrecking ball to that wall.

One of our favorite quotes is Viktor Frankl's: "Between stimulus and response there is a space. In that space is our power to choose our response. In our response lies our growth and our freedom." This skill is all about intentionally creating that space. To help you respond productively, we created the PEAR model, which stands for pause, explicitly acknowledge, ask questions, and reflect. Let's take a closer look at each step.

Pause

When someone points out a blind spot or criticizes a decision you've made, the first step is to pause and take a deep breath. When we think about emotional regulation, we often think about the big things we do to feel better, like going for a walk or engaging in a favorite hobby, and forget about strategies we need in the moment. Taking a deep breath deactivates our fight-or-flight response and helps us create that space between stimulus (receiving difficult feedback, for example) and response (being intentional about what you say and do).

Explicitly Acknowledge

Next, thank the person for speaking up. When someone raises a concern, they are being vulnerable and taking a big risk. By thanking them for saying something, you are reinforcing and rewarding behaviors that build trust and psychological safety. If their perspective catches you off guard, you can say something like, "Thank you for speaking up. I am really surprised to hear this and need a little time to process." Such response to candid feedback reinforces a culture where everyone feels empowered to share their perspectives, ultimately leading to fewer mistakes, more innovations, and better decisions.

Ask Questions

The next step is to ask follow-up questions to better understand their perspective. Lead with curiosity rather than defensiveness. You can say things like, "I hadn't thought about it this way. Can you say more?" or "That's an interesting point. How did you come to this conclusion?" By actively listening and seeking additional insights, you signal that their input is valued and that their contribution has the potential to shape positive outcomes. This approach not only encourages honest communication but also reinforces the idea that diverse perspectives are essential for informed decision-making and team growth.

Reflect

After engaging in a conversation where someone shared an authentic idea, perspective, or feedback, take the time to reflect on the exchange. Consider what was said, how it was received, and the impact it may have had. Reflecting allows you to gain deeper insights into your own reactions, biases, and areas for growth. It's an opportunity to integrate new perspectives, learn from experiences, and refine your approach for future interactions. By embracing reflection as a regular practice, you cultivate self-awareness, enhance communication skills, and contribute to a culture of continuous improvement within your team and organization.

By embracing the PEAR approach—pausing to create space, explicitly acknowledging contributions, asking questions with curiosity, and reflecting on the exchange—we lay the foundation for constructive dialogue, meaningful collaboration, and transformative innovation. Each intentional response, each brick in the wall of community, reinforces a psychologically safe environment where authentic ideas flourish and diverse perspectives are welcomed. This not only leads to individual growth but also strengthens belonging and elevates the collective potential of teams and organizations.

FROM MUSCLES TO BRAINS TO HEARTS

Fostering a workplace culture that embraces and values each individual's authentic identities and ideas is not just a commendable goal but also a strategic imperative. In a recent interview, Minouche Shafik, former president of Columbia University, stated, "In the past, jobs were about muscles. Now they're about brains. But in the future, they'll be about the heart."

That future is here, and it demands that leaders step forward with empathy, recognizing that your team members are individuals with multifaceted lives. Do you care about what's happening in your team's personal life outside work? Do you ask about and remember personal details about your team? When someone on your team is personally struggling, can they tell you? These are not just rhetorical questions but essential reflections for any leader.

The future of work calls for leaders who are not only intelligent but compassionate, not just skilled but understanding. It's a future we must embrace now. In her powerful memoir *The Choice: Embrace the Possible*, Holocaust survivor Edith Eva Eger shares the harrowing account of her experience in Nazi concentration camps and her remarkable recovery and journey to becoming a world-renowned clinical psychologist. She writes that the most common diagnosis among the people she treats is not depression or posttraumatic stress disorder but hunger. Hunger to be our true selves. In her practice, Dr. Eger has worked with patients afflicted by many different types of conditions, yet the longing to be one's true self has stood out to her as underlying all human struggle.

As leaders, we can help satiate this hunger. By recognizing, appreciating, and supporting the entirety of each individual, leaders enable authenticity. When this happens, our research clearly shows that work becomes infused with meaning. It's possible for leaders to foster this kind of environment even before a person joins their organization.

When a seed takes root in an old-growth forest, it immediately taps into an extensive underground community of diverse species. This allows the new seed to thrive and grow strong. Like this seed, new employees can also benefit from the collective knowledge and support network that exists within your organization. In the next chapter, we will dive into hiring and onboarding practices that make work truly meaningful.

6

BEGINNINGS MATTER

You never get a second chance to make a first impression.
—WILL ROGERS

Have you ever walked into a new place and instantly felt a sense of excitement or anticipation? Or met someone new and immediately sensed a connection? Or maybe you started a job and quickly formed an impression about what it would be like to work there? These are examples of what is known as *first impression bias*. Our initial experiences and perceptions profoundly impact our long-term attitudes and behaviors toward people, places, and situations.

At the start of a relationship with an organization, new employees form immediate impressions based on their initial interactions and experiences. These early impressions are critical because they set the tone for the entire duration of the employee's tenure. In these first moments, leaders have the opportunity to show new employees that this is going to be a meaningful place to work.

Our research clearly revealed that how you start the relationship with a new team member highly impacts how meaningful their work becomes. Nurturing these first impression moments is key to building a meaningful and successful long-term partnership.

Leaders can set the stage for a meaningful relationship by creating a meaningful hiring and onboarding experience. This starts with **hiring carefully for values alignment** and continues through an **intentional social and cultural onboarding process**. In this final chapter on community, we will explore these practices, starting with hiring for values alignment.

VALUES-ALIGNED RECRUITMENT

"It was the greatest job in the world. I remember in a three-year stretch going from boarding blockade-running cargo ships off the coast of the Korean peninsula in the Yellow Sea to looking for potential war criminals in Albania to driving mini-submersibles on and off nuclear-powered submarines in the Mediterranean." This is how Jeff Gibson describes his time as a Navy SEAL. Jeff grew up in St. Louis as the youngest of four children. His childhood was marked by adventure—playing sports, exploring the woods and rivers, canoeing, and camping—all activities that would later shape his career. When the time came for Jeff to attend college, he chose the University of Missouri and joined the Navy ROTC to reduce the financial burden of his education and to serve his country. Throughout his college years, Jeff dedicated his summers to intensive four-week training sessions, which exposed him to various facets of the navy, including the submarine and aviation communities. It was during one of these summers that Jeff first encountered the Navy SEALs.

The Navy Sea, Air, and Land teams, commonly known as Navy SEALs, are the US Navy's primary special operations force. The

SEALs are a highly elite and specialized group, trained and equipped to carry out a wide range of unconventional and high-risk military operations. Two years after graduating from college, Jeff joined the SEALs, where he spent the next ten years.

Becoming a Navy SEAL is a highly selective process, starting with the initial training called BUD/S, which stands for Basic Underwater Demolition/SEAL. This training, which spans about six months, is known for its extreme physical and mental challenges, designed to sift out all but the most resilient and determined individuals. Completing BUD/S is a major accomplishment. Only 20 to 25 percent of individuals complete the training, and by the time they make it through, not only have their skills been assessed but also their values and character. While the physical and mental challenges of BUD/S are well known, less recognized is the SEALs' emphasis on character. During the training, they look beyond a potential candidate's physical and mental prowess to determine if they also possess the right qualities to join the organization.

For the SEALs, it is not enough to have a high level of technical skills; it is equally as important to demonstrate a high level of trust—the quality that the SEALs care most about. Because SEALs operate in small units in remote and high-risk environments, they are required to depend on each other to ensure their safety and mission success. This includes the mission readiness of their equipment such as weapons, diving gear, parachutes, and radios. Within those units, different teammates are assigned the responsibility of one of the equipment groups. They are responsible for ensuring that equipment is maintained properly, fully operational, and stored appropriately so that it is fully ready when needed. For example, the air operations lead ensures that the parachutes, various harnesses, and climbing equipment are mission ready. When it comes time to use that equipment, the rest of the team needs to trust that their equipment is ready, tested, and fully operational. This trust is literally a life-and-death decision.

The SEALs—one of the most elite and high-performing organizations in the world—have learned that a high-performing individual who demonstrates a low level of trust can become a toxic team member, leading to terrible outcomes, especially in the high-stakes business of combat. So, no matter how high-performing someone is, if they don't demonstrate a high level of trustworthiness, they don't get assigned to a team. This evaluation continues even after candidates make it through BUD/S.

After completing BUD/S, prospective SEALs get assigned to a team for a six-month probation period. During that period, they are watched to see if they're proficient in the skills they were taught but also, most importantly, to see how they interact and engage with others. Five to 10 percent of the probational SEALs don't end up getting their SEAL certification because they lack qualities like trust.

Research supports the SEALs' practice. Earlier, we highlighted the importance of values alignment in fostering meaningful work. When making hiring decisions, alignment is especially critical. Assuming they are competent, hiring a candidate whose values are aligned with the organization's generally enhances performance across the board. However, hiring someone who doesn't share the organization's values, even if they are a top performer, creates a net loss for the organization.

Ensuring values alignment *before* someone joins an organization matters because a person's character at work—their values in action—is highly stable over time. A meta-analysis of over twenty-eight thousand people showed that work-related values change very little across a person's career, especially after they have been in the workforce for a few years. This means that, except for entry-level hires, you are generally getting someone with a fully established set of values about how they approach work. People can evolve, of course, but it rarely happens without a significant investment of time and energy. It is highly unlikely that a high performer whose values don't align with an organization's values will change. On the other hand, candidates who share the vision and values of an organization are likely to remain aligned for the long term.

Jeff's first operational assignment after completing BUD/S and his six-month probationary period was assistant officer in charge (AOIC) of a SEAL platoon. His SEAL platoon was assigned to go through a year's worth of training, which included all the operational mission responsibilities assigned to special operations units in various environments, such as desert, jungle, woodland, urban, and extreme cold. Upon completing the year's training, his platoon would then deploy overseas and be the on-call SEAL platoon to respond as directed by the US military leadership. However, about eight months into the training period, the platoon's officer in charge (OIC) was reassigned due to unforeseen circumstances. Instead of his platoon getting a replacement, the SEAL team commanding officer selected and promoted Jeff as the new OIC of that platoon—a position usually reserved for more experienced officers. Jeff was specifically selected because he had already proven himself operationally, but more importantly he had earned the trust and respect of his platoon during the training phases that he had already completed.

Whether your team is fighting terrorism in life-and-death situations, like Jeff's SEAL teams, or whether your team is driving forward the purpose-driven mission of your company, the lesson is the same: skills are important, but values are the key to sustained success.

THE NBA OF FAST FOOD

At Chick-fil-A, the fast-food chain famous for its chicken sandwiches and waffle fries, your chance of becoming a franchise operator is only slightly better than your chance of getting drafted into the NBA. Every year, sixty thousand candidates apply for a franchise but only about eighty are selected. The company has an arduous vetting process that can take up to twelve months, including a detailed application form and a series of phone, video, and in-person interviews. They go as far as interviewing family members of prospective operators to learn more about the candidates, their relationships, and, ultimately, their character.

Until his death in 2014, founder Truett Cathy interviewed every single franchise candidate before they were accepted. He believed that selecting the right team members was critical for the company's success. Dee Ann Turner, former vice president of talent at Chick-fil-A, told us, "Deciding who could run a franchise was Truett's most important decision because the company's reputation was going to ride on it. Truett would carefully select the right person to become a franchise operator, knowing that they would then select the right people to work in the stores."

Chick-fil-A has grown from a single store in 1946 to a massive franchise with yearly revenue estimated at more than $20 billion. They have one of the lowest turnover rates among franchisees, at just 5 percent each year. Among hourly workers, turnover is nearly half of industry average. They attribute this success in large part to their emphasis on character in their selection process. Dee Ann continued, "Character is the most important thing to look for in hiring. Your culture is the sum total of the character of the individuals in your organization. People can be taught to do a lot, but if they have poor character, skill and talent will not compensate for the negative impact they can have on an organization." At Chick-fil-A, character is assessed by a demonstrated commitment to its four core values: "We're Here to Serve, We're Better Together, We Are Purpose-Driven, We Pursue What's Next." Interviewers ask candidates for specific examples of times when each of these values drove their decisions. As we'll see, these types of interview questions can help you select candidates that are aligned with your core values.

Why does it work so much better to hire in this way? It would be tempting for Chick-fil-A to recruit a top manager who has done well at another fast-food chain, regardless of their values. This is how hiring in most companies happens. But research shows that Chick-fil-A is wise to take a different path. Even if someone joins an organization as a top performer, a misalignment of values can be devastating. After joining, research shows that the values-misaligned employee's performance plunges and so does the effectiveness of the entire team. This is because other team members lose motivation and confidence in leadership, resulting in significant loss of productivity. Eventually, critical members of the team leave, creating turnover and further damaging morale.

On top of that, the importance of someone's existing skills has a shorter shelf life than ever. In the face of continuous technological advancement, global pandemics, and ongoing uncertainty, even if you did manage to hire the Michael Jordan of your field, you may find that instead of basketball the market now demands baseball, and well, we know how that turned out. The good news is that new skills can be developed, while character is mostly fixed.

By making values, not just skills, a focal point in your recruitment process, you gain insights into the candidate's character and also provide them with a transparent view of your organization's culture. This alignment is crucial for fostering a work environment where individuals feel a sense of belonging and are inspired by the shared values that drive the organization forward.

When we work with growing companies and talent acquisition leaders, we're often asked, "Why would you hire someone who doesn't demonstrate the highest level of skills and experience to do the job?" What we found is that *who someone is* (their character) is more important than *what they know* (their capabilities) when it comes to inviting them to join your organization.

WHO WOULD YOU CHOOSE?

Imagine the following situation: You have an incredible opportunity to take a year-long trip around the world. You'll have the chance to explore diverse cultures, countries, and experiences. As you prepare for your journey, you face a crucial decision: Who will you invite to join you on this adventure? You ask a few friends and relatives and narrow it down to two choices.

The first is a well-traveled friend who possesses in-depth knowledge of geography, languages, and planning skills. However, there have been times when their self-centeredness led to disappointment. They always insist on choosing restaurants without considering your food preferences. When you were going through a difficult situation and needed emotional support, they were dismissive and failed to offer empathy and understanding.

Your other option is a friend who has always wanted to explore the world but has never had the chance to leave the country. While lacking travel experience, this person embodies exceptional compassion and the ability to genuinely listen and connect. They are the friend you can always count on for support, whether in times of need or moments of joy.

As you weigh the decision, you consider the challenges you're likely to face—language barriers, unfamiliar foods, unexpected setbacks, and cultural differences. Your highly skilled friend might be proficient in handling logistical aspects of the trip, but their controlling tendencies could create a lot of conflict. The tensions might even prevent you from ultimately getting to your destination.

On the other hand, your values-aligned friend will face a steep learning curve on their first trip out of the country. With their kindness and compassion, however, you expect that they will be adept at forging genuine connections, defusing potential conflicts, and fostering goodwill throughout journey.

Who would you invite on your adventure? Most of us are likely to choose the second friend. A typical interview process, however, would most likely select the first friend for the job.

Most organizations today place greater value on a person's résumé, past experiences, and achievements than on who they are, what they value, and how they act. Just as your highly skilled friend lacks the traits that foster harmony and success, organizations that prioritize skills over values might find themselves dealing with internal tensions, cultural clashes, and increased turnover. All these issues erode meaning at work.

But the question remains: How do you correctly assess someone's character in an interview? We turn to this next.

CHARACTER COUNTS TWICE

In graduate school, one of our favorite professors was Angela Duckworth. She somehow managed to make statistics approachable and, dare we say, fun. Angela's research focuses on factors that contribute to achievement and success, particularly the role of grit. She defines grit as a combination of passion and perseverance for long-term goals. Grit is our capacity to invest sustained effort over time.

One of her lessons about grit really stood out to the two of us. When predicting success, we tend to focus on a person's innate talents. Our culture prizes the idea that people are born with gifts in certain areas. "She's a natural" or "He was born to do this." Angela's research shows, however, that "no matter how talented you are, effort counts twice." While we may start with different levels of innate talent, we must invest effort to turn that talent into practical skills. Then, we again have to apply effort to use those skills to achieve our goals. Angela represents this with a formula:

$$\text{Talent} \times \text{Effort} = \text{Skill}$$
$$\text{Skill} \times \text{Effort} = \text{Achievement}$$

Effort factors into the achievement calculation twice. With effort, talent becomes skill and skill becomes achievement. This is why, over time, passion and hard work often trump raw talent.

During our research, as we heard story after story of organizations prioritizing character when hiring, we couldn't stop thinking about Angela's formula. Slowly, we came to realize that when it comes to hiring for meaningful work, no matter how skilled you are, character counts twice. Borrowing from Angela again, we define character as your *values in action*. Here's what we mean—someone might say that they value respect, for example. However, unless they *act* respectfully, this value is not actually part of their character. A person's character is the sum total of their values in action.

This means that when trying to hire for character, you need to understand how a candidate's values show up in their day-to-day lives. We have found that the best way to do that is with a **values interview.**

THE VALUES INTERVIEW

When the late Tony Hsieh took over as CEO of the online retailer Zappos in 2000, the company was struggling. Tony knew that the organization needed a complete transformation, starting with its culture. That's when he engaged the team to create a set of core values for the company. He made it a priority to build a culture around shared values and commitment to delivering exceptional customer service. This commitment contributed to the organization's renowned culture and meteoric success. Zappos experienced exponential growth and was bought by Amazon in 2009 for over $1 billion. Part of Tony's transformation started with selecting for values alignment.

Zappos developed a deeply institutionalized values interview process. At the time of our study, the organization's human resources team interviewed every single candidate for values alignment and had the final say in whether or not someone was hired. Christa Foley, former senior director of brand vision and culture and head of talent acquisition, told us, "If we have an amazing software engineer with skills that the entire software development team loves, and they're going to really help us go to the next technical level, but they show red flags in the core values interview, we won't move forward."

While experience and skills are important, values are critical for Zappos, where character counts twice. Even after someone is hired, Zappos goes as far as offering them a month's salary to leave if they don't believe the company is a good fit for them. Hsieh said, "We have passed on a lot of really smart, talented people that we know could have made an immediate impact on our top or bottom line, but if they are not good for our culture, which is more of a long-term play, then we won't hire them. We are willing to sacrifice the short-term benefits for the long-term gains."

Zappos has a unique and quirky culture, and one of their values is "Create Fun and a Little Weirdness." A question that gets asked of every candidate in their values interview is, "On a scale of one to ten, how weird are you?" Tony Hsieh explained, "If you're a one, you're probably too strait-laced for the Zappos culture; if you're a ten, you might be too psychotic for us. But it's not so much the number that we actually care about—it's more how people answer. . . . Our belief is that everyone is a little weird somehow, and this is more just a fun way of saying, 'We really recognize and celebrate each *person's* individuality, and we want their true personality to shine in the workplace.'" Some additional questions Zappos asks to assess that specific core value are, What is something weird that makes you happy? In your current or previous work environment, what did you do to make it more fun?

Our research indicates that simply asking about a candidate's values in the interview process is tied to greater performance, retention, and meaning down the road. Discussing values signals that character matters in your organization. This is particularly significant to attract Gen Z workers, a group that places a high importance on values alignment when choosing where to work. Discussing values during the interview process sends the message that you have a strong, intentional culture and that candidates are expected to contribute to it. Those whose values align become more strongly attracted to your organization. Those whose values don't, can self-select out of the process or be screened out by your team.

Adding a values interview to your recruiting process can help keep out misaligned candidates and focus your team on hiring for long-term value. Here are three ways to create an effective values interview:

1. **Ask candidates about their values.**

   Start by developing several interview questions focused on your organization's core values. As we learned in Chapter 3, having clear organizational values and acting in line with those values is a requirement for meaningful work. To assess a candidate's values during the interview, you can use a behavioral interviewing style in which you ask for specific examples about past values-driven actions. Behavioral interviewing involves probing candidates to provide concrete examples from their past experiences, such as times when they faced ethical dilemmas or demonstrated integrity in challenging situations. This approach not only helps you assess how well the candidate's values align with your organization's but also provides a more nuanced understanding of their character.

At Patagonia, the renowned retailer of outdoor recreation clothing, leaders believe that the heart of their impact lies in demonstrating that businesses can and should live by their values. One way Patagonia does that is by hiring people who are committed to the same values. Patagonia actively seeks candidates who are passionate about their communities, the environment, and caring for others. They seek individuals who dedicate themselves to spending as much time as possible in the mountains, the ocean, and the wild.

This was evident to Theresita Richard, Patagonia's chief people and culture officer, from her very first meeting with the organization, when her interviewing panel tried to understand how a commitment to the planet manifests in her daily life. During her interview, Theresita wasn't just asked, "Why Patagonia?" but also, "What's your personal relationship with environmental work and how does it show up in your own life?" One of Patagonia's values— "not being bound by convention"—deeply resonates with Theresita. For her, this value gives the team permission to experiment, which really fuels her. During her interview, they talked at length about this value, and Theresita shared many examples of times in her life when she led with curiosity and experimentation. Theresita told us that having conversations about the organization's values—which clearly aligned with hers—really helped confirm that Patagonia was the right place for her.

An easy way to start incorporating values into your recruitment process is to simply ask candidates, What are your top three to five values when it comes to work? Can you give me an example of how these showed up in your last job? You'll learn a lot from how candidates answer (or struggle with) this question. At the same time, they will learn if your organization is the right fit for them.

2. Create a scorecard.

We are full of biases—many of which are difficult to consciously recognize. We think we are great judges of character based on intuition, but without objective criteria, we are more likely to make decisions based on unconscious biases and stereotypes. Creating a scorecard, one with clear instructions on what to ask candidates to assess each value and how to rate them based on their answers, helps reduce interviewer bias. It also makes it easier to compare candidates who have been interviewed by different people.

At Zappos, recruiters check for overall values alignment during their core values interview. As the candidate responds to questions about their values, like the questions mentioned above for their value of "Create Fun and a Little Weirdness," the recruiter rates them on a scale of one (strongly disagree that the candidate is a culture match) to five (strongly agree that the candidate is a culture match), using specific criteria provided. The recruiter then submits their notes to the hiring manager along with a summary and recommendation of whether or not they believe that candidate's values align.

3. Look for values-added, not just values-conformity.

When emphasizing character in the hiring process, it is possible to go too far. As Katie Burke from HubSpot told us, "We are not looking to hire clones—we want people who share our values *and* will challenge us to live them more fully." As we shared in the last chapter, research shows that diversity of perspectives is a huge asset in organizations. The more that people from diverse backgrounds and experiences engage around shared values, the more innovative thinking and creativity are ignited.

At Patagonia, they look for candidates who are activists but recognize that activism can show up in many different ways. Theresita explains, "We want to find out, 'What's that thing that is important to you?' It could be tied to the environment or climate change or something totally different. What we really want to know is how you are advancing the issues you care about." For Theresita, her activism showed up through involvement in her local community, where she provided free leadership coaching and team development training to local nonprofit organizations whose missions she supported.

Theresita told us that Patagonia doesn't just want to honor the history and legacy that it has built, it also wants to grow into the Patagonia of the future. This requires that the company have an openness and receptivity to different voices and to different lived experiences. Hiring people with diverse perspectives is a critical ingredient for this to become a reality.

Hiring for character is good business. Candidates are hungry to join organizations where they can do meaningful, values-aligned work. Additionally, prioritizing character broadens the candidate pool and opens the doors for individuals with limited experience. There are a lot of people out there like your second friend—eager to travel and waiting for a chance to join the adventure.

Hubert Joly, former chair and CEO of Best Buy who led the company's turnaround, emphasized the importance of hiring for character in a recent interview: "A mistake I made for too many years was putting too much emphasis on expertise and experience when recruiting somebody. Over time, I [put] more and more emphasis on who is this person? And being clear about our leadership expectations. . . . I told the officers at Best Buy if you don't agree with these principles, that's okay. Except, oh, you cannot work here."

Hiring people based on who they are and what they value is the first ingredient of a meaningful beginning. Next, leaders can leverage onboarding to prepare a new hire for a lengthy, meaningful career in the organization.

THE INGREDIENTS OF A MEANINGFUL ONBOARDING

Mise en place is a French culinary term that translates to "everything in its place." It refers to the practice of preparing and organizing all the ingredients, tools, and equipment needed for a particular recipe before starting to cook. Mise en place ensures that a chef has everything ready and easily accessible, making the cooking process more efficient, organized, and fun.

By investing the time to do the prep work before they begin cooking, chefs can more effectively move through the steps of their recipes. One of our favorite chefs, Kelcy Scolnick, has a great mantra: "Start as you mean to go on." She believes that mise en place sets the stage for a successful cooking experience.

Intentionally onboarding new employees into your organization is like using mise en place to prepare a meal. Except that instead of chopped vegetables and spices, the critical ingredients for a meaningful onboarding are authentic relationship building and cultural immersion. By doing the prep work ahead of time, you are setting the stage for your new team members to have a successful and meaningful career in your organization. You are starting as you mean to go on.

Many companies invest significant time, resources, and money recruiting new talent. When it comes to their first day, however, new employees are handed a laptop and expected to hit the ground running. An intentionally designed and carefully executed onboarding experience can ensure your new team members have all the ingredients they need for a successful start. It also ensures that all the time and money you spend recruiting, vetting, and hiring new employees isn't wasted.

The early cues employees receive when they start their tenure with a new organization carry great weight in the creation of meaning at work. A new employee's introduction during that period significantly impacts engagement across their entire tenure at an organization. Twenty percent of employee turnover happens within the first forty-five days. On the other hand, employees who are onboarded effectively are up to eighteen times more committed to their workplace, 89 percent more engaged, and thirty times more likely to be satisfied at work.

This is a largely untapped opportunity. Typical onboarding processes focus heavily on general compliance and mundane topics such as technology and paperwork. This can leave new hires feeling overwhelmed by a volume of information that is impossible to process in a short period of time.

In contrast, onboarding can be what one of the leaders in our research called a "sacred moment"—the perfect time to create a strong foundation for a long-term relationship. An intentionally designed onboarding experience—like the mise en place—matters because it sets the stage for the new employee's future experience.

Leaders who want to start as they mean to go on, focus on two essential (and mostly overlooked) ingredients to create a meaningful onboarding experience—**cultural mastery**, which involves orienting employees to their unique culture through storytelling and shared rituals, and **authentic relationship building**, which includes helping new employees show up authentically and cultivate connections right away.

Cultural Mastery

Vincent Stanley was one of Patagonia's original employees. He intended to work at the organization for six months, save some money, and then backpack around Europe. However, the chance to be a part of something bigger has kept him at Patagonia for more than fifty years. In the early days, he and founder Yvon Chouinard would sit around and hash out how they wanted to do business, what they stood for, and how they wanted to grow. Vincent helped put these philosophies down on paper, and those philosophies became the heart of Yvon Chouinard's bestselling book *Let My People Go Surfing*.

Vincent is now Patagonia's director of philosophy and, informally, the company's chief storyteller. Part of his role is to onboard new employees to the organization by sharing stories that illustrate how each of their five values—quality, integrity, environmentalism, justice, and not bound by convention—comes to life at Patagonia. He said, "It strikes me as amazing, 50 years after I got here, that the best qualities of the company persist today."

Patagonia's emphasis on storytelling was a memorable part of Theresita's onboarding. Vincent was one of the first people that Theresita met when she joined. During the first week, she took a philosophy course with him, where a particular story he shared about revitalizing the Ventura River really stood out to her. In the story, Patagonia employees helped bring life back to a river that was thought to be dead. Through small actions, like providing a desk, phone, and mailbox to local organizations, they helped bring about significant environmental change. To Theresita, it highlighted the power of activism, one of Patagonia's core values, and showed how little investments from passionate people could make a big difference.

Meaning-driven leaders use stories like this to create a rite of initiation for new employees. The process of sharing the stories becomes a kind of ritual that each person experiences as part of their acceptance into the community.

Although we often think of rituals as formal ceremonies or religious events like weddings or graduations, they can also be smaller practices that are infused with meaning. Rituals like Vincent's philosophy course for new employees bring culture to life, bind people together, and help everyone move toward a shared purpose. They help transform the ordinary into something meaningful. Rituals can transform your onboarding from a mundane process to a sacred moment. During onboarding, these rituals signify acceptance to the team and create a sense of belonging.

Storytelling is an effective mechanism to reflect and reinforce strong cultures. Like Vincent at Patagonia, meaning-driven leaders use stories to teach new employees about the organization's values and desired behaviors or "how things are done around here." Research finds that when employees strongly agree that their onboarding provides a good understanding of the organization's culture, they're nearly five times more likely to praise their onboarding experience.

After hiring for character, leaders at Zappos start a four-week onboarding process by doing a deep dive on their values. Their goal is to clarify for new employees the exact meaning and expectations for each of their ten core values. They invite individuals from across the organization to share a story about a particular value, why that value is personally important to them, and how it has helped their career at Zappos. One famous story comes from Tony Hsieh about Zappos's first core value, "Deliver WOW Through Service."

Tony shared about a time when he took clients out for a night on the town. When the bar closed, they all went back to their hotel rooms. One of his clients was hungry and craving pizza, but the hotel's room service was closed for the night. Tony suggested that this client call Zappos customer service. Even though his company was a shoe retailer, Tony was confident about his team's ability to deliver WOW. The customer service representative took the call at 2 a.m., found three pizza shops that were still open near the hotel, and made the order for the client.

By sharing stories that animate the company's core values, leaders not only bring those values to life but also create a space for new employees to contribute their own stories. This exchange begins during the interview process with behavioral questions that probe how candidates embody these values in their daily lives. Extending this into onboarding enriches the experience, transforming it from a standard procedure into a deeply meaningful journey.

In addition to storytelling, meaning-driven leaders engage new employees in a variety of other shared rituals during onboarding, transforming them from mere observers of the culture into fully immersed participants. For example, some organizations make it a practice to give new team members a physical object that symbolizes their acceptance into the group. At Google, new employees, or "Nooglers," receive a baseball hat with a propellor on top, symbolizing Google's quirky culture. Nooglers will often proudly take pictures of themselves wearing the hat to share on LinkedIn or other social media and dig it up years later when they receive a big promotion or move on to an exciting new job. At Airbnb, people from across the organization form a human tunnel through which new employees run. This ritual was created to welcome colleagues and represents the company's mission to "create a world where anyone can belong anywhere."

The best rituals are simple, unique to the organization's culture, and create a shared identity that makes new hires feel "like one of us." These rituals can be designed to be just as effective in remote onboarding experiences as they are in in-person ones. While remote work has many benefits, it has also brought many challenges for organizations, including reimagining their onboarding experience. Without the traditional rituals that signal new beginnings, employees might be leaving a previous job on a Friday and starting the new job the next Monday from the same desk, in the same home office. Additionally, without in-person contact and shared experiences, the ability to form new relationships can be compromised.

Humu, a behavioral change technology company, adapted their onboarding to a fully remote experience in 2020. Part of the redesign involved developing rituals to increase belonging for "Numus" (what they call their new hires—even these silly names have a significance in immediately binding people together who are in on the joke). Lynn Chikasuye, the organization's head of IT, shared, "The official 2-week Numu onboarding ends with a company-wide 'graduation' ceremony, where each manager talks about their Numu graduate and their personal accomplishments so far. Celebrating small wins like graduation helps new hires feel like they're already part of the team, and also helps build rapport between managers and their direct reports."

When designing cultural mastery rituals for your onboarding process, consider the following questions:

- How can you integrate storytelling around your organizational values and culture into the onboarding process to ensure new employees understand "how things are done around here"?
- What specific activities and rituals can be incorporated to foster strong interpersonal connections among new hires and existing team members?
- In what ways can you make the onboarding experience more interactive and engaging to help new employees feel connected and motivated from the start?

Incorporating storytelling and other meaningful rituals during onboarding is an effective way of cultivating a sense of shared purpose and belonging. Starting with a small yet purposeful gesture, like a goofy hat or running through a human tunnel, can set the tone for a welcoming employee experience.

In addition to ensuring that new hires develop cultural mastery by learning about the organization's purpose, values, and expected behaviors, a meaningful onboarding process is intentionally designed to foster authentic relationship building.

Authentic Relationship Building

When Tamara's children were ten, nine, and seven years old, she and her husband made the difficult decision to leave the small town that had been their cherished home for many years. A new job opportunity took them to a new community more than fifty miles away. The weight of this decision pressed upon them for months. Tamara and her husband, Ted, struggled with the idea of leaving a beloved community where their children thrived to move to a town where they didn't know anyone. Would the kids make new friends easily? Would the community share the values that they prized as a family? Would they feel like they belonged?

The kids were entering fifth, fourth, and second grades. Tamara and Ted knew that their experiences at the new school would be a key factor in adjusting to the new town. Although the school system had a great reputation, they were all nervous. Then something remarkable happened.

One week before school started, Tamara received an email from the principal, Mrs. Fernandez, inviting them for a private tour of the school. Mrs. Fernandez showed them around, highlighting areas that she knew were of special significance for the kids. She pointed out each of their classrooms, the cafeteria, the gym, and, most importantly, the playground. While she guided the family around the school, Mrs. Fernandez was intentional about prompting and answering questions that she knew would be on the children's minds—things like how to buy lunch, whether they needed a bathroom pass (yes), and how many recesses they would get each day (at least two, but sometimes more depending on the teacher). By the end of the tour, the kids were excited to start school. Then Mrs. Fernandez had another surprise. She told the family that the school has an onboarding program for new students called the New Family Program, which involves pairing each new child with a buddy from their class.

Mrs. Fernandez had meticulously reviewed the information packets Tamara completed upon enrolling the children. She then carefully handpicked a buddy for each of them based on shared interests and what she believed were complementary personalities. She told them to expect a call from the buddies' parents within the next day. The kids would meet their buddies before the first day of school so they would have a friendly face in the classroom, someone to sit with at lunch, and a friend to play with at recess.

It is hard to describe, even all these years later, how much that moment meant to Tamara's family. In that instant, all their anxiety and fear dissolved, and they knew they had chosen the right community. By caring enough to get to know her children before they walked through the door and taking the extra step to introduce them to families in the community, the school leadership made them feel like they belonged.

That week, after exchanging emails with the three families, they met with the buddies in a nearby park. The kids all played together while the parents chatted. Meeting these families was a lifeline not only for the kids but also for Tamara and Ted. They now had friends they could call with questions about activities and local resources: How do we sign up for soccer? Is there a good theater program? What is your favorite local sushi restaurant? These families also invited them to social events and introduced them to other friends in the community.

The New Family Program was, in essence, an onboarding buddy program. Mrs. Fernandez designed it to foster relationships and a network of support for incoming students and their families. It was a very meaningful experience not only for the first day of school but for years to come. One of the families has become very close friends. They travel together frequently, celebrate each other's milestones, and reminisce about that first awkward meeting in the park.

ONBOARDING BUDDIES

After a few years of working to improve their onboarding process, Microsoft piloted an onboarding buddy program in 2018. The company began assigning a dedicated current employee to help each new hire's transition. The program proved to be extremely successful, positively impacting the new employees' productivity, satisfaction, and cultural mastery. In Microsoft's pilot, new hires with buddies were 23 percent more satisfied with their overall onboarding experience compared to those without buddies. Buddies provide support for new employees, which is one of the most important things a new hire needs for success. This can lead to a positive and productive first few months on the job, which has ripple effects throughout an employee's career.

Evelyn* is a senior program manager in culture and employee experience at Microsoft. Her formal onboarding buddy process lasted only a few weeks, but she and her buddy stayed casually connected for several months. Evelyn shared, "My buddy kept an open door for me, which I preferred over a formal scheduled meeting. This meant I could reach out to her with questions in real time."

When she first started with Microsoft, Evelyn had a huge learning curve when it came to establishing her own rhythms with the senior leaders who were sponsoring her programs. This involved learning how to build relationships with business managers, which was something Evelyn hadn't been familiar with at her previous company. Her onboarding buddy took the time to walk her through examples of times she worked well with business managers and common challenges that she or her colleagues faced. This helped Evelyn build a strong relationship with her sponsor's business manager, which is a relationship she still maintains and leverages several years later. Ultimately, she felt far more confident stepping into her role than she would have without her buddy's support. A few years later, Evelyn and her buddy are still in touch. They catch up every few weeks and continue to support each other's work.

An onboarding buddy is your first office friend—someone whom you can ask questions from the trivial, such as where to find the bathroom or where to eat lunch, to more nuanced questions about cultural norms and office dynamics. Research suggests that 65 percent of new

---

* Name changed to protect anonymity.

hires feel frustrated because they don't have a clear point of contact for questions. A buddy also helps new employees forge relationships across the organization.

Although growing in popularity, fewer than half of organizations today have a formal onboarding buddy program in place. However, you don't need a formal buddy program in your organization to facilitate relationship building during onboarding. Simply helping your new hires make intentional connections can be powerful. At Patagonia, Theresita's leaders focused on helping her build relationships and get to know an array of people across the organization. Although they didn't have a formal onboarding buddy program in place, they helped Theresita set up meetings with "people she should know." In this way, they jump-started the process of building her internal network.

Fostering relationship building during onboarding is crucial for new employees to integrate smoothly into the organization and hit the ground running. It's like chopping the onions and garlic for a recipe's mise en place. But meaning-driven leaders don't stop there. They carefully add spices and seasoning to enhance the flavor even more.

AUTHENTICITY IN ONBOARDING

As you learned earlier, authenticity—being able to show up fully—increases belonging and meaning. The faster a new employee can show up authentically, the faster they can build meaningful relationships.

Researchers conducted a study at Wipro BPO, an India-based organization that provides telephone and chat support, to see if encouraging authenticity during onboarding would lead to greater performance and retention. They chose an Indian call center because those employees are often expected to be less authentic in their jobs by adopting a Western accent while on the phone with customers. The researchers randomly assigned new Wipro employees to one of three conditions during their onboarding.

The first condition focused on how new employees could bring their unique perspectives and strengths to the job. First, a senior leader discussed how working at Wipro would give newcomers the opportunity to express themselves and create individual opportunities for career growth. Then, new employees performed an individual problem-solving exercise and were asked to spend the next fifteen minutes reflecting on the decisions they made in the exercise and on how to apply their strengths to the job. The new employees then spent fifteen minutes introducing themselves and their decisions to the group so they could get to know each other better. Finally, they were given an employee badge and a sweatshirt with their own names on both.

The second condition started with the assumption that new employees would perform best when they developed pride in their connection to the organization and accepted the organization's norms and values. This time, a senior leader discussed Wipro's values and why Wipro is an outstanding organization, followed by a star performer doing the same. Then, the new hires were asked to spend fifteen minutes reflecting on what they heard and an additional fifteen minutes discussing their answers within their group. Finally, they were given a badge and sweatshirt with the company's name on both.

In the third condition, the control group, new employees went through Wipro's traditional onboarding process, which focused primarily on skills training and general compliance.

The results were remarkable. Participants who onboarded in the first condition—the one which encouraged authentic expression of their unique perspectives and strengths—reported higher job satisfaction and had over 33 percent greater retention during the first six months on the job. Their customers were also happier.

The researchers have replicated these findings in different settings and have found, again and again, that the sooner new employees are encouraged to authentically show who they are, the better they perform. They are also more likely to collaborate with colleagues, more creative and innovative, and more satisfied with their jobs.

During her onboarding at Patagonia, Theresita was asked to create a personal user manual, referred to internally as *Read Me*, which would be shared with her team. A *Read Me* is a deck that each employee puts together in which they share who they are, what is important to them, and the things that bring them joy. In addition, the *Read Me* includes personal work styles and preferences—the nitty-gritty of work details like, are you someone who sends bullet points, or do you send a narrative with paragraphs? Are you the person who would rather pick up the phone and talk, or do you prefer a quick text or message from your team?

For Theresita, it was important to share her early rising nature. She wanted her team to know that she starts her days early, around 4:30 a.m., before the sun and her family are up. This allows Theresita to have what she calls her "sacred time" to do her morning rituals and have space to think deeply before the world wakes up. On the flip side, it means that she goes to bed very early and will likely not see messages that are sent later in the evening. Theresita made a point to emphasize that this is *her* practice, and she has no expectations for others on her team to do the same.

Patagonia's *Read Me* is designed to accelerate the process of building relationships and getting to know each other's authentic selves. Like the forms Mrs. Fernandez used to match buddies for Tamara's children, these personalized user manuals allow individuals to share their work styles, interests, sources of energy, and communication preferences.

Personal user manuals can be a powerful tool to expedite team integration and authentic relationship building by offering insights into both a person's blind spots and their bright spots. To help you design your own personal user manuals, we included some examples from different organizations and a template on our website, www.makeworkmeaningful.com.

Relationship building during onboarding is not just about making friends. It also expedites the time it takes for new hires to get up to speed. The New Family Program wasn't only about having someone to sit with at lunch, although that was meaningful and crucial. Having this small network also helped Tamara's family sign up for activities, find local resources, and integrate into the community faster. Similarly, by looking through others' *Read Me* decks, Theresita was able to do more than build connections. She was also able to quickly learn her team's work preferences and reduce the time it took to collaborate with them effectively. Whether through structured programs or organic connections, fostering these initial relationships sets the stage for a smoother and more meaningful start.

Often, we only think of onboarding when new employees join the organization. However, these practices can be valuable anytime you have the opportunity to make a first impression. Even if you don't have control of your organization's onboarding process, you can still use cultural mastery and authentic relationship-building practices when new people join your team, when you kick off a new project, or even when hosting a special event.

SHOW, DON'T TELL

When we recently had the opportunity to share our onboarding research during a conference of MAPP alumni at Penn, we saw an opportunity to put some of these leadership practices to work. Instead of *telling* them about our research, we thought it would be more impactful and more fun to *show* them what a great onboarding looks like. We designed a mini onboarding program for the conference focused on cultural mastery and authentic relationship building.

We started by enlisting our colleague Jan Stanley, a world expert on rituals. She designed a beautiful meditative experience focused on grounding us in place, people, and presence for the day. To bring our community's values of engagement, connection, and fun to life, we invited three colleagues to share stories of those values in action to paint a picture of our culture and how different people live our values in different ways.

Finally, to build authentic connection, we designed an activity for individuals to connect and deepen their relationships with each other. Before participants arrived, we placed dice on all the tables and created a list of six discussion prompts to facilitate authentic relationship building. The prompts were playful (in keeping with our value of fun) and included things like, "You can learn the answer to one secret in history. Which do you choose and why?" and "Tell the story of your first live music concert." These were numbered one through six. Participants formed pairs with someone at their table, rolled the die, and took turns answering the question on the corresponding number. In a few minutes, the room was buzzing with excitement and connection.

These simple onboarding practices helped our colleagues build new relationships, gain a sense of what our weekend together was going to be like, and know what behaviors were expected of them. Throughout the weekend, we heard from people that this process of cultural and community onboarding had kick-started their excitement and helped them make meaningful connections that blossomed throughout the conference. Fostering this meaningful start took us less than an hour.

Although the practices we presented in this chapter are simple, they are not commonly used. Research from Gallup shows that only 12 percent of workers think their organization does a great job of onboarding new employees. One of the biggest obstacles we hear from leaders when we suggest redesigning their onboarding process for increased meaning is lack of time. They tell us there is an urgent need to get new employees up to speed quickly so they can start producing. We believe that is a short-sighted view. As we have seen, investing in a meaningful onboarding experience increases engagement and productivity.

Just like the mise en place is a time investment that can ensure a seamless cooking experience, investing time and energy in a thoughtfully designed onboarding process can ensure your new team members have all the ingredients they need to succeed in your organization. By intentionally recrafting the onboarding process to include authentic relationship building and cultural mastery, you can make work meaningful, build community, and set the stage for new employees to become highly engaged and productive.

In Part II of the book, we explored how practices that create community make work meaningful. From creating a values-aligned culture to authentic relationship building to creating opportunities for shared experiences, practices that build belonging are crucial to increasing meaning. In the next part, we turn our focus to practices that increase our sense of contribution at work.

PART III

CREATING MEANING THROUGH CONTRIBUTION

During the development of the Apollo space program, President John F. Kennedy visited NASA headquarters in Houston, Texas. It is rumored that, during a tour of the facility, he came across a janitor mopping the floor and walked over to introduce himself. After shaking the man's hand, he asked the janitor what he was doing. The janitor replied, "Putting a man on the moon."

The janitor's response was not a fluke. For years, NASA had invested in connecting every employee's work to the organization's larger purpose. In a study of NASA employees in the 1960s, psychologist Andrew Carton found that these efforts to highlight their contributions to the organization increased employees' sense of meaning at work. As leaders shifted from managing daily tasks, such as fixing electrical circuits, to telling the story of how those tasks laddered up to the organization's larger aspirations, such as expanding the boundaries of human knowledge, people saw that they were contributing to something bigger than themselves.

Community drives meaning by helping people understand how they matter to others in their organizations. Our second C, contribution, drives meaning by helping people understand how their work matters—to the people within the organization, as well as its customers, partners, and members of the local community.

Earlier, we noted that the idea of having an organizational purpose is well-worn territory at this point. We wholeheartedly support efforts to articulate your organization's bigger impact, but that vision alone does not create meaning. A clear purpose will help inspire others to join your cause and can build community by giving them common goals to work toward, but that is only part of the equation. A sense of contribution comes from seeing progress toward those goals—from advancing that purpose. Those goals might ladder up to a noble mission like NASA's work to put a man on the moon. They could also be as simple as saving people a little time in their day, the mission of scheduling software company Calendly. As you'll see, a strong sense of contribution can be found just as easily in both organizations when leaders frame the work effectively.

Contribution also comes from receiving positive feedback from leaders and coworkers. Positive feedback validates the effort we put into our work and provides a sense of accomplishment. Although it is an often overlooked and underutilized practice, recognition from a leader or team member can be incredibly meaningful.

When people see the impact of the tasks they perform each day and understand how those tasks benefit something larger than themselves, their work becomes meaningful. Those contributions can be found in a few words, such as a customer letting their sales rep know how the company's product helped them land a new deal, a Slack message from a colleague thanking a team member for their help on a recent project, or an email from a manager praising a direct report for helping take the company to the next level. Meaning-driven leaders show people that their work matters in two ways—by giving positive feedback that highlights their contributions to the team and by connecting their work to the bigger impact of the organization.

7

THE POWER OF
POSITIVE FEEDBACK

The deepest principle in human nature is the craving to be
appreciated.

—WILLIAM JAMES

Every Friday around 4 p.m., Kathy Rollins* faithfully performs a ritual to close out the week. Kathy, a managing director in the audit
practice of a large accounting firm, blocks off thirty minutes to reflect
on her team's progress. She looks back over her calendar to identify
the significant moments of the week. Then she writes and sends brief
emails to five of her teammates. In these "gratitude notes," as Kathy
calls them, she recognizes each person for something they did to support the team that week. Kathy focuses on a specific action that person

_____

* Name changed to protect anonymity.

took and shares the positive impact that action had. She closes each note by thanking them for their contribution before closing her laptop for the weekend.

Several years ago, Kathy realized something was missing. As an auditor, Kathy spends a lot of her time looking for mistakes. Clients hire her team to comb through their books to identify errors and irregularities that need to be fixed. Kathy found she was spending all of her time looking for what was wrong but never acknowledging or celebrating when things went well.

Although most of us don't work in the audit department, we all have a natural drive to focus on what's wrong. Research shows that we tend to notice negative events at three times the rate we do positive ones. This innate negativity bias has served us well from an evolutionary perspective. Staying alive depends largely on identifying and successfully navigating threats. Those ancestors who kept an eye out for leopards lurking in the trees lived longer than those who admired the beautiful wildflowers on the forest floor. At work, however, our negativity bias can often work against us. It can keep us so focused on highlighting what's wrong that we forget to acknowledge what's right. Kathy resolved to change this and started the weekly gratitude notes to remind herself and her team of what they were doing well. She hoped it would give her a boost and that the team might also benefit, but she didn't expect what happened next.

Just a few weeks after Kathy's notes started landing in inboxes, they began to multiply. Unprompted, other members of the team began sending out gratitude notes as well. Kathy saw that team members became more intentional about thanking each other throughout the week. Meetings, Microsoft Teams chats, and informal conversations were suddenly peppered with praise. Kathy's simple practice had snowballed into a teamwide culture of positive feedback.

By letting her team members know that their efforts mattered to her, Kathy showed them that their work was valued. With a newly bolstered sense of contribution, team members brought increased energy and engagement to their work. That energy spread as they, in turn, showed others that their work was valued. Instead of just auditing their work for mistakes, they started accounting for their wins.

We crave positive feedback from others because it lets us know that our work matters. When employees receive positive feedback from their leaders and colleagues, their sense of contribution increases and their work becomes more meaningful. Whether your organization calls it recognition, gratitude, appreciation, celebration, or something else, positive feedback serves as a significant signpost of a meaningful contribution.

Dan Ariely, professor of behavioral economics at Duke University and author of multiple bestselling books, designed an unusual study to understand how recognizing someone's work impacts their desire to keep doing it. Dan's team paid three groups of participants to examine a string of letters on a piece of paper and circle duplicate letters. The experiment really began, however, when the participants handed in their assignments. For the first group, there was explicit acknowledgment of their work—the researchers examined the paper and said "uh-huh" before setting it aside. The second group's papers were placed in a pile with no acknowledgment. In the third group, there was explicit devaluing of the work—the papers were immediately shredded in front of the participants. Once finished, all the participants had the option of completing another assignment for additional pay.

Not surprisingly, the group whose work was acknowledged opted to complete more papers. But what's truly fascinating about the study is what Dan found with the second group. The group whose initial assignments were placed in a pile with no acknowledgment completed roughly the same number of additional papers as the third group. They reacted in almost the same way as the group whose work was shredded. Knowing that our work matters to the team—that our contributions to the group are acknowledged and appreciated—makes work meaningful and motivates us to do more. Telling us nothing, however, is nearly as bad as trashing our work.

Recent reports show that less than 40 percent of employees believe they are adequately recognized for their work. Without positive feedback, employees are 74 percent more likely to leave within the year. When our efforts go unacknowledged, like those of the participants in Dan's study, we don't have the necessary feedback to make meaning from them. We're left to wonder whether our work was worthwhile.

Feedback is any information we receive about the impact of something that we did. At work, it typically comes from managers, colleagues, and customers. Feedback is how we learn whether or not our actions are achieving our desired goals. Fifty years of research on goal setting and achievement shows that feedback plays a critical role in success. Without regular information on how we're doing, it's incredibly difficult to know how we're progressing or when we need to adjust our behavior.

When we hear the word *feedback*, many of us cringe in anticipation of hearing a list of our mistakes or personal faults. Or worse, we prepare to be handed a "feedback sandwich"—criticism of our behavior sandwiched between two inauthentic compliments in an attempt to soften the blow. In many organizations, feedback is given poorly and focuses almost exclusively on what went wrong.

Receiving constructive feedback is an important part of improving performance when delivered effectively—given with context, tied to a specific behavior, and focused on how to do things better in the future. But constructive feedback isn't what we need most to meet our goals. Constructive feedback tells us we might need to stop or change a particular behavior. Like pulling weeds, constructive feedback can help us remove the things that are getting in our way. Positive feedback, like Dan Ariely's "uh-huh" or Kathy's gratitude notes, lets us know that our efforts are worthwhile. Like sunlight, it is a source of energy that helps us grow and thrive. We naturally move toward the sun.

Imagine you are on a road trip from New York to Los Angeles. You rent a convertible, gas up the tank, and kick off your cross-country journey. A few miles in, the GPS on your phone dies. And for some crazy reason, the Department of Transportation has taken down all of the highway road signs. You're pretty sure you have to keep going west, but as the hours pass by, it's less and less clear whether you're getting closer to LA. Without any signs of progress, it's hard to know if you're headed in the right direction. Positive feedback, like the mile markers on the highway, lets us know we're making progress toward our destination. Without those markers, it's easy to get lost. Constructive feedback helps us avoid roadblocks, but only positive feedback keeps us moving on the right track.

Leaders can inspire us to greater heights when they let us know what we've done well. Research shows that people are more likely to learn from positive feedback than they are from critical feedback. A series of studies showed that participants who took a knowledge test learned more and subsequently performed better after receiving positive feedback on their efforts. When they were told what they got right, they remembered information more clearly and scored higher on a second test of the same material. The researchers noted that "our society celebrates failure as a teachable moment. Yet we find that [focusing only on] failure does the opposite: it undermines learning. It causes participants to tune out and stop processing information."

Pete Berridge, coauthor of *Feedback Reimagined* and designer of the ShiftPositive feedback method, said, "Telling people what went wrong doesn't give them a way to productively move forward. They know what *not* to do next time, but they don't get information about how to perform better. There is no opportunity to learn, and it feels like the work they did was wasted effort." When we tell people what they did right, however, we validate their work and give them a road map to continued success. Behavior that is recognized is repeated.

Despite this, people consistently undervalue giving positive feedback. One study found that participants who were asked to give positive feedback significantly underestimated how much it would matter to the person receiving it and also how surprised the recipients would be to hear it. Participants assumed their gratitude would be more obvious and less meaningful to the recipient than it actually was. We tend to think that others know how much we appreciate their work, so we don't actually tell them. Often, this leaves them wondering.

In the same study, participants hesitated to give positive feedback because they believed recipients would feel awkward receiving it. It turned out that the awkwardness was more on the part of the givers, not the receivers. This reluctance to share positive feedback with others can siphon gas from their tanks. Before she started the weekly gratitude notes, Kathy took for granted that her team members knew she appreciated their work. She thought people might feel uncomfortable if she made a big deal out of recognizing them. But as she learned, she had underestimated the power of positive feedback.

There are two ways that leaders can tap into the power of contribution through positive feedback—by **giving positive feedback directly** and by **creating structures for peers to give positive feedback** to each other.

POSITIVE FEEDBACK FROM LEADERS

Tunde Oyeneyin is one of the most popular cycling instructors on the global fitness platform Peloton. Her classes regularly draw more than twenty thousand riders who are inspired by her engaging attitude and by the encouragement that she gives them. If you clip in to a ride with Tunde, you'll quickly understand why riders keep coming back. While she has a reputation for being one of the toughest instructors, she also makes you feel that the work is worth it. Tunde recognizes riders for making it through each tough stretch. She also gives shout-outs to those who are hitting milestones of ten, one hundred, or even one thousand rides, as well as those who are getting on the bike for the first time. Tunde's shout-outs are even more powerful because riders know she understands the effort each of them is putting in. She regularly shares her own stories of struggle and success to let them know she's been in their shoes.

Tunde grew up the daughter of Nigerian immigrants in a suburb of Houston. From a young age, she had challenges with her weight and struggled with self-esteem. She didn't always feel like she fit in. In a particularly poignant moment, her mother had to sew together two dresses so that she could be a bridesmaid at a family member's wedding. Seeing her frustration, her mother looked at her, saying, "If you want to change things, *you* have got to change things." Determined, Tunde joined the local gym and set to work. The road was long, but she eventually lost seventy pounds and remade herself physically and mentally. Along the way, her mother gave her positive feedback, which helped keep her going.

"I had three brothers, and they were going to make fun of me at any size," Tunde laughs, "so I don't think that they were helpful." Her mother, however, encouraged her, letting her know that her hard work and determination were noticed. "From my mom, it was just acknowledgment. She saw me, she acknowledged the work that I was doing, and she told me I was doing a good job." By providing positive feedback, Tunde's mother showed her that the effort she was putting in was worth it. Without criticizing her past behavior or making her feel inadequate, Tunde's mom helped her learn that focusing on what was going well, putting her energy into what she was doing to get better, was the thing that would help her succeed.

Eventually, Tunde left for Los Angeles to pursue an opportunity to work for a beauty company she admired. As a makeup artist, she took a similar approach to her clients, focusing on their strengths. "My mom taught me that the purpose of makeup isn't to cover who you are but rather to bring who you are out. You want to enhance the natural beauty that's already there. And so that was my philosophy." We often think about makeup as a way to hide blemishes or fix things that we don't like about ourselves, but Tunde believes that cosmetics have the most powerful effect when they amplify what's special and unique about a person. As an instructor for the company, Tunde brought that same mentality to her teaching style. When training new sales representatives, she had them practice applying makeup on each other. Trainees could be easily frustrated when they made mistakes, but when Tunde called out small successes, she saw them light up immediately.

On a company trip to New York, Tunde decided to take a cycling class she had heard about from a friend. Being on the bike for the first time was transformative and she was hooked. After returning to LA, she joined a local cycling studio and eventually began teaching there. In her book *Speak: Find Your Voice, Trust Your Gut, and Get from Where You Are to Where You Want to Be*, Tunde writes, "As a trainer, your job is to get the best out of people, and I knew how to do that, whether I was working with makeup artists or cyclists. I knew how to give feedback and motivate people." She soon left her cosmetics career to focus on cycling full-time. It wasn't long before her reputation as an inspiring instructor caught the attention of Peloton. They reached out to ask her if she'd be interested in joining the team.

In her first audition for Peloton, Tunde didn't make the cut. For weeks after, she played the audition over and over again in her mind, trying to understand what had gone wrong. Was it her music? Her look? Her vibe? Eight months later, when she got another chance to audition, she sought feedback from lead instructor Cody Rigsby on how she could improve her performance. Instead of focusing on what she might have done wrong, Cody told her to lean into what she had done well the first time. The Peloton team was dazzled by her authenticity and her relentless focus on bringing an encouraging atmosphere to the class. They offered her a coveted spot on the Peloton roster—and she didn't disappoint.

Tunde's motivating style and use of positive feedback have earned her a dedicated following. Lisa Richardson, a longtime Peloton rider and positive psychology researcher who has studied the company, finds Tunde's feedback inspiring. "Like everyone, I've got a lot going on. It's not easy to get up early and find time to get on the bike. But when I get a shout-out from Tunde, it makes me want to give my best and come back for more." Lisa, who recently celebrated her 2,500th ride, gets her motivation and her meaning from knowing that someone sees her and appreciates her hard work.

"At the start of a recent class, Tunde gave me some praise for just being there, for making the effort to show up and get on the bike," shared Lisa. "It's a small thing, but I needed it in that moment. There are so many other things I could have been doing, and I was thinking about clipping off. That positive feedback from her acknowledged the effort I put in to get myself there. It kept me locked in."

Tunde has built on the practice of positive feedback she learned from her mother and passes it along to her riders. She recognizes that encouragement is what keeps us going: it's like fuel. "I am a pretty tough instructor, and I know that in order to get people to come with me, they have to know that they're doing a good job. Or else, who wants to go? What is it for?" said Tunde.

In a study that Lisa conducted on the experiences of Peloton riders, they cited encouragement from instructors as a top factor for staying with the platform. The more positive feedback instructors gave, the more likely riders were to work harder and keep coming back.

To fuel meaning and motivation at work, we need leaders like Tunde. When we're on the right track, meaning-driven leaders let us know by praising our efforts and encouraging us to keep moving in the right direction. They see and validate our work. They are there to redirect us when we get off track, but their biggest impact comes from pushing us to do more of what's working. Whether we're putting in miles on the bike or hours at the office, we need positive feedback from others to know that our efforts are paying off. Calling out someone's contributions creates meaning. Meaning fuels motivation. At work, like on the bike, behavior that is appreciated is amplified.

"Fitness is hard," said Tom Cortese, cofounder of Peloton. "We certainly have the capability to outrun animals who are chasing us down in the forest. But when we don't have to, sitting on the couch and watching Netflix is just lovely. We use so much of our willpower in our day-to-day to raise our kids, to get our ass to work, to do a great job, to be a good spouse, to be a good friend. We're using so much willpower to do all these other things on a daily basis. And so, we've got to summon it. We need help."

As Tom and his team launched and scaled Peloton from a scrappy start-up to a billion-dollar public company, he developed his corporate team with the same mindset. Just like Peloton riders, Tom wanted his team to feel recognized. In the early days of Peloton, long before there were any customers, the founders made a point to acknowledge the contributions that each team member made to the company.

"We would take videos of simple milestones—like when a technical glitch was fixed and the digital leaderboard finally showed up on two bikes at the same time the way it was supposed to," Tom laughs. John Foley, another cofounder and former CEO of Peloton, would take those videos and share them with investors to update them on the company's progress but also to recognize the work of the team. John would write celebratory, detailed emails and name everybody who contributed to achieving a new milestone. This helped draw them closer as a team and get everybody pumped to go and do it again. "As a leader, you can forget how that celebration, those little moments of positive feedback, can have such a big impact," said Tom.

Tom was responsible for designing all of Peloton's products, including the bike and the software that powered it. As he worked to design positive feedback into the customer experience, he learned lessons that informed his design of the employee experience as well. Early on, he learned that Peloton customers would initially use the bike in fits and starts. While some outliers would take a class every day at the same time, few were that disciplined, especially at the beginning. Tom and his team experimented with adding "streaks" to the Peloton platform. If you used the bike for two days in a row, you would start a streak, which would earn you a badge, the platform's equivalent of positive feedback. Your streak would grow until you missed a day, and then you'd lose it.

Tom was surprised to find that, instead of getting riders to exercise more, streaks actually had the opposite effect. Tying the badges to getting on the bike every single day made the risk of failing too high. Few people were able to keep their streaks for long. Instead of a positive reminder of progress, the first version of streaks served as a reminder that people weren't meeting their goals. It ended up being more frustrating than inspiring. Tom and his team redesigned the functionality around weekly streaks to make them more achievable. Then they added additional rewards for moving up to twice a week, and then three times a week and more. Tom realized that Peloton needed to meet people where they were and recognize them for accomplishing something rather than call them out for failing. The updated streaks were a success and helped motivate riders to stay on the right track.

As the company scaled up, it became impossible for Peloton's founders to call out every good piece of work that employees were doing. At the same time, the organization grew to include a diverse set of employees with different experiences and skill levels. A one-size-fits-all system of feedback didn't work for the corporate team any more than it did for the customers. If they only rewarded salespeople who were hitting huge targets, the ones who were just starting out had little motivation to get there. It would be very discouraging. It was important to recognize that different people were starting from different places. Tom helped design the right amount of positive feedback into Peloton's culture by developing a set of recommendations for people managers. Managers were encouraged to regularly recognize each of their people for accomplishments that were appropriate to their skill level. To ensure the process was effective, employees were surveyed several times a year to ask about the amount of recognition they received and make sure everyone was on the right track.

As Tom learned, every acknowledgment from a leader was a mile marker on the road to meaning for members of the team.

BEST FEEDBACK

Expressing gratitude, the act of thanking someone for their actions, is one way to share positive feedback. In Dan Ariely's experiment, a simple uh-huh was enough to let participants know that their efforts mattered. Recent research found that just one thank-you from a manager once a week was enough to double engagement at work and cut turnover in half. Employees who receive gratitude regularly are 90 percent less likely to report being burned out. Organizations with high levels of gratitude are more resilient and perform better financially.

To explore the impact that positive feedback from a leader has on productivity, researchers set up a simple experiment at a call center. They split the employees into two groups. For the first group, it was business as usual. For the second, a senior manager came in to thank them for their work. Over the next week, the second group increased their efforts by more than 50 percent. Like adding fuel to the tank, positive feedback from leaders powers performance.

While acknowledgment of mile markers makes a huge difference, the journey becomes even more meaningful when leaders call out specifically what's going well. You can amplify the impact of a simple thank-you by giving positive feedback that is behavioral, explicit, strengths-based, and timely. We developed the BEST feedback model as a framework for leaders to give high-impact positive feedback to their teams. It helps someone understand and do more of the things that are working well. Let's take a closer look at the components of **BEST feedback**.

Behavioral

The feedback focuses on the actions someone took. Instead of praising an outcome ("Thanks for delivering that report"), behavioral feedback highlights the specific actions you observed that led to that successful outcome ("You did excellent market research for this report. You went above and beyond by adding in the various customer personas to bring the research to life"). Focusing on specific behaviors improves future performance by giving someone a road map for what to do more of next time.

Explicit

The feedback is explicit about the impact the person's behavior had on you and others. As we shared earlier, we often underestimate the power of telling people why what they did mattered to us. Be explicit about the impact that the person's behavior had on you. In an illuminating *Harvard Business Review* article on feedback, leadership experts Marcus Buckingham and Ashley Goodall emphasize the importance of giving explicit praise: "Describe what you experienced when [someone's] moment of excellence caught your attention. There's nothing more believable and more authoritative than sharing what you saw from [them] and how it made you feel."

To continue with the previous behavior example, you could add, "I was impressed by your work on the report. It really helped me understand the potential customers better. We ended up landing the account in part because of your efforts." This additional context helps communicate the value that the behavior brought to you and the team.

Strengths-Based

The feedback references a strength that the person showed. When we recognize others' strengths, it makes them feel seen and appreciated for who they are and lets them know their contributions matter. Highlighting a strength that someone has used makes the feedback feel more personal and helps someone understand what you value about them, in addition to what you value about their actions. For example, you could say, "You showed creativity by providing in-depth profiles of potential customers and initiative for going beyond the original assignment."

Timely

The feedback is delivered as soon as possible after the behavior occurred. Don't wait until an annual review to tell someone what they are doing well. The sooner you reinforce the behavior, the sooner you'll see more of it. Research shows that feedback works best when it is timely. It's much more effective to share feedback about what someone did this week than provide feedback on something they did last month.

A complete example of BEST feedback would be, "Lena, thanks for the extra research you did yesterday to support our client pitch. I was impressed by your work, and it really helped me understand the potential customers better. It was creative of you to bring the profiles to life with illustrations. The clients loved it, and we landed the account in large part because of you."

You can find additional examples and tools for crafting BEST feedback on our website at www.makeworkmeaningful.com.

Take a minute to think about how you can incorporate more positive feedback into your workplace. Here are some questions to help you identify opportunities:

- How could you get in the habit of saying thank you to people on your team more often? Where could you design this into your existing business process?
- How could you use the BEST feedback model to go beyond a simple thank-you to highlight the specific behaviors you want to see more of?
- What weekly or monthly team meetings are already on your calendar? How could you add time to call out team members for a job well done?
- When you finish a project, how are you recognizing team members who contributed?

As we saw with Kathy's gratitude notes, leaders who model positive feedback can inspire others to follow suit. When Kathy made a weekly practice of writing gratitude notes, it didn't take long to see the impact spread across her entire team. The consistency of the notes created a new culture of positive feedback, and soon others had adopted the practice.

In addition to setting an example and inspiring others, leaders can create a teamwide culture of positive feedback by designing programs that encourage coworkers to recognize one another. We found that meaning-driven leaders do this by creating infrastructure for peer recognition and by celebrating big moments.

POSITIVE FEEDBACK FROM COLLEAGUES

Peer recognition, like recognition from leaders, satisfies our deep desire to know that our work matters. Unfortunately, just like positive feedback from leaders, positive feedback from peers is a missed opportunity in most organizations. Research has found that a paltry 10 percent of people express gratitude to their colleagues daily. Sixty percent reported rarely or never expressing it at all.

By formalizing peer recognition programs and gratitude practices, leaders can create self-sustaining sources of contribution that require less of their personal time and energy. Giving positive feedback yourself has a big impact. Building a culture of positive feedback amplifies it. Like a cell dividing into two, then four, then eight, then sixteen, the growth becomes exponential when the practice of positive feedback spreads to team members. Positive feedback from peers provides a low-cost, renewable source of meaning for people across your organization.

Peer feedback activates contribution at the same time that it helps strengthen community. Employees who believe that recognition is an important part of their organization's culture are nearly four times more likely to be engaged and about half as likely to experience burnout than those who do not. In one study, when employees gave positive feedback to a peer, the strength of the connection between them increased 55 percent.

Think about a time when you received positive feedback from one of your colleagues. How did you feel when you received it? How did it impact your relationship with that person? For Lisa, the Peloton rider, gratitude from a work colleague lets her know that something she did made a difference and added value. In one of her past roles, Lisa was responsible for facilitating weekly meetings with senior executives. After a particularly high-stakes conversation, Lisa got an email from a member of her team saying he was very impressed with how she navigated the discussion and cited her unflappable attitude.

"Not only did it call out my work, but the feedback also named a specific skill and a strength. It was meaningful to have that recognized, and now I know how to effectively navigate a similar situation the next time."

Peer feedback doesn't just benefit the people who receive it. Sharing positive feedback also benefits the giver. Expressing gratitude causes our brains to release dopamine and serotonin, neurotransmitters that are responsible for positive emotion. In addition to making us feel good immediately, repeated release of these neurotransmitters can permanently change the wiring of our brains, leading to a long-term increase in well-being. One study found that expressing gratitude regularly increased the gray matter in the region of the brain associated with visual processing and memory. Another found that people who expressed gratitude had lower indications of stress and better cardiovascular performance and were more resilient. More research shows that employees who give positive feedback to others also work harder to achieve their own goals.

Even just witnessing an act of gratitude between other people can move us emotionally and cause us to feel greater satisfaction in our own lives. Think of the last time you watched the Oscars, the Grammys, or another awards show. The most poignant moments tend to be the speeches from award winners. They express gratitude to their families, friends, and colleagues who helped them make the long journey to the stage. We watch these shows less to see who will win and more to experience the emotion and sense of possibility that comes from the winners' words of thanks.

When Eimear Marrinan, vice president of culture at HubSpot, is having a rough day, she reaches for the glass mason jar that sits on the corner of her desk. She unscrews the seal, pops the top off, and pulls out one of the dozens of folded pieces of paper inside. On each is a note of thanks from one of her colleagues at HubSpot. Today's note is from a colleague thanking her for being supportive and helping him find his feet when he first joined the company.

Many HubSpot teams have formalized the practice of creating gratitude jars at the start of every year. Employees write short notes of gratitude for each of their colleagues and place them in a mason jar. Any time throughout the year, a HubSpotter can reach into the jar and pull out a note for a dose of positive feedback. For Eimear, these notes help to renew the sense that her work matters. The team at Hub-Spot has quite literally devised a way to bank positive feedback that employees can withdraw when they need it most.

The easiest way to begin encouraging positive feedback in your own organization is to build it into existing communication channels. Where are people in your organization already gathering and sharing information? If you use Slack or Teams or something similar, it could be as easy as starting a new #gratitude channel and asking your team to shout out their colleagues. You might also create space for people to recognize each other in existing meetings by setting aside five minutes at the beginning or the end.

Performance management platforms like 15Five can help formalize the practice of sharing positive feedback with work colleagues who aren't often in the same room. 15Five developed a feature they call High Fives. As hybrid and remote work has become the norm in many companies, 15Five has seen the use of this feature among its clients skyrocket as a way to share gratitude no matter where people are located. Designed using evidence-based positive psychology practices, High Fives focus on strengths- and values-based recognition in a similar way to the BEST feedback model.

Courtney Bigony, former director of people science at 15Five, helped design High Fives to nudge people toward more specific and meaningful feedback. The platform has a weekly check-in where people can give a High Five to a coworker to acknowledge something positive they did that week. The feature encourages people to share the specific impact that this person had on them rather than simply communicating that the person did a good job. The High Fives go into a feed that everyone—from associates to the CEO—can contribute to and see.

This feed allows everyone to experience the lift that comes from witnessing gratitude and shows that recognition is core to the culture. It also makes the feedback visible to those that might not be in the same room or the same office.

Once you have incorporated positive feedback like High Fives into your existing communication channels, you can add new practices to focus on recognition and gratitude. At clothing retailer Kenneth Cole, peer recognition is part of the company's monthly Wine Wednesday event. Once a month, the full team comes into the office to share gratitude and toast the things, big and small, that people have done for one another and the organization.

Ingrid Yan, the Kenneth Cole employee we met earlier, was one of the first people recognized by her peers at the inaugural Wine Wednesday. Colleagues talked about how valuable her work was to the company and how much they respected her. As someone who usually operates behind the scenes, it was a meaningful moment for Ingrid. "I usually grind through the week going from one thing to the next, trying to get it all done. It was nice to get that recognition from my peers because it made me pause and realize, wow, I've done a lot. It confirmed that I was doing a good job." Investing in consistent gatherings like Wine Wednesday sends the message that recognizing colleagues is valued in your organization and encourages more positive feedback in day-to-day operation.

Focusing consistently on small wins through digital channels, physical notes, or regular gatherings helps us keep moving down the right path. Every now and then, however, it's worth celebrating in a bigger way. Research indicates that big events can have a large and long-lasting impact on someone's sense of contribution. These big events inspire us to travel even further together.

CELEBRATING BIG MOMENTS

At KPMG, the Award of Distinction is the highest honor that an employee can receive. A handful of people each year are recognized for exemplifying the firm's values and positively impacting their teams. Of KPMG's thirty-five thousand North American employees, just twenty-four are honored—less than 0.07 percent of the community. Potential recipients are nominated by their peers, and final recipients are selected by a committee of senior team members.

"Day-to-day recognition is very important. It helps to sustain you over time," said Kyle Bodt, a recent recipient of the award. "But to be recognized with this award was so powerful. It means a lot when you work so hard to make an impact. If I showed up to work just to get a paycheck, I don't think that I would be fulfilled. I want to spend my time doing something that's meaningful. I want to know I really made a difference. I want to care about the work that I did."

At the awards ceremony, Kyle was recognized by the company's senior leaders, including the CEO. It was a landmark moment for him to get positive feedback at that level, but what stuck with him the most were the words of the people that recommended him in the first place. At the end of the process, award recipients are given the original nominations from their coworkers. Oftentimes those write-ups are the most important part of the award. For Kyle, the recommendations from his coworkers made him feel seen and that his efforts were noticed. It also gave him a feeling of intense gratitude for his peers, given that they appreciated his work so much. He could see firsthand how much his work was valued.

Big moments of celebration help cement a long-term sense of contribution for people like Kyle. They make clear which behaviors are valued and show employees across the company that efforts are recognized and rewarded. By highlighting employees who are living the organization's values and making outsized contributions, these big events also provide aspirational models for others in the organization. The effect of these moments tends to stay with us and can help us navigate tougher times.

As Kyle shared, "Work isn't always perfect. Sometimes things don't go well, and it can be tough. We know this, and that's part of the messiness of solving hard problems. Big moments like the Award of

Distinction are a huge motivator. To be able to look back on that and remind myself why I'm here, and to feel that other people see that, is really powerful. It continues to energize me, for sure."

These big moments are possible even for organizations that aren't able to bring people together in person. At the end of each year, Hub-Spot, which has employees across the world, has devised a peer-led positive feedback event that spans the globe. The Great Gratitude Relay is a twenty-four-hour marathon. A HubSpotter will share notes of gratitude for their colleagues in a dedicated Slack channel and tag them in the post. The baton is then passed to the people tagged, the ones receiving gratitude, to share their own notes of gratitude with others. Over the course of the day, the relay pulls in nearly every HubSpotter on the planet, from Dublin to Tokyo to Toronto. Leaders also pop in at various times throughout the relay to share videos expressing gratitude.

In addition to incorporating positive feedback into your organization's daily work, investing in big, celebratory moments can create big doses of contribution that last all year long. In the hustle of the day-to-day, an event like the Great Gratitude Relay helps break through the noise. It creates an opportunity for everyone to step back and appreciate individuals who have made significant contributions to their peers.

We encourage you to design your own positive feedback practices both big and small. Each organization is different, and positive feedback practices should align with the particular style and culture of yours. The most important thing is that it feels authentic to your team and is designed in a way that encourages broad participation.

In the next chapter, we'll explore strategies for showing people how the work that they do each day contributes to the organization's bigger mission and its impact on customers, partners, and community members.

8

COMMUNICATE BIGGER IMPACT

Making a positive impact on others is at the core of what we do. I want to have a meaningful impact not just on people's wardrobes, but also on their lives. At the end of the day, work has to be about more than just a paycheck.

—KENNETH COLE

Toward the end of the twentieth century, as the personal computer spread to homes across the country and Windows 95 was replaced by Windows 98, software was developed in a highly structured and siloed process. Companies employed the waterfall method, which involved each department gathering requirements, building a plan, and then handing things off to the next department for implementation. Much like a relay race, each business unit completed its section of the process and passed the baton, never to see it again.

Business analysts would research the market and write the business requirements for the software, including functional and design needs. Then the tech team would take those requirements, which were usually in the form of long, detailed documents, and translate them into a set of longer, more detailed documents outlining the architecture, features, and data tables needed. When software engineers were finally brought in, they were handed several hundred pages of instructions to code and implement. They were essentially order-takers with little say in product design.

This process of building software was expensive and slow, usually taking several years between major releases—hence the three-year gap between Windows 95 and Windows 98. Often, in the time between writing the original requirements and completing the software, the needs of the customers had changed. Engineers might labor away for years on software that was irrelevant by the time it was released. Sometimes projects were abandoned before completion, and an engineer's work was shelved, never to be used. Even when software did finally make it to market successfully, engineers had already moved on to the next project. The engineers building the software were separated from the people who used it by several layers of bureaucracy. They never had contact with one another. Similar to the second group of participants in Dan Ariely's feedback study, the work of many engineers was essentially ignored.

As cloud-based software replaced CD-ROMs, the need for innovation and speed eclipsed the value of the bureaucratic waterfall process. In February of 2001, a group of leading engineers met in Snowbird, Utah, to figure out a better way. Fed up with the inefficient and demoralizing waterfall process, they discussed and debated a new model. After three days, they had drafted what is now known as the Agile Manifesto. Their vision for a new model of software development was guided by four main values:

1. Individuals and interactions over processes and tools
2. Working software over comprehensive documentation

3. Customer collaboration over contract negotiation
4. Responding to change over following a plan

The third value—prioritizing customer collaboration over the rigid documentation process of waterfall—put the software's users at the center of the agile model. It changed everything. Instead of a relay race, engineers and customers began running side by side.

The Agile Manifesto quickly caught fire and ignited a revolution in the tech industry. Agile development powered the rise of companies like Google, Amazon, and Salesforce from scrappy start-ups to world-dominating tech titans. Nearly every piece of software you use today, from the iOS that powers your iPhone to the Netflix interface on your TV, was built and is continuously updated by engineers following an agile process.

Agile differs from waterfall in two major ways. The first is the shorter cycle between concept and development. Instead of taking years to develop complex software, agile teams break things down into smaller chunks and have working prototypes within days. The second difference is that the whole team is involved from start to finish. From the beginning, engineers help gather information and write requirements. Most importantly, they actually meet the people who will be using the software they create. The founders of agile wisely made customer interaction a core part of the model.

Hamish Cook became an agile evangelist during his time as a product manager at Pivotal Labs (now VMware Tanzu Labs), a software consultancy that was one of the early champions of the agile method. Pivotal doesn't just build software for its clients; it helps clients rebuild their internal software development teams using an agile framework. Hamish traveled from company to company, spreading the gospel of agile and reorienting engineers around people instead of process. He has seen firsthand how someone's work can be transformed by understanding how they contribute to others.

Hamish told us about a project he led for a client in the trucking industry. The trucking company needed to rebuild their fleet management system—the software that allows the corporate office to track the location, cargo, and maintenance needs of the thousands of trucks they operate. For people in the company headquarters, getting this information on the fleet in real time was critical to efficient business operation. It also helped them anticipate potential issues with trucks that might cause them to break down on the road. Needless to say, this software had the potential to make a huge impact on the business and also the truckers who drove for it.

Hamish partnered with the trucking company's engineering team to rebuild the software and teach them the agile way. When he arrived, the company was still using a waterfall process, and it wasn't going well. In the company's legacy model, someone from the business would say to the engineers, "Go build this thing." The engineers would then sit in a cubicle by themselves and code late into the night. Sometimes the person giving the orders would communicate the value of the product to the engineer, but most times they didn't. The engineers were order-takers.

Hamish remembers one software engineer in particular who was clearly struggling. "This guy hated his job," Hamish recalls. "He was stuffed away in a back office, didn't feel connected to the customer, and didn't feel his work was valued. In all the years he worked there, he had never had the opportunity to talk to one of the people that used his software. He couldn't see the impact of his work."

Hamish took the engineer and his team to a distribution site to meet the fleet manager and talk with some of the truckers. As the engineer interacted with the people using his software and began to understand the value it added to their jobs every day, his whole attitude shifted. Using the agile process, Hamish showed him a new way where he actually connected with the operators who were using his software and the truckers who rely on it. "It utterly blew his mind," Hamish told us. "Seeing that impact changed the game for him." By the time Hamish left, the engineer had found a new love for his job because he saw the value of his work.

Earlier in the book, we shared that our brains are wired to be social, which drives our desire to be authentically included in our social group.

This wiring also drives our need to know that our work matters to others. Work that is prosocial, that benefits others in some way, is highly meaningful. When we understand the impact of our work, it activates our sense of purpose. It boosts our motivation, performance, and dedication to our jobs. Prosocial work supports our own feelings of self-worth and the sense that we are contributing to others.

In addition to the sense of contribution we feel from receiving positive feedback from our colleagues, knowing that our work benefits customers or the larger goals of the organization, what we call work's *bigger impact*, shows us that our work matters. We all want to see how our work helps put a man on the moon. The more closely we connect with the bigger impact that our work has, the more meaningful our work becomes.

Connecting with work's bigger impact can happen naturally when employees regularly interact with customers. If you work in a restaurant or a retail store, you likely hear from customers every day. Many people, however, have little or no contact with customers in their day-to-day work. In fact, the layers of bureaucracy between our daily tasks and the people we impact have probably increased in recent years. Hybrid work has given many of us valuable flexibility, but we spend most days staring at a screen instead of into the eyes of another person. The value of our work can seem far away. When this is the case, leaders have to invest intentionally in connecting daily tasks to work's bigger impact.

Meaning-driven leaders do this in several ways—by directly **connecting employees with customers and other stakeholders**, by **capturing and sharing stories of moments that matter**, and by **reframing daily tasks as opportunities for positive impact**.

CONNECTING WITH CUSTOMERS

Organizational psychologist Adam Grant was curious to see what would happen if he showed people the bigger impact of their work.

In a landmark study, he worked with fundraisers at a university who were charged with calling alumni to solicit donations for the university's scholarship fund. You have likely received a similar call from one of these folks, usually a current student, at your own university. If you have, you know how unwelcome these calls can be. One examination of these types of fundraising calls found a 99 percent failure rate, making the job a pretty frustrating one. For the people making these high-volume cold calls, it can feel like their work doesn't really matter.

Adam separated the fundraisers into three groups. The first group met a scholarship recipient, the fundraisers' "customer," who spent five minutes talking about the impact that the scholarship had on his university career and life in general. In the second group, a manager read a letter from a scholarship recipient also sharing how the program allowed him to attend the university and improve his life. The third group, the control group, got nothing. One month later, the second and third groups showed no significant changes in the time they spent on the phone (the study's measure of engagement) or the total money raised (the measure of performance). In contrast to the others, something magical happened with the first group that met the scholarship student in person.

While the first group worked the same number of hours as the other two, they spent 142 percent more time on the phone and raised a whopping 171 percent more money. Understanding the bigger impact of their work through just a brief interaction with someone who benefited from it was enough to supercharge their engagement and nearly triple their revenue.

It took just a few short minutes with a scholarship student for participants to find meaning in their previously defeating tasks. That small interaction was powerful enough to connect the fundraisers with the bigger impact their efforts had on another person's life. This sense of contribution motivated them every time they picked up the phone. The return on that investment for the fundraisers and for the school was staggering. Adam Grant and other researchers have replicated this study in several forms. In each case, direct contact with beneficiaries dramatically improved outcomes.

Meaning-driven leaders look for ways to leverage the power of contribution by increasing contact with customers and other beneficiaries. The founders of agile recognized the value of direct contact and reimagined the entire software development process around it. For those of us who aren't in a position to redesign the way our organizations operate, there are still many opportunities to create connection with customers.

One study suggested that something much simpler than redesigning a workflow process—such as simply seeing a picture of someone who benefits from our job—can activate our sense of contribution and improve performance. This study focused on the connection between radiologists who worked remotely and their patients. The radiologists selected for the study rarely saw their patients in person: the hospital sent them X-rays, MRI images, and CT scans electronically to review. The researchers sent the radiologists two CT scans: one they received right away, and the other three months later. The radiologists weren't told that the scans were identical. The only difference between the two scans was that one came with a photograph of the patient. The same radiologists, looking at the same scans, made more accurate diagnoses and wrote more detailed reports when the photo was included. Simply being reminded that there is a person behind the scans helped turn their tasks from transactions into contributions.

Customer contact doesn't need to happen every day to be effective. In the fundraiser experiment, a few minutes with a customer was enough to drive a sense of contribution for a month afterward. Some research even indicates that less frequent but more significant moments may even be more effective than small, regular doses. As a leader, consider how you might create these connections at regular intervals by planning a team field day to visit a customer's business or bringing a business partner to speak at your annual retreat. While it's an investment to organize, the returns are worth it. Finding the right balance of inspiration and impact for your team will require some experimentation. What matters most is making sure that you are helping to connect employees directly with the bigger impact of their work.

Although customer connection is powerful, it isn't possible or financially feasible to facilitate it all the time. When that's the case, leaders have another way to create a sense of contribution—by capturing and sharing moments that matter.

MOMENTS THAT MATTER

We invite you to pause for a few minutes and think about a time that you found your work especially meaningful. Choose a moment that stands out to you—one when you were able to see the bigger impact that your work had on the life of a client, customer, or community member. Perhaps it was when you received an email from a customer thanking you for going the extra mile to help them out. Maybe it was an unexpected conversation at the grocery store with a neighbor who loves your company's products.

Write down the details of this meaningful moment of contribution using the Moments That Matter Canvas on the following page. Where were you when it happened? What changed for the person who was impacted by your work? What role did you play in making that change happen? Why is this moment meaningful to you?

You can also go to our website at www.makeworkmeaningful.com to fill out and download a digital version of the Moments That Matter Canvas.

Notice how you feel as you recall this moment. Are you proud of the experience you've mapped out on the canvas? If you take a step back, how do you feel about the job that this experience was a part of?

When we facilitate this exercise, the meaningfulness of these moments shows clearly on the faces of the participants. These interactions, though many of them are very brief, can be powerful sources of meaning. When the software engineer at the trucking company

MOMENTS THAT MATTER

Complete each part of the canvas to capture and reflect on a specific moment in time that your work was particularly meaningful to you.

When exactly did this happen? What was the context of the story? What happened leading up to it?	Who did you interact with? Was it a customer, business partner, or other stakeholder? What role did they play?
What did you do that resulted in this moment? How did you contribute?	What did you learn that made the moment meaningful? What will you carry forward with you?

finally connected with a customer who used and got value from his work, everything changed for him. Taking time to engage with these moments that matter can have a staggering impact on the meaning of our work.

Reflecting on your own moments that matter, like we just did, is a powerful way to build a sense of contribution in your own work. As a leader, an effective way to help others connect with the bigger impact of their work is to start by sharing how you are connecting with the bigger impact of your own. Sharing your moments that matter gives your team an opportunity to look at work through your eyes. It helps them see bigger impacts that they might not have considered. By exploring the bigger impact of your own work with the team, you are also modeling a meaningful practice and encouraging others to emulate it. Sharing a personally meaningful moment demonstrates authenticity and builds trust, helping to build community as well.

Wes had one of these experiences in his first corporate job. After graduating from college, he moved to New York, excited about the opportunity to live in the big city. Unfortunately, he arrived in the aftermath of the dot-com bust, and the economy was lagging. Jobs weren't so easy to come by, but he was fortunate to land a full-time role at a large insurance agency where he had been temping for several months. The new job was in the compliance department, where Wes spent most of his day reviewing contracts. This was before the technology to track changes in a document became widespread, so he was reading these contracts manually. People in each of the company's fifty US offices would fax him newly signed client contracts, and he would review them to flag any potential issues for the legal department. All contracts were supposed to follow the standard template unless changes had been approved ahead of time. Essentially, Wes read the same contract over and over, looking for changes. In the first six months he was there, he reviewed more than three thousand of them.

As you might imagine, Wes found this work mind-numbingly boring. It was also hard to see how it added any value to the company beyond getting other people in trouble for breaking the rules. One day, a couple of months in, his boss's boss came by and struck up a conversation with him. He asked Wes how he was doing and what he thought about the job. Being young and inexperienced with office politics, Wes cracked a joke about every day being Groundhog Day. The senior leader was generous enough to chuckle, but then he did something unexpected. He told Wes what he found meaningful about his work.

The legal department at the insurance company had crafted the standard client contract to make sure that both businesses, the insurer and the insured, were adequately protected. As an insurance company, the team was safeguarding clients against excessive risk and giving them the protection they needed to grow and thrive in the face of unexpected challenges. If the contracts weren't solid, that not only endangered the insurance company, but also threatened the security of its clients. The senior leader saw the tedious work as a service to those clients. He helped Wes understand that his tasks might not always be exciting, but they were still adding value. After he left, Wes felt a new appreciation for his job. He never loved it, but thinking about the value he was creating for clients motivated him to do better work.

The moment the senior leader shared made Wes's work more meaningful and gave him the energy to get through some challenging days. When leaders make a practice of sharing their own moments that matter with their teams, it can help build their sense of contribution.

SHARING MOMENTS THAT MATTER

Tope Awotona grew up as the third of four brothers in a middle-class family in Lagos, Nigeria. Tope's mother was the chief pharmacist for the Central Bank of Nigeria. She was a driven and focused woman who taught the value of hard work and appreciated it in those around her. While she came from a family with resources, Tope's father had worked his way up from poverty to become a microbiologist at Unilever. His father had dreams of being an entrepreneur and fostered a sense of possibility and potential in his sons. Sadly, he didn't live to see that dream realized.

When Tope was twelve, his father was tragically murdered in a carjacking. Devastated, his mother relocated the family to an area near Atlanta, Georgia, where relatives were already established, for a fresh start. Tope attended high school there and later the University of Georgia, where he majored in business. After graduation, he worked a few corporate sales jobs, but his father's dream of running his own company stayed with him. While he worked elsewhere, Tope started several businesses but achieved limited success.

A dating site called Single to Taken never got off the ground. Another business selling projectors online faltered. An e-commerce site hawking gardening tools and grills eked out a small profit. None of them came close to fulfilling the big dreams that Tope had inherited from his father. He just wasn't passionate about projectors, and yard supplies were a yawn. He realized that something was missing. To succeed, Tope needed to find a business idea that was meaningful to him.

In his day job, Tope worked as a sales representative for a software company. He found he was spending a huge amount of time trying to schedule meetings with prospective clients. The back-and-forth was maddening, and the process kept Tope from spending his time on more productive work. He thought there must be a better way—so he made one. Using his life savings and maxing out his credit cards, he founded the scheduling software company Calendly with the mission to "take the work out of meetings so our customers can do more in their daily lives." He believed, and still does, that it's a mission that matters. Finally, Tope had a product that he was passionate about.

Tope is relentless in his focus on making Calendly easy to use and efficient for customers. Where most of us dread the back-and-forth process of scheduling meetings, he sees an opportunity to facilitate and streamline the critical connections that fuel an organization's success. Calendly estimates that the product saves users between two and four hours per month, potentially adding up to a full workweek over the course of a year. In Tope's view, he and his team aren't just saving their customers the frustration of scheduling. Every hour that a Calendly customer saves is an hour that they can spend advancing strategic business priorities or, better yet, an extra hour they can spend with their families. For the Calendly team, that's a meaningful contribution.

Like the software developer at the trucking company, many of Calendly's employees work behind the scenes. Although these team members aren't externally facing, Tope connects them to the bigger impact of their work by regularly sharing his own experiences with customers. He shares these moments that matter by recording videos for the team in which he talks about significant interactions he's had with people who use the product. By sharing his own stories of bigger impact, Tope helps others on the team see their contributions as well.

For Michael Biggs, the lead developer of Calendly's iPhone app, Tope's videos help to reinforce that he's building something that other people value. Michael spends most of his days working from home writing and tweaking code. When he hears one of Tope's stories of bigger impact, it reminds him how much his work matters, even though he didn't meet the customer himself.

"It's motivating to see the videos," he said. "It helps us see how what we built is being used and how it's providing value to customers. We're not just building features that are forgotten about. It motivates us to build quality products because we know that people are relying on Calendly for their livelihood."

Tope's focus on contribution has translated into standout success in the market. The iPhone app that Michael oversees has an impressive rating of 4.9 out of 5 stars in the App Store. Less than a decade after founding, Calendly was valued at an estimated $3 billion and served ten million users globally. That makes Calendly one of the 0.00006 percent of start-ups that achieve unicorn status and one of just a handful to do so in its hometown of Atlanta. Tope is the first Nigerian American to become a billionaire and only the second Black tech billionaire ever in the United States. His focus on contributing to others has helped him realize his father's entrepreneurial dreams in a way that neither could have imagined.

Understanding our bigger impact isn't just important to people who work in customer-facing departments. Employees in finance, legal, accounting, and other operational roles still care about the impact of their work, even when they may be several layers removed from the people they eventually benefit. Like the engineers who developed agile, it is sometimes possible to refine a business process to physically connect those people with customers and other beneficiaries of their work. When an in-person meeting isn't possible, meaning-driven leaders can share their own stories to help people make those connections in their minds.

This practice of sharing moments that matter is an integral part of Rob Waldron's leadership approach. Rob, the CEO of Curriculum Associates whom you met earlier, is responsible for 2,500 employees at a company that grosses nearly one billion dollars a year. When the pandemic hit, Rob knew employees were facing many challenges at work and at home. At the same time, the company's role in supporting education was more important than ever as schools closed and classes went remote. The team was no longer in the same room and couldn't hear what was happening with others in casual conversation.

To keep his people connected to the impact of their critical work, Rob started making three or four short videos on his iPhone every week to share the different ways he saw the team supporting children during the pandemic. For many in the organization, these videos were a lifeline that kept them connected to the meaning of their work. During that critical period, Rob's videos also inspired his team to share their own moments that matter. As the stories multiplied, the team's sense of contribution did as well.

MULTIPLYING MOMENTS THAT MATTER

In addition to sharing your own moments that matter, you can make it a practice to collect and reflect on the moments that matter to members of your team. What is compelling to one person may not motivate another, so we've designed the Moments That Matter Canvas to surface stories at the individual level.

When we take teams through this exercise, like we did with Keisha at Microsoft whom you met earlier, we ask each person to think of a specific experience in their current role that stands out to them—something that gives them a sense of meaning or pride. We clarify that they aren't meant to share a general answer, such as "when I get good feedback from a client." Instead, we push them to share in detail the story of a specific moment that stands out to them. Then we ask them to fill out the Moments That Matter Canvas with as much detail as they can.

Although people sometimes share big wins, just as often the stories they tell are about small moments that stuck with them. We recently received a LinkedIn message from someone who attended one of our workshops several years ago. The message simply said, "Just wanted to let you know that what I learned in your workshop really changed the way I interact with my team. It has helped me be a better leader. I use those tools every day." That brief communication let us know that, even after a couple of years had passed, the work that we had done was still valued. Those few words meant the world.

After each person fills out the Moments That Matter Canvas, we ask them to share their story with the group and discuss what resonated. It's at this point that the feeling in the room changes significantly. As people tell their stories, their faces and body language transform. The energy generated from tapping into contribution doesn't just affect the teller; it also impacts the listeners as well. They light up and the energy in the room elevates.

A study that followed nearly five thousand people across twenty years shows that this spread of positive energy isn't anecdotal. Scientists tracked the spread of emotions in the community of participants and found that they could be measured up to three degrees of separation. This phenomenon, called social contagion or emotional contagion, can be seen very clearly in organizations. This means that the excitement you feel when you share a meaningful moment affects your coworkers, and it even affects their families and the friends of their family members.

The practice of capturing and sharing moments that matter is easy, accessible, and requires no budget. We've seen leaders at every level use this practice to reinvigorate their teams, deepen engagement, and fuel motivation. As a single intervention, this practice is powerful. It's even better, however, if it becomes an institutional practice. In the same way that facilitating peer positive feedback can amplify contribution, we've seen leaders formalize the practice of sharing moments that matter in a variety of ways.

Tools like Slack, Zoom, and Loom that help us collaborate when we're apart can also help keep us connected to bigger impact. You can leverage these tools to share moments that matter from your entire team. Calendly has a Slack channel where leaders and employees can share stories of bigger impact. At Kabbage, a small business loan provider now part of American Express, the "Voice of the Customer" is a part of every all-hands meeting. Each week, a recording of a customer service call is played for the full organization. Hearing the calls firsthand allows everyone to experience the struggles and the appreciation of Kabbage customers. The weekly reminder helps people who aren't on the front lines stay connected to the bigger impact of their work by bringing customers' words to them.

Whether through direct customer contact or stories of moments that matter, we need to know the work we've done has added value to others. Being aware of this need for contribution can also help us shift the way we think about our future work by putting customers front and center. By reframing tasks with bigger impact in mind, everyday work can take on more meaning from the start.

REFRAMING WORK AS AN OPPORTUNITY FOR POSITIVE IMPACT

Brianne Goguen is a hairstylist in an Aveda salon near Boston. While each of her clients receives slightly different services, the tasks she performs on a given day are generally the same—cut and color, wash and blow out. If asked for a list of the most meaningful occupations, it's unlikely that most of us would put hairstylist in the top ten. Brianne, however, couldn't imagine work that's more fulfilling. For her, being a stylist isn't just about cutting and coloring hair—it's also an opportunity to make someone's day.

Brianne is a popular stylist and has a packed schedule every week. People sometimes come to see her before job interviews, in anticipation of a big social event, or even for their weddings. Mostly, however, she sees them during the course of their day-to-day lives. When Brianne styles one of her clients, her goal isn't just to make their hair look good. She wants to make them feel confident and powerful. She helps her clients show up at their everyday best. While she is a highly skilled professional and takes pride in the quality of her work, she sees herself not as a hairstylist but as a "Daymaker."

Brianne believes each appointment is an opportunity to have a bigger impact by creating a little joy for her clients. She asks them about their personal lives and takes notes so she can follow up on significant events when they come in next. She uses what she learns to adjust her services for each client. Some receive personalized aromatherapy. Others who are coming from a stressful job get a relaxing warm towel on the back of their necks. "I get my satisfaction from the impact that I have on people," Brianne told us. "It's not about the haircut as much as it is the feeling they walk out with."

Brianne's Daymaker mindset is no accident. Leaders at the Aveda Institute, where Brianne was trained, encourage this approach to work. David Wagner, an early Aveda salon owner, launched the Daymaker Movement after a poignant experience with one of his clients. David was working at his salon one day when a client came in to have her hair done. He gave her a cut and color. He styled her hair. They joked and laughed during the appointment. At the end, she smiled and hugged David good-bye.

A few days later, he received a letter from this client with a shocking revelation—she had been planning to commit suicide later that day. The reason she'd come to the salon was to have her hair styled for her funeral. But the connection she'd experienced during the appointment with David had given her hope. She decided to check herself into the hospital to get professional help. Through that experience, David realized the potential impact that a brief appointment could have on a client's life. He was inspired to make the most of his clients' time in the chair, and the Daymaker Movement was born. The Daymaker mindset spread rapidly through the Aveda community and has become a pillar of its culture. David's Daymaker story is shared with each new cohort of stylists trained at the Aveda Institute.

Brianne's Daymaker mindset is an example of cognitive job crafting, the practice of reframing tasks to connect them to meaningful outcomes. Researchers of this phenomenon have found that individuals often cognitively craft their work on their own. However, like the leaders at Aveda, you can help create contribution by encouraging the reframing process.

Instead of seeing an appointment as a transaction, meaning-driven leaders at Aveda teach new stylists to see it as an opportunity for contribution. They show stylists how their tasks can add up to something larger. To develop this mindset, leaders at the Aveda Institute have formalized a Daymaker practice as part of the training curriculum. Every Monday during the training program, leaders solicit Daymaker stories from each of the trainees. They kick off the meeting with calls of "Who's got a Daymaker? Who did something that made your day last week?"

Students are encouraged to share interactions with others that had a positive impact on their day. Kaitlin Desselle, a former trainer at the Aveda Institute, explains, "Our goal is for students to experience what it's like to be on the *receiving* end of a Daymaker moment so that, when they graduate and work in a salon, they know how the little things they do can have a bigger impact on clients. We want students to pay attention to when someone was a Daymaker for them, which helps them focus on being a Daymaker for someone else. You will hear things like, 'I had a brutal day Wednesday that totally exhausted me. I was so busy I skipped lunch. When I got home, I found my partner had picked up food from my favorite Thai place so we could just chill together. That made my day.'"

By making it a practice each week during training, Aveda students get in the habit of looking for the little moments where they can have a bigger impact on clients. It boosts morale, improves client service, and keeps stylists focused on the bigger impact of their work. This Daymaker training shifted Brianne's understanding of her job. Brianne takes pride in her styling ability, but she finds the most meaning in the smiles on the faces of clients who sit in her chair. Whether your company sells insurance, makes scheduling software, provides styling services, or something in between, you can help your team reframe their work as an opportunity for positive impact.

An easy place to start is by asking yourself and your team a few questions about your work:

- Who is your work helping today? What are the potential positive impacts on them?
- Why do you think this task matters to other people?
- How would people be impacted if you didn't do this?
- How could you approach this differently to add more value to your customers or partners?

With the right mindset, many of our daily tasks can be a source of contribution. In the next section, we'll look at how work that helps us strive toward our full potential creates meaning. Challenging your team to learn and grow and helping them see how work positively impacts their own development is the final component of meaningful work.

PART IV

CREATING MEANING THROUGH CHALLENGE

Leaders harness the power of our final C, challenge, to create meaning by satisfying our inherent need to learn and to grow. While community comes from understanding that we matter to others in our organization and contribution comes from the belief that our work adds value, challenge comes from doing work that pushes us to become better versions of ourselves.

Viktor Frankl, psychiatrist, Holocaust survivor, and author of *Man's Search for Meaning*, wrote, "What man actually needs is not a tensionless state but rather the striving and struggling for some goal worthy of him. What he needs is not the discharge of tension at any cost, but the call of a potential meaning waiting to be fulfilled by him." To Frankl, whom many consider one of the foremost experts on meaning, life's challenges were fertile ground for meaningful experiences.

The struggle required to move toward a personally significant goal helps us grow and move closer to our full potential. Making progress toward that potential is a core driver of meaning. Reaching big goals requires us to stretch our capabilities—to do more than what we're already doing and learn more than what we already know. Work that helps us develop our potential, to become a version of ourselves that is closer to the one we want to be, fosters meaning.

As Frankl noted, the growth we seek inevitably comes through challenge. To provide challenge, leaders must give people the space to spread their wings, along with a push out of the nest when needed. To maximize our development opportunities, leaders must give us autonomy while also providing guidance. Assignments that stretch people must be balanced with support, and freedom must be given within clear boundaries.

Leaders who give members of their team the freedom to pursue their own paths and the support to expand their capabilities help create meaning in their work. Our research shows that meaning-driven leaders facilitate challenge in two ways—by empowering people within the bounds of organizational values, and by supportively stretching their capabilities. As we'll see in the next two chapters, doing this effectively requires leaders to play several roles at the same time—guide, advocate, mentor, and coach.

9

BALANCED AUTONOMY

If you want to build a ship, don't drum up the people to gather wood, divide the work, and give orders. Instead, teach them to yearn for the vast and endless sea.

—ANTOINE DE SAINT-EXUPÉRY

Our innate desire to make our own decisions is evident at an early age. Tamara found this out when her oldest daughter turned three. All of a sudden, getting her dressed and out the door in the morning became a struggle. Tamara, who was used to selecting her daughter's clothes, getting her dressed, and calmly taking her to preschool, found that her daughter was no longer willing to have her outfits chosen for her. One day shortly after her birthday, she refused to wear the dress Tamara had chosen. She insisted on dressing herself, and the outfit she chose was a princess costume over pajama pants accented by sparkly sandals.

It wasn't the most appropriate choice for school, but Tamara was running late and gave in. Feeling embarrassed, she walked her daughter into class that morning with her head down. She was surprised, however, by the looks of understanding and support she got from the other parents. Each of them had faced similar experiences as their own children began to demonstrate their innate needs for independence.

To support her daughter's autonomy, but also guide her toward more context-appropriate outfits, Tamara reorganized her daughter's closet into different sections—school clothes, play clothes, and dressy clothes. From then on, she gave her daughter the freedom to select what she wanted to wear within the boundaries of each section. Her daughter felt empowered and was able to choose clothes appropriate for the occasion. She was excited about the opportunity to make decisions on her own and, in the process, learned how to dress herself.

Autonomy, the freedom to determine our own actions and make our own choices, is an essential human need. Our ability to learn and develop a sense of self-efficacy relies largely on the challenges of having to choose our own way forward. When we are able to navigate these challenges independently, we feel a sense of accomplishment that makes the effort meaningful. Like Tamara's daughter, we prefer to choose our own outfits both as a way to assert our unique individuality and also to demonstrate to ourselves that we can accomplish tasks on our own.

As adults, our need for autonomy only grows. We want more freedom and control over our own actions and our own lives. This need extends beyond our choice of clothes to encompass all of the decisions we face each day, including those we make at work.

Decades of research show that autonomy is a critical component of a healthy and productive job. Autonomy leads to increased productivity, satisfaction, and well-being. The more autonomy a person has, the more engaged and invested they are in their work. In one study, in fact, autonomy emerged as the strongest predictor of meaning at work. By encouraging autonomy, leaders tap into people's core psychological need for self-determination. They provide an environment where employees can grow and find meaning in their work.

Unlike some of the other practices we've shared, giving autonomy often requires leaders to do less, not more. They must step back and create the space for self-directed growth. They set goals and then challenge employees to find their own way. When we have a say in how we do our jobs, we access authentic passion and internal motivation, which drive meaningful growth and development. We are able to work toward goals that matter to us and gain the satisfaction that comes from figuring out how to get there on our own. Our ability to choose makes the effort meaningful to us.

When leaders fail to give us autonomy, however, they rob us of the meaning that comes from finding our own way. Without the autonomy to decide, we can feel like robots simply executing a preprogrammed set of tasks. We follow a process without the opportunity to explore or experiment. Challenge is limited and we don't have space to grow.

In an effort to exert control over business outcomes, leaders often impose excessive control over their employees. They compose long lists of rules and requirements. They lean too heavily on process instead of empowering people. They give their teams rigid instructions on how to do their jobs instead of trusting them to get things done. This practice, known as micromanagement, is a meaning killer.

Brain-imaging studies find that micromanagement triggers a fight-or-flight response in the brain—the same neurological impulse we feel when our physical safety is at risk. When leaders threaten our autonomy, we go into survival mode. Stress levels shoot up, and our capacity to productively engage with our tasks and our colleagues shrinks. This frustrates collaboration, reduces well-being, and leads to poor business outcomes across the board. Think about the last time a passenger in your car shared their opinions on your driving. In the same way no one likes a backseat driver, no one wants to be micromanaged at work.

Micromanagement also limits individual learning and growth. Research shows that the less autonomy we have, the worse we integrate new concepts into our existing knowledge base. On the other hand, teachers who support autonomy in the classroom have students who are more motivated, feel more competent, and have an increased desire to challenge themselves to learn.

All this leaves leaders in a tricky position. For an organization to operate effectively, leaders must limit freedom and choice to some degree. Without clear goals and boundaries to guide behavior, confusion and chaos can quickly ensue. At the same time, when leaders take away freedom, they erode meaning and, in turn, well-being and potential. How can leaders find the right balance? We believe our research has identified the sweet spot.

BALANCED AUTONOMY

As we discussed earlier, alignment around shared values is a prerequisite for meaning at work. Values alignment provides the foundation for community by informing whom we hire and how we treat each other, and it shapes contribution by directing our shared goals and guiding our efforts to reach them. Finally, values alignment facilitates challenge by providing the necessary boundaries for meaningful learning, growth, and achievement. Rather than limiting us, these particular boundaries allow for an optimal level of autonomy.

Balanced autonomy exists when leaders empower employees to make decisions within the boundaries of organizational values. They hand employees the keys to the car, while being clear about the rules of the road. Values provide a shared set of guidelines that shape desired behavior and hold people accountable. At the same time, because values are not specific instructions, they allow employees to exercise their own judgment in the way they pursue goals. Values keep people from crashing into each other on the road while still allowing them to map their own course.

By providing balanced autonomy to make our own decisions about how we do our jobs, leaders tap into the power of challenge and unlock more meaning across many areas of work. We're going to focus on three different ways that leaders can give balanced autonomy to drive challenge and build meaning:

First, leaders can **empower employees to do their work and accomplish goals in their own way.** This allows them to take ownership of the work and challenge themselves to do things differently.

Second, leaders can **give people flexibility to choose a work environment that is most effective for them,** such as at home or at an office. Different types of work are done more effectively in different environments, and different people work best in different ways. When flexibility is balanced with values alignment, it helps employees optimize their work to devote maximum energy to tackling challenges.

Third, leaders can **provide people with self-directed opportunities to learn and grow by taking on new roles within the company.** This practice allows an employee to pursue a more challenging job or set of tasks that they are passionate about.

We'll look at examples of how leaders give balanced autonomy in each of these three areas and how you can leverage it to drive challenge in your own organization.

EMPOWERING EMPLOYEES

Chris Hurn didn't make it to his family vacation. Instead of joining his wife and kids for a few glorious days at the Ritz-Carlton in Amelia Island, he got stuck in a conference room in California on business. He arrived home just in time to help unpack the car that his wife had driven to the beach. Disappointed to have missed the holiday but grateful to be reunited with his family, he took a deep breath and let the stress of the last few days leave his body. That's when the screaming started.

"Where's Joshie? I can't find Joshie!" wailed Reilly, Chris's young son. Chris looked at his wife, and they shared a moment of panic. Reilly's beloved stuffed animal, Joshie, was nowhere to be found. His wife was certain the plush giraffe had been in the hotel room last night. Reilly never went to bed without Joshie by his side. He never went anywhere without Joshie by his side. This was not good. After digging through the car and turning their bags upside down, it was clear that Joshie had been left behind.

Reilly was inconsolable. As any parent can attest, the loss of a beloved stuffed animal can be devastating. When bedtime came, Reilly refused to go down without his giraffe. In an effort to calm him, Chris told him that Joshie must have stayed behind for some extra vacation days. Reilly looked at Chris with wide, teary eyes, but the idea of Joshie enjoying a longer holiday seemed to satisfy him and he eventually fell asleep.

Chris's little white lie bought him some time, but he knew he had to retrieve Joshie and get him home as soon as possible. Chris called the Ritz-Carlton, praying that Joshie had turned up. Fortunately, the cleaning staff had found Joshie under the bed. He was safe and sound in lost and found. Chris was relieved and let the staff know he was grateful. During the conversation, he mentioned the story he had told Reilly about Joshie's "extended vacation" and asked the manager if he could snap a quick picture to back him up. The desk manager said he was happy to help and promised to mail Joshie back right away.

The next day, the errant giraffe arrived. When Chris opened the shipping box, however, he found that Joshie wasn't the only thing in it. There was also a photo album, along with some other gifts from the Ritz-Carlton. Instead of simply mailing Joshie back, the staff decided to turn Chris's little white lie into a true story. The photo album contained pictures of Joshie enjoying the best of the Ritz-Carlton's many amenities on his extended vacation: Joshie getting a massage in the spa. Joshie sitting in a lounge chair at the pool. Joshie driving a golf cart to the beach. Joshie socializing with other stuffed animal friends in the hotel lounge. They even created a Ritz-Carlton ID badge for Joshie and made the giraffe an honorary member of the Loss Prevention Team.

Needless to say, Chris was blown away by the time and care the staff invested in making sure his story was airtight. Reilly was thrilled to finally have Joshie back, and he enjoyed the album, but Chris was the one who appreciated it most. The employees at the Ritz-Carlton didn't just help Chris out of a jam; they went above and beyond to create an unforgettable experience for him and his family.

The experience was meaningful for Chris, but it was just as meaningful for the employees who made it happen. The idea for the album was entirely their own—thought up and executed without following any guidelines or getting approval from any managers. This team saw an opportunity to put a smile on someone's face, and they knew that their own initiative was responsible for making someone's day.

The Ritz-Carlton, part of the Marriott family of hotels, is renowned for its legendary customer service. Given that the Ritz-Carlton has been a leader in the luxury hotel market for more than a century, you might expect them to have developed an encyclopedic set of rules for dealing with customers. Leaders at the Ritz-Carlton, however, have taken a balanced autonomy approach.

Joshie's vacation is an example of what sets the Ritz-Carlton apart when it comes to empowering individuals to make their own decisions. At another hotel, the staff member who found Joshie would have had to follow a strict policy for tracking and returning lost items. If they wanted to take Joshie out of the lost-and-found locker, let alone make a photo album, they would have had to fill out a form and get a senior manager to sign off on it. Even if the request was approved, spending the money to create an album would have required an expense report and a whole lot of other work outside the manager's normal job description. It probably would have taken days before the staff member heard back on it. Knowing all the hoops they would have to jump through, it's unlikely the staff member would have bothered at all.

Instead of micromanaging employees with rules or a cumbersome approvals process, leaders at the Ritz-Carlton empower them with the autonomy to engage and delight customers in the way they believe is best. They begin by creating alignment around the organization's values. Then, they give employees the space to find their own way forward. As long as employees stay aligned with the organization's Gold Standards, such as "creating Ritz-Carlton guests for life," they are given the freedom to choose the best path.

When staff members join, they are trained extensively on each value and its aligned behaviors during a three-day orientation. To build cultural mastery during onboarding, a practice we explored earlier, leaders give examples of how employees have brought the company's values to life. In one example, a manager at the Ritz-Carlton in Washington, DC, found out that a couple was celebrating their wedding anniversary during their stay. The staff worked with the Ritz-Carlton in Tokyo, where their wedding was held ten years earlier, to get the full details of their special day. The staff surprised the couple with an evening that included photos from their wedding and an exact replica of the bride's bouquet. They even remade their wedding cake. The couple was delighted, and the staff successfully created Ritz-Carlton guests for life. Sharing these "wow stories" is a regular part of the culture at the Ritz-Carlton. Leaders continue to highlight them each week to reinforce the organization's values and to emphasize the autonomy that employees have to bring those values to life every day.

Amanda Joiner remembers her first role at the Ritz-Carlton in Atlanta as a turn-down manager, the person in charge of nighttime housekeeping. Soon after she started, she learned that her responsibilities went beyond keeping the rooms clean. Her formal tasks might have included vacuuming floors and turning down beds, but the true purpose of her job was to help create unique and memorable experiences for every guest. "The Ritz-Carlton didn't teach me how to clean rooms. It taught me how to make good decisions. When a new challenge came up, it didn't matter if I didn't know what to do. I knew all I had to do was look at our Gold Standards, and I could figure out the best way to serve our guests," she told us. That empowerment has been incredibly meaningful to Amanda—so much so that she's been with the Ritz-Carlton for more than thirty years.

Amanda is now the global vice president of the Ritz-Carlton Leadership Center, where she teaches other organizations how to implement the Ritz-Carlton's approach to empowerment. Amanda cautions that this feeling of empowerment doesn't develop overnight. In her experience, many employees have heard these words before. They've had previous leaders tell them they were empowered, only to find themselves in trouble when they made their own decisions. To build a culture of balanced autonomy, the Ritz-Carlton focuses on recognizing positive examples through wow stories as well as things like First Class cards, their version of peer-to-peer gratitude notes. By leaning on some of the practices we explored in the contribution section, the Ritz-Carlton also rewards people for taking advantage of balanced autonomy. Seeing these examples highlighted encourages others to do the same.

In addition to giving employees the space and support to make their own decisions, leaders at the Ritz-Carlton also encourage autonomy by giving them the resources to bring their ideas to life. Every employee, from the janitor to the general manager, has access to a budget of $2,000 that they can spend on guests, no questions asked. What employees do with this ranges from small things, like a housekeeper buying ingredients for soup that she made and brought to a sick guest, to over-the-top gestures like Joshie's vacation album or the Tokyo wedding redux.

While most organizations don't have the capacity to give large budgets to employees like the Ritz-Carlton does, giving autonomy, even in small ways, can be meaningful. Other leaders frequently ask Amanda how they can empower people when they don't have huge budgets. "I say, you're missing the point. It's not about the money," she tells them. "The money is just a signal of trust. Empowerment is about trusting your people and teaching them to make good decisions."

Other organizations find creative ways to encourage autonomy in smaller tasks. Southwest Airlines, for example, has a storied reputation for empowering its employees. Even within the strict safety guidelines of the airline industry, Southwest has found room for balanced autonomy. Flight attendants are encouraged to embody the organization's value of a "Fun-LUVing Attitude" by bringing their own style to the standard procedures. For example, their safety announcements must cover the same key points on every flight, but no two are ever the same. If a flight attendant sees that there are some first-time passengers who are nervous about the flight, they may turn the safety demonstration into a runway show to make them smile. Or they could deliver the announcements like an emcee of a variety show. One flight attendant has been known to lighten the mood with jokes: "Do you know Robin Hood's favorite way to travel? By arrow-plane!" When that gets an inevitable groan from the cabin, they throw up their hands and respond with, "That's OK. My airplane jokes never seem to land."

While small, these moments are significant for employees. The ability to make our own decisions signals that we are learning and growing in a direction that we find personally significant. When we have a voice in the direction of our work, we feel more ownership of it. Our sense of challenge is increased when we're able to choose our own path forward.

For Kahlil Shepard, the team member at A–B Partners whom you met earlier, this empowerment is important. He said, "I'm afforded a lot of bandwidth in how I navigate my work, and that's really valuable. Solving a problem on your own is how you evolve and grow. It requires going in your own direction. You can't just follow instructions because you'll never actually learn that way."

Part of A–B's mission is to cultivate new leaders, and the organization values an experiential approach to learning. Leaders at A–B make an intentional effort to empower employees like Kahlil with opportunities to grow. It's company policy for the person who came up with a strategic idea to present it to the client. Often, that means a junior employee like Kahlil will take the lead in a client meeting—something practically unheard of in other agencies. While A–B leaders always make sure these employees are properly prepared, they don't tell them what to say. Using the organization's values as a guide, employees are empowered to present in their own way. When leaders trust us and empower us to make decisions, we tend to rise to the occasion.

Schneider Electric, an energy management company with more than 160,000 employees globally, is another company that provides balanced autonomy in day-to-day work. They operate using a decentralized decision-making model. Teams in different functions or different countries have the autonomy to do their work in the way they believe will be most effective. To help facilitate this, the company focuses on setting clear goals without mandating specific processes to achieve them.

Tina Mylon, chief talent and diversity officer at Schneider, is a strong believer in hardwiring values into the company's culture and workplace. Like the Ritz-Carlton, Schneider provides extensive values training to employees to guide their behavior. During annual reviews at Schneider, employees are rated on their adherence to values such as "Act like an owner." That rating factors into their overall performance evaluation, which is tied to their annual bonus. At Schneider, leaders prioritize outcomes over processes and genuinely trust their employees to perform at their best. Leaders focus on the destination rather than the directions to get there. At the same time, they emphasize the need to follow the rules of the road.

To achieve this balance, Tina advises leaders to adopt a coaching mentality. Instead of a traditional command-and-control approach, she encourages leaders to focus on asking powerful questions. When employees bring leaders a challenge, leaders can give them guidance and the opportunity to learn by helping them find their own answers.

Autonomy-supporting questions seek information without being instructive. They are not veiled suggestions in the form of questions (Do you think you should . . . ?). They are open-ended questions designed to help individuals chart a path forward. These types of questions help people stay focused on values (Which of our values are important here? How might you prioritize them?), address pain points (What's your biggest obstacle at the moment? How could you navigate it?), surface helpful information (What have you learned so far about this project? What do you think is most important here?), and identify potential resources (Who do you know that's done something like this? What could you learn from them?).

Below, we've provided a bank of balanced autonomy–supporting questions for you to draw from when supporting someone to find their own way to accomplish a task.

Balanced Autonomy-Supporting Question Bank

- What have you learned about this issue so far?
- What would be most helpful to know?
- Who else in the organization has done this?
- What could you learn from their experience?
- Which of our values can guide your decisions?
- What does your experience tell you to do?
- What options do you have? What will the impact be of each one?
- What are the pros and cons of your idea?
- What problems or obstacles are you facing? What are some ways you've thought of to deal with them? What else could you do?
- What assumptions do you have about this issue? How can you test them?
- Who are the other people involved? How might they look at this?

The next time someone shares a challenge with you, instead of providing a potential solution, try asking balanced autonomy–supporting questions. If you're able to do this with curiosity and an open mind, you may be pleasantly surprised with answers you may not have thought of yourself.

GIVING FLEXIBILITY

Before the COVID pandemic, the act of commuting to an office was assumed to be a normal part of having a job. It was also taken for granted that employees would absorb the costs of time and resources that were required to travel to a central work location. During the pandemic, we learned that many of us could complete our tasks just as effectively without making that daily journey. Since then, the calculus of coming to an office has changed. For better or worse, instead of assuming that commuting is part of the employee's job, the burden now falls on the employer to justify the effort.

Leaders continue to struggle with the practical implications of workplace flexibility. Many organizations have attempted to resolve the tension by mandating a set number of days each week in the office. For some, this is working well. For others, it continues to cause friction with employees. Many workers now have the tools and experience to complete their tasks effectively wherever and whenever they want. Why would they want to come into the office if they can get their jobs done remotely?

Hybrid design and remote work policies have huge implications for autonomy. Each of us works best in different ways. We all have styles, preferences, and other commitments in our lives to navigate. Having some autonomy to choose when and where we work allows us to tackle challenges more effectively. Without a values-aligned reason, mandated time in the office can feel like micromanagement. Without any structure, however, remote work can feel to leaders like a free-for-all.

Instead of arbitrarily mandating in-office days, we encourage leaders to consider a balanced autonomy approach. We believe that every organization must find a model that works best for its unique team. We start with questions like, Why is it important to you for the team to meet in person? Why is it important for people to be in the office? What are you hoping to accomplish? What is the least amount of control you can exert to stay aligned with your values?

Instead of mandating time in the office, we believe meaning-driven leaders can best support balanced autonomy by keeping office time focused on the parts of work that are best executed when we're in person. Research shows that those things include creative ideation, relationship building, learning and development, and big-picture inspiration. For other work—such as task execution, process and project management, and research—leaders can give people the autonomy to do it wherever they will be most productive. Both employees and organizations benefit from giving employees balanced autonomy to work wherever is best for them.

Gustavo Razzetti, author of *Remote, Not Distant*, frames this as a shift from head trust to heart trust. Head trust is the belief that people have the capabilities to fulfill their roles effectively and will do what's expected. Heart trust, however, is the belief that people will continue to advance the shared interests and values of the group, even in ambiguous circumstances or when those people aren't right in front of you. Heart trust involves leaning fully into balanced autonomy, especially when it comes to where people work.

HubSpot, the company you met earlier that is famous for its Culture Code, leaned into its values of empathy and adaptability to design a fully empowered hybrid model for its global team of eight thousand employees. When HubSpot launched the program, leaders gave everyone in the organization the freedom to choose one of three options: @office, @flex, or @home. Employees who chose @office would be assigned to one of HubSpot's physical offices and agreed to come in at least three days a week. Those who chose @flex would also be based out of an office and would come in about eight times a month. The @home employees would be fully remote with no expectation to gather with other HubSpotters but would have the opportunity to come into the office once or twice a quarter. From the CEO to the most junior new hire, every employee was given the autonomy to choose the model that worked best for them, no questions asked.

When the program launched, HubSpotters were asked to commit to the choice for a year to see how things went—and it didn't always go smoothly. At first, leaders wanted everything to feel exactly the same whether people were @home, @flex, or @office. Eimear Marrinan, HubSpot's vice president of culture whom you met earlier, recalls an event she planned for St. Patrick's Day in the Dublin office: "We had a load of employees having the time of their lives in

Dublin. And then we had a Zoom screen with a ton of folks at home. We were trying to recreate the same experience for them. What we did was we created a massively inequitable experience. Imagine being at home looking at a Zoom screen with all these people having fun. Major FOMO," she laughs.

Eimear realized that it wasn't enough to give everyone a choice of where to work and then limit autonomy by forcing them into the same structures. She discovered that, to support balanced autonomy, leaders can't just sit back and wait to see how things turn out. To stay aligned with HubSpot's values of empathy and adaptability, her team also had to develop new capabilities and structures to support new choices.

Eimear and her team learned from their early fumbles and adapted quickly. They took a step back and reevaluated their approach. Instead of trying to make everything the same, they now focus on providing an equitable experience wherever people are located. In the same way that the company views their culture as a family recipe, they see their employees as "siblings, not twins." They share the same values and have the autonomy to operate within them, but what one of them needs to be successful may be very different from another. Eimear recognized that to truly lean into their value of empathy meant recognizing that an @home employee needed different resources than those who chose @office. In the office, employees wanted more face time with colleagues. For those working from home, it didn't make sense to try to include them in office events. Instead, it was more valuable to connect them with other @home employees who were in a similar situation. These employees also wanted the flexibility to connect with other people in their local communities who work from home as well. Eimear's team now focuses on supporting everyone's choices, while ensuring that they have the tools they need to succeed.

As HubSpot leaders iterated on their new model, they made sure to hold themselves and their employees accountable. Eimear's team carefully tracked engagement, performance, and retention. They also paid attention to things like promotion velocity—how quickly individuals were getting promoted—to make sure that there wasn't a bias toward team members with more in-person interactions. After a year of experimenting, HubSpot's efforts had paid off. Overall engagement from @home and @flex employees was actually higher than those who were @office. Sales numbers were equivalent across the board. Giving people the autonomy to choose where they worked allowed them to tap a more diverse talent pool and was a financial win for the business. It also made work more meaningful for HubSpot employees. Eimear believes it has truly empowered their team. For her own part, she has three small kids and can now flex her schedule around them—something that is incredibly meaningful to her. Other organizations have developed their own ways to provide balanced autonomy around where and when people work.

At the J.M. Smucker Co., the storied food company that produces Jif peanut butter, Twinkies, and many eponymous jams, leaders have adopted a Core Weeks model for corporate employees. Two weeks a month, teams are expected to be in the office in Orrville, Ohio. The rest of the time, employees are free to work and live wherever they like. Some employees live or have relocated to places as far off as San Francisco and make the trip to Ohio on their own dime. The company created its Core Weeks model as a way to help encourage meaningful shared time in the office, while trusting employees to work the rest of the month wherever made the most sense for them. They've empowered their leaders to apply the company's guiding principles in a way that best supports the business needs and operating rhythms of their teams. "We've created guiding principles, not rules," said Lindsey Tomaszewski, head of human resources. "When you start from a place of trust and positive intent—with employees who are motivated to do the right things—the best results are often achieved by providing guidelines that individuals can flexibly work within."

For employees who don't have the opportunity to work remotely—those in retail, hospitality, health care, manufacturing, and other industries—autonomy around their schedules is still important. Research shows that one of the biggest retention factors for frontline workers is the ability to choose their own working days and work a reliable schedule. This gives them the flexibility to get their work done and the ability to attend to other priorities in their lives. Although they don't have the flexibility to choose *where* they work, there is an increased expectation for employees in these industries to have a say in *when* they work.

Smucker employees who work in the company's manufacturing plants don't have the same opportunities to work remotely as the corporate employees. Because the requirements of their roles are different, leaders at Smucker have focused on giving them different forms of autonomy. They recognize that they need to meet the unique needs of both their corporate employees and the operations segment of their workforce. To start, they directly acknowledge that these groups are different and that the support they need to provide will look different too. Smucker empowers the plant manager in each location to make and adjust the shift schedule for their site based on the production needs of the business unit, as well as the input of the team. They are free to adjust shift hours or schedules as needed to accommodate individual employees. Plant workers are given generous paid time off, family leave, and other benefits to provide as much autonomy and support as possible.

While HubSpot and Smucker have developed models that work for them, workplace flexibility continues to be hotly contested in many organizations. We believe that there is no one-size-fits-all solution. Each organization must build a structure that meets their unique needs. To be successful, however, we believe that the structure and accompanying support must include balanced autonomy. Our research found that, regardless of your industry, work location, or how many days you spend in the office, balanced autonomy remains an important part of challenge. Whether you're working from home, the office, the plant, or the plane, balanced autonomy is critical to creating meaning.

SELF-DIRECTED CAREER DEVELOPMENT

It will come as no surprise that when people have an active role in shaping their own careers, they are more likely to report higher levels of meaning at work. Giving people a voice in their own development allows them to pursue challenges that are meaningful to them. On the other hand, when employees don't have an opportunity to determine their own way forward, meaning erodes, engagement declines, and people are more likely to leave their jobs.

In our work with Matt Fishman and the team at Barking Hound Village (BHV), whom you met in the Introduction, it became clear that employees were leaving because they weren't able to set a clear path ahead for themselves. Senior management roles were few and far between, which left most of the staff without a way to grow within the organization and no option but to languish in their existing roles. As a result, turnover was incredibly high. Without the option to decide their own futures, their jobs had an expiration date. To solve this at BHV, we focused on building more balanced autonomy in their career growth.

One of BHV's core values is "Room to Run." When dogs are in BHV's care, the team gives them as much time to play as they can. The team at BHV believes that dogs shouldn't be locked away in cages. Instead, dogs should be as free as possible to explore and engage with other dogs. It was important to the team that their pups weren't penned in—and that their people weren't either. When we took a hard look at the opportunities that most employees had though, it was clear they were on a short leash.

To give employees more autonomy in their careers, we leaned into the Room to Run value and created several development tracks. We worked closely with leaders to outline three ways that employees could grow in the organization—by becoming an expert dog handler, by growing into a people leadership role, or by becoming a master dog trainer. For each step in those tracks, we outlined the requirements that employees would have to meet. We clearly listed trainings they would have to complete, length of time they could expect to reach each stage, and the compensation they would receive. Then we gave them a choice.

Managers met with each employee to explain the tracks and gave the employee a voice in their own path forward. Because they were able to choose a track that resonated with them and they knew exactly how to move up the ladder, employees found a renewed sense of excitement for their jobs. The average tenure of employees has skyrocketed, and the rate of internal promotions has jumped significantly. With more Room to Run, employees at BHV have a meaningful voice in their path forward.

Leaders don't have to wait until a person's next promotion to provide choice in growth opportunities. Another way to support employee-led development is to allow team members to spend some of their time learning from other departments or pursuing passion projects within the organization.

During a period when HubSpot's hiring slowed down and their recruiters weren't at full capacity, leaders developed TalentHub, an internal talent marketplace where team leaders across the company could pull recruiters into other projects. Functioning like a Craigslist for internal job opportunities, employees volunteered for the program and outlined the types of projects they wanted to work on. Eimear recruited three employees who had indicated an interest in learning more about culture work to join her on a new project. Adding capacity to her team worked out well for Eimear, and the recruiters gained some fantastic experience in another part of the company. They were able to broaden their skill set in an area they cared about, and the business benefited immensely. Two of them eventually moved to Eimear's team full-time.

Earlier in the book, we explored cognitive crafting, the process of shifting the way you think about your work as a way to increase contribution. Similar to cognitive crafting, *task crafting* is a way to reshape your existing job in ways that are more meaningful to you. Task crafting happens when employees have the opportunity to focus more on tasks they find meaningful and less on tasks they don't. It is an employee-led process that gives people a degree of autonomy in both the work they do day-to-day and the trajectory of their careers within a company. By allowing employees to craft their own tasks, leaders can foster meaning by allowing them to choose activities that align with their strengths and interests. It can also help them develop their capabilities in ways that are personally meaningful.

Google, another company known for providing self-directed opportunities to employees, is famous for its "20 percent time" policy, which allows employees to spend one day a week pursuing a project of their choosing. Popular products like Gmail, Google Maps, and AdSense all got their start as someone's passion project. This practice of giving employees significant amounts of time to encourage innovation was originally popularized at 3M Company, and is reportedly responsible for inventions like the Post-it Note.

In a similar fashion, Pinterest hosts an annual Makeathon, a two-day event where employees across the company are given the freedom to tackle challenges or explore opportunities they choose. They are empowered to pursue any project they like as long as it aligns with company goals. During Makeathon, employees establish small teams and work on topics that they are passionate about. At the end of the two days, each team presents a video and a prototype of their proposal. Through several rounds of competition, judges eventually choose a few winning projects. The projects that win are then funded to be fully developed. Sometimes projects that don't win also end up in the product road map. At one Makeathon, a team inspired by Pinterest's "create belonging" value wanted to figure out how to make the product's search feature more inclusive. They pitched an idea to add options like skin tone, hair type, and body type to the search functionality. The idea was picked up, and now users looking to build community, find fashion tips, or discover other forms of inspiration can more easily search for images of people who look like them.

During the rest of the year, Pinterest employees who are passionate about issues like sustainability and internet safety can opt to spend some of their time on cross-functional working groups. Those groups help direct the company's work in those issue areas. For example, members of the mental health working group Pinside-Out recently worked with the People team to develop training for managers to help them to spot when people are having mental health issues and address them. The group helped facilitate a pilot training and contributed to rolling it out across the company. The training was driven by employees who wanted to be involved, and they got a chance to spend their time on something meaningful to them.

Christine Deputy, Pinterest's former chief people officer, believes that leaders have to get more and more comfortable with giving employees autonomy. In her view, employees today want more transparency around choice and control. If you can guide them with values and give them choices, it creates meaningful opportunities that keep people engaged at your organization.

In addition to empowering us to choose our own way forward, leaders also create challenge by taking us down paths we may not yet see for ourselves. In our next chapter, we'll explore the ways that leaders bring meaning to our work by nurturing our potential and by strategically stretching our capabilities.

10

THE ZONE OF POSSIBILITY

Treat people as if they were what they ought to be and you help them become what they are capable of being.
—JOHANN WOLFGANG VON GOETHE

Christopher Wheeldon is one of the world's most influential and in-demand ballet choreographers. From Chicago to London to Moscow, top ballet companies hire Chris to develop new works and regularly perform his critically acclaimed dances to sold-out theaters. After a performance, you can watch fans rush over to Chris with the enthusiasm of Swifties (but, of course, with the reserve and sophistication befitting a ballet crowd). Looking at the arc of Chris's career, with a résumé punctuated by success after smashing success, you couldn't be faulted for thinking he was a virtuoso from the start. The truth, however, is that all along, Chris was challenged by leaders who believed in him.

At nineteen years old, while at home in London rehabbing from a dance injury, Chris caught a TV commercial for Hoover vacuum cleaners. In a bid to boost sales, Hoover was offering free round-trip tickets to the United States for anyone who spent at least a hundred pounds on their products. "It was a no-brainer," Chris recalls. "Everyone went out and bought a vacuum cleaner." Facing a flood of buyers, Hoover subsequently canceled their offer, but Chris was among the fortunate few early birds who secured his ticket to New York.

As he prepared for the trip, Chris wrote to the New York City Ballet to ask if he could take a class with them. Chris had joined the Royal Ballet School in London at age eight and had long admired the dancers at the New York City Ballet, whom he had been reading about in dance magazines since he was a kid.

On his first morning in the city, Chris packed his dance kit and walked nervously to the theater to attend class. Halfway through, he noticed the company's director, Peter Martins, whom he recognized from magazines, closely watching him. Chris put on a good show, trying to jump higher and turn faster than he normally would. At the end of class, Chris was summoned to Peter's office. Peter had mistaken Chris for another dancer who was auditioning for the company that day. To Chris's utter surprise, Peter invited him to join the New York City Ballet. "It was midday on my first day in America. I haven't seen any sights in New York. I've only gone from 34th Street to the theater, and I had a job offer," he recalled, still in disbelief over his luck years later.

For the rest of the week, Chris watched rehearsals, performances, and Broadway shows. He fell in love with the city. He was thrilled about the job offer but also nervous—it was a big decision. However, Peter Martin's belief in his potential buoyed him and inspired him to say yes.

After four years with the company, Chris was ready for another challenge. The New York City Ballet is renowned for being the home of new work, and he knew that Peter liked to champion new choreographers. He marched into Peter's office with a stack of choreography tapes and said, "Here, I'm a choreographer." Peter again saw potential in Chris and gave him a chance to prove himself.

Chris's debut ballet, *Slavonic Dances*, premiered to wide acclaim. Clive Barnes, the *New York Post* critic at the time, hailed him as a "diamond in the rough." Chris recalls, "I thought, *OK, I can be that. I can polish myself up and get better.*" Shortly after, Chris choreographed his second ballet, *Polyphonia*. That was the ballet that truly launched his career. Chris started choreographing for the top companies in the world, from the San Francisco Ballet to the Bolshoi Ballet, garnering wide acclaim and prestigious awards for his work. Despite all this success as a choreographer, Chris hesitated when he was offered the chance to direct a new Broadway musical.

Broadway producer Stuart Oken had obtained the rights for a new stage musical, *An American in Paris*, based on the Oscar-winning movie. He approached Chris to direct and choreograph the show. The shift from ballet to Broadway was terrifying, so Chris turned him down. He thought he had no business directing actors and worried he had no idea how to do it. Chris didn't believe he could be a director. Stuart, however, had other ideas. He had seen a performance of *Alice in Wonderland*, a ballet Chris had choreographed for the National Ballet of Canada, and believed in his ability to convincingly tell a story. Stuart told him that directing dancers in narrative ballets was not so different from directing actors.

The opportunity was exciting, but with no formal directing experience and facing a huge learning curve, Chris still wasn't sure. Undeterred, Stuart encouraged him. He reassured Chris that they would navigate the process one step at a time, and if at any point it wasn't working out, they could part ways amicably. This understanding took a lot of pressure off Chris.

For Chris, the process was far from comfortable. He had cold sweats all the time. Each time he was working with the actors, a voice in his head said, *You have no right to be here. You don't know what you're doing.* It was terrifying. Stuart kept pushing, however, and his belief in Chris was contagious.

In the end, Chris lived up to Stuart's expectations. *An American in Paris* was nominated for eleven Tony Awards. Chris was nominated for Best Director. Both lead actors, neither of whom had acted professionally before, were nominated for Best Actor and Best Actress—a strong validation of Chris's work over the many months he spent developing the show.

Yet, until the opening on Broadway, he remembers feeling like a fraud. He was doing the work, but he wasn't sure if it was any good. What kept Chris going was the steadfast belief that Stuart and the other producers had in him. They invested so much in his potential that he was inspired to reach a new level of performance. Because the producers believed in him, identified possibilities that he had never envisioned for himself, pushed him beyond his comfort zone, and supported him along the way, Chris had one of the most meaningful and successful experiences of his career.

Our research has found that nurturing potential and challenging people to grow—like Peter and Stuart did for Chris—creates meaning at work. When leaders push people beyond their comfort zones while giving them the support they need to succeed, they lift them into what we call the Zone of Possibility.

WHEN HIGH EXPECTATIONS MEET HIGH SUPPORT

Take a moment to think about someone who has profoundly influenced your life in a positive way. It could be a mentor, a friend, a family member, or even a colleague. Consider the specific ways in which this person has made a positive impact on your journey. What qualities or actions stand out to you? How did they encourage your growth? Chances are this person had high expectations of you and pushed you to grow beyond your existing capabilities. It's likely that this person did more than push—they also supported you through the challenging process of developing new skills.

When Chris choreographs new ballets, he often includes several dance lifts that elevate the entire performance. In a dance lift, one dancer lifts the second up into the air, taking them to heights greater than they could achieve on their own. Although these lifts look graceful from the audience, they require immense focus and control. The first dancer doesn't just throw the other up in the air; they provide steady support and guidance from below. Similarly, leaders who believe in our potential to reach new heights *and* provide the support we need to reach them challenge us in ways that lead to meaningful growth.

To illustrate this relationship between expectations and support and the different outcomes that can result, we developed the Zone of Possibility Matrix.

A leader with high expectations believes in someone's potential and challenges them to reach their full capabilities. These leaders raise the bar by providing meaningful opportunities for someone's development. Giving high support involves providing the necessary guidance, feedback, and resources to help them meet those expectations. Remember Michigan University professor Robert Quinn's description of a leader

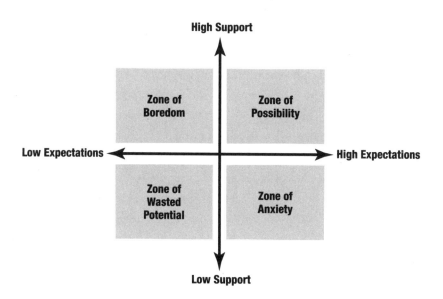

having one hand on your back, pushing you to be the best possible version of yourself, and the other hand under your arm, supporting you to navigate the challenging terrain. Like in a successful dance lift, the two must happen simultaneously.

High expectations without adequate support can thrust people into the Zone of Anxiety. In this zone, people feel like the challenge is too high and they don't have the resources to meet it. Perhaps the timeline is too short, they don't have access to the right information, or they are afraid to make a mistake and be fired. They second-guess themselves, lose confidence, and are fearful. Staying in the Zone of Anxiety for too long can lead to disengagement and eventual burnout. Without proper support, people are likely to fail and could even end up resenting the leader for pushing them into a project they weren't prepared for.

On the other hand, high support without high expectations can lead individuals to the Zone of Boredom. Here, individuals lack challenge and feel disengaged, often leading to complacency and low motivation.

In the Zone of Wasted Potential, where low support meets low expectations, people are deprived of the opportunities, challenges, and care needed to grow. Lack of challenge and growth opportunities has been a common problem for many younger workers. In a recent study, 74 percent of millennial and Gen Z employees said they were likely to quit their jobs within the next year due to a lack of development opportunities. Many of the Gen Z workers we have interviewed feel bored or stagnant at work. They are either in the Zone of Boredom or the Zone of Wasted Potential, leading to what's known as "boreout."

Boreout describes feeling bored at work, often because there's not enough to do. The employee feels like their job doesn't matter, or they have no opportunities to grow. As humans, we are wired to grow and develop. Like burnout, boreout can cause exhaustion, low self-esteem, lack of motivation, and decreased productivity. Surprisingly, according to psychologist Robert Kegan and educator Lisa Laskow Lahey, coauthors of An Everyone Culture, "one of the biggest causes of work burnout is not work overload but working too long without experiencing your own personal development." If you have ever felt like you're stuck in a rut, you're not learning and growing, and work is meaningless, you have probably experienced boreout.

In a global survey of more than thirteen thousand people, the number-one reason individuals quit their previous job was a lack of career development. Another study revealed that 94 percent of employees would stay at their company longer if they had better learning opportunities. The importance of having a leader who sincerely prioritizes the development of their workers cannot be overstated. Leaders who facilitate growth are more than seven times more likely to engage and retain employees.

When we feel like our efforts are contributing to the organization *and* to our personal growth and development, we come alive. Only in the Zone of Possibility—where high expectations meet high support—do we experience increased engagement, motivation, and meaning. Research shows that, in any field, leaders who believe in someone's potential and invest in helping them develop new skills are rewarded with outstanding performance.

There are many ways in which leaders signal their high expectations and confidence in their employees' ability to reach them. Challenging projects that leverage an employee's unique strengths are explicit expressions of high expectations. High support includes ongoing development conversations and a growth mindset that treats setbacks as opportunities for learning and improvement. This combination of **high expectations** and **high support** keeps individuals in the Zone of Possibility and creates a powerful foundation for them to achieve their highest potential.

What If We Believed That Everyone Is High Potential?

In the early 1960s, psychologist Robert Rosenthal made a startling discovery. Interested in investigating the effects of expectations on individual achievement, he designed a clever study. He labeled sixty-five rats in his lab either "bright" or "dull" to indicate their level of intelligence. When his research students came in the next morning, Rosenthal told them that the rats had either been bred for maze-brightness or maze-dullness, according to the labels. For the next week, his research team put the different rats through multiple mazes and recorded the outcomes. The results weren't even close. The "bright" rats did almost twice as well as the "dull" rats.

What Rosenthal hadn't told his students was that he hadn't bred or tested the rats for intelligence. They were all the same stock of average lab rats, which he had randomly labeled bright or dull. Rosenthal concluded that the expectations of the students must have shaped their behavior toward the rats, which helped the bright rats perform better. The results of the study were so astounding that Rosenthal initially had a hard time publishing them because no one believed him.

If rats demonstrated superior performance when their trainer expected it, Rosenthal found it plausible that children might also exhibit superior performance when their teacher expected it. In a landmark follow-up study, Rosenthal partnered with California school principal Lenore Jacobson to investigate whether information given to teachers about the intellectual ability of their elementary school students would affect the students' academic performance. They wanted to know if the students would benefit from their teacher's high expectations. Rosenthal and Jacobson started by administering a test to all the students entering first through fifth grades, which they called the Harvard Test of Inflected Acquisition. They claimed the test would predict academic improvement, but it was in fact just a standard IQ test.

Before the new school year started, Rosenthal told teachers that some of the students entering their classes were expected to do well that year. He said that the test had identified these students as having exceptional intellectual potential that had not yet been evident in their school performance. He told each teacher the names of these high-potential students, whom he called "academic spurters." However, like the bright rats, the students identified as spurters had been randomly selected by the researchers. The only difference between the spurters and the rest of the students was their teachers' expectations. At the end of the school year, Rosenthal and Jacobson readministered the same IQ test to the children. They found a large effect on performance. Students who had been identified as spurters gained, on average, 4 IQ points more than the other students. In younger grades, the gains were even larger, averaging 15 IQ points.

Rosenthal and Jacobson concluded that the teachers had unknowingly treated the high-potential students differently. Teachers' high expectations most likely caused them to give spurters extra attention, encouragement, and opportunities for intellectual growth. This may have come in the form of subtle gestures or extended eye contact, as well as increased positive feedback and greater patience. This extra attention, even if subtle and subconscious, influenced the students' confidence and motivation, driving higher levels of academic performance. (It should be noted that there are obvious ethical issues with this study—treating some students better than others is ill advised, even for a short period of time. It's not likely this study would be approved today. We can still learn from it, but we wouldn't advocate repeating it.)

Rosenthal and Jacobson dubbed this phenomenon the Pygmalion effect, a reference to the sculptor Pygmalion from Greek mythology. According to the myth, Pygmalion fell so much in love with the statue of a beautiful woman he had carved, that the statue came to life. Like the sculptor, the teachers' special attention and encouragement brought the spurters' potential to life.

The Pygmalion effect highlights the powerful impact of expectations on a person's performance. When others believe in our potential and have high expectations for our growth, we rise to meet those expectations. Higher expectations lead to higher performance. Many subsequent experiments have validated the Pygmalion effect not only in the classroom, but also in the military, in sports, and at work. When someone believes in us, we are motivated to prove them right. Researcher Dov Eden, who studies the Pygmalion effect in management, went as far as stating that the old adage "managers get the subordinates they deserve" should be updated to "managers get the performance they expect."

Research finds that the opposite is also true—lower expectations lead to lower performance. This is bad news for the way we lead today. Most organizations aren't great at recognizing and nurturing the potential of every employee. That's because most development efforts are directed toward people identified as high-potential employees, or HIPOs—usually the top 5 to 10 percent of employees in an organization. That leaves a whopping 90 to 95 percent of employees in the Zone of Wasted Potential or the Zone of Boredom.

To help employees reach their full potential, leaders must recognize everyone's capacity for growth and development, not just that of a small subset of HIPOs. We all need someone who believes in us. No one should be made to feel like a second-class, low-potential member of the organization. Even if they don't explicitly know that they're not considered a HIPO, this vast majority can be made to feel like the dull rats—overlooked and unsupported. This leads to decreased motivation, productivity, engagement, and retention.

On the other hand, higher leader expectations lead to stronger employee confidence, which leads to greater achievement, productivity, and, of course, more meaning. Viewing every individual as high potential is a small but powerful mindset shift that can have a transformative impact.

How can you demonstrate that you believe in someone's potential? One way is by simply telling them, like Peter and Stuart did for Chris. In a study exploring the impact of feedback on trust and performance, a team of researchers attached different notes to the feedback that teachers gave middle school students on their essays. In the first group, the note stated, "I'm giving you these comments because I have very high expectations and I know that you can reach them." In the second group, the note simply stated, "I'm giving you these comments so that you'll have feedback on your paper." The notes were otherwise identical.

The researchers found that communicating high standards and assuring students of their potential to reach those standards significantly increased effort and performance. Students in the first group put in 40 percent more effort to revise their essays than the students in the second group, leading to increased performance. The researchers deemed this framing "magical feedback." These nineteen words—*I'm giving you these comments because I have very high expectations and I know that you can reach them*—convey not only your high expectations but also your belief in their ability to reach them. It is a great way to lift individuals into the Zone of Possibility and unlock their effort and performance.

In addition to explicitly telling people you believe in their potential, you can demonstrate high expectations by focusing on and developing their strengths.

WHAT'S STRONG WITH YOU?

Spencer Durden is a manager in Mergers & Acquisitions Tax at KPMG, the global professional services firm. He is part of what KPMG calls their Culture Champions Network, a self-selected group of over four thousand employees committed to strengthening the firm's culture. The Culture Champions help every employee live the firm's values of integrity, excellence, courage, together, and for better. KPMG asked us to run a series of trainings for the Culture Champions, and Spencer was one of the participants.

One of the sessions we designed focused on identifying and applying character strengths at work. Character strengths are the positive parts of our personality that make us feel authentic and engaged. In the field of positive psychology, we typically use the empirically researched and validated VIA Survey of Character Strengths and Virtues to discover our strengths. Developed by positive psychology's founders, Marty Seligman and Chris Peterson, the VIA represents a departure from traditional psychology's focus on pathology and disorders—what's *wrong* with us. Instead, the VIA Survey explores human potential and virtue—what's *strong* with us. By offering a language to describe and appreciate our positive traits, the VIA Survey serves as a valuable tool for those seeking to tap into the best of who they are.

The survey classifies twenty-four character strengths that are valued across cultures and time. Some examples include creativity, curiosity, honesty, humor, and perseverance. The graphic below visually represents all twenty-four strengths. The survey is available in over forty languages and has been taken by over thirty million people worldwide. You can access it for free at https://makeworkmeaningful.pro.viasurvey.org/.

When you take the assessment, the top five to seven strengths in your report are considered your signature strengths. These are your most prominent and authentic character strengths and have three key qualities, known as the three E's. First, a signature strength is **essential** to who you are as a person. Second, it is **effortless**—using it is second nature. Finally, a signature strength is **energizing**, bringing joy and vitality when used. If you're unable to take the assessment, you can still identify your signature strengths by examining the list of twenty-four strengths on the next page and applying the three E's criteria. Any strength that meets all three criteria can be considered a signature strength.

People flourish at work when they're able to use their signature strengths. In a study of ten thousand people, those who used their strengths consistently were eighteen times more likely to be thriving at work than those who didn't. Additionally, people who use their strengths at work tend to find their jobs more meaningful, enjoyable, and engaging. When leaders recognize employees' strengths and give them opportunities to develop those strengths, they increase their employees' motivation, maximize their productivity, and improve their performance. It is a powerful way to move employees toward the Zone of Possibility.

Many leaders adopt a deficit-based approach to management by focusing only on correcting what employees are doing wrong. While this approach can help minimize mistakes and prevent failures, it is only half of the equation. Correcting what's wrong is like pulling weeds—necessary but not sufficient for a thriving garden. In contrast,

THE VIA CLASSIFICATION OF
CHARACTER STRENGTHS AND VIRTUES

VIRTUE OF WISDOM

CREATIVITY
Original & Adaptive, Clever, A problem solver, Sees and does things in different ways

CURIOSITY
Interested, Explores new things, Open to new ideas

JUDGMENT
A critical thinker, Thinks things through, Open minded

LOVE OF LEARNING
Masters new skills & topics, Systematically adds to knowledge

PERSPECTIVE
Wise, Provides wise counsel, Takes the big picture view

VIRTUE OF COURAGE

BRAVERY
Shows valor, Doesn't shrink from fear, Speaks up for what's right

PERSEVERANCE
Persistent, Industrious, Finishes what one starts

HONESTY
Authentic, Trustworthy, Sincere

ZEST
Enthusiastic, Energetic, Doesn't do things half-heartedly

VIRTUE OF HUMANITY

LOVE
Warm and genuine, Values close relationships

KINDNESS
Generous, Nurturing, Caring, Compassionate, Altruistic

SOCIAL INTELLIGENCE
Aware of the motives and feelings of others, Knows what makes others tick

VIRTUE OF JUSTICE

TEAMWORK
Team player, Socially responsible, Loyal

FAIRNESS
Just, Doesn't let feelings bias decisions about others

LEADERSHIP
Organizes group activities, Encourages a group to get things done

VIRTUE OF TEMPERANCE

FORGIVENESS
Merciful, Accepts others' shortcomings, Gives people a second chance

HUMILITY
Modest, Lets one's accomplishments speak for themselves

PRUDENCE
Careful, Cautious, Doesn't take undue risk

SELF-REGULATION
Self-controlled, Manages impulses and emotions

VIRTUE OF TRANSCENDENCE

APPRECIATION OF BEAUTY & EXCELLENCE
Feels awe & wonder in beauty, Inspired by goodness of others

GRATITUDE
Thankful for the good, Expresses thanks, Feels blessed

HOPE
Optimistic, Future-minded

HUMOR
Playful, Brings smiles to others, Lighthearted

SPIRITUALITY
Searches for meaning Feels a sense of purpose, Senses a relationship with the sacred

leaders who focus on what's *strong* create meaning and, in turn, a high-performance culture.

At a recent gathering of Masters of Applied Positive Psychology students, Marty Seligman shared, "I spent the first half of my life looking at what's wrong. I've come to think of that as child's play. It's much easier to look at what's wrong. It is much more challenging to look at what's right and try to replicate it." Similarly, we have grown accustomed to focusing on our weaknesses. We are frequently confronted with challenges at work, from meeting tight deadlines to resolving conflicts with colleagues to adapting to new technologies. These situations demand our best performance. However, if we focus exclusively on correcting our weaknesses, we don't bring the best of who we are to these challenges and our performance suffers. To unlock high performance, we must leverage our strengths. By using our existing strengths, we can tackle challenges more effectively, even if we approach them differently from others. It's a different approach to achieving peak performance—and a better one.

Prior to our Culture Champions session at KPMG, we asked all the participants, including Spencer, to take the VIA Survey and bring their results to the session. During the workshop, we invited a few of them to share one of their signature strengths with the group and discuss how it shows up in their lives. One participant shared how they use their love-of-learning strength to continually read and take online courses. Another participant shared how their creativity signature strength manifests in their innovative problem-solving at work. As participants shared their stories, they came alive and the whole room was buzzing.

We then led the group through a series of exercises designed to help them innovate, problem-solve, and increase resilience. The exercises included thinking about different ways to use one of their signature strengths each day for a week. This is one of the most empirically validated exercises in positive psychology that is shown to improve well-being. For example, if someone has curiosity as one of their signature strengths, they could apply it to get to know their new project team by reaching out and asking questions to build their relationship. Or they could explore a new hobby or learn about a topic outside their comfort zone.

During the session, we noticed that Spencer looked doubtful and reserved. We invited him to share his thoughts. Spencer raised an important concern, stating, "Two of my signature strengths are kindness and forgiveness. They are truly core to how I conduct myself and an important part of who I am. Unfortunately, I don't think these 'soft' strengths are valued at work." Spencer shared that during goal-setting and performance reviews with his manager, kindness and forgiveness are rarely something that they discuss. Everyone in the group agreed.

Spencer's insight led to a great conversation about what is truly valued at work and how we can leverage our strengths to help us perform at our best. Even when we are incentivized to drive specific business outcomes and acquire job-related skills, our character strengths shape *how* we work. For instance, Spencer could give feedback *with kindness*; if someone on his team makes a mistake, he could respond *with forgiveness*. He left the session feeling skeptical but agreed to try the exercises discussed.

Two weeks later, we met with the group again and asked for examples of how they had applied their signature strengths at work. Spencer's hand immediately shot up. He enthusiastically shared that when he saw that forgiveness and kindness were his top two signature strengths, he had initially thought, *How am I going to bring that to work when I've got tight deadlines and am managing multiple projects?* But Spencer wanted to express these strengths at work. For him, the idea of leveraging your strengths to improve in areas where you may not be as skilled was a completely different way of thinking. The day after our first session, Spencer had an opportunity to apply his strengths when he received an email from his manager.

He said that the content of the email would stymie anyone in their quest to be resilient and productive. There were many aspects to the email that undermined his ability to perform—he wasn't included until the very last second and the overall tone was unpleasant and distressing. Before responding, Spencer considered what it would be like to use his strengths of kindness and forgiveness. It completely changed the way he wrote back to his manager. Spencer told us that it wasn't just the text of his email that changed. Leaning into his strength of forgiveness also made the tough task of responding to his manager's email a little easier. He told us that "thinking about forgiveness while writing an email worked like magic." Spencer's relationship with his manager was a difficult one, but leaning into his strengths completely changed the way he engaged.

Learning about character strengths gave Spencer a new way to think about work and what really matters. He regularly introduces this strengths-based approach to colleagues and mentees and intentionally creates opportunities for them to use their strengths at work every day.

In Chapter 7, you learned the powerful practice of strengths spotting when giving positive feedback with the BEST model. When others notice our strengths, it makes us feel appreciated and lets us know that our contributions matter. But meaning-driven leaders go beyond merely recognizing strengths. They also give their team ample opportunities to use their strengths. Leveraging strengths to develop your team's potential is a great way to keep them in the Zone of Possibility.

In Chris Wheeldon's early days on Broadway, he leaned on his strengths as a choreographer while learning to direct. Chris particularly recalls the "29-hour reading" for *An American in Paris*. This is a phase in the development of a new Broadway production that allows producers to test the rhythm of a show with live actors before moving forward. Actors are allowed to participate without a contract but are restricted to twenty-nine hours of work, thus its name. The reading has no choreography, props, or costumes. Actors are reading from the script and typically sitting behind music stands with very minimal staging.

This was Chris's first time directing a 29-hour reading. He didn't know how to direct the actors, so he just made them move around the room a lot, like dancers. He remembers them being frustrated, looking at him with an expression that said, *This is a 29-hour reading. Why are you making us move?* But Chris kept leaning on his strengths as a choreographer, asking the actors to stand up and move, despite their horrified expressions. None of the producers shot this unusual approach down, which gave Chris the space to figure it out as he went along. It worked. They ended up with the most staged 29-hour reading anyone had ever seen on Broadway. It was dynamic and engaging. The producers got excited about the show. Even the actors ultimately thought it was fun. By allowing Chris to access directing through movement, the producers let him use his current strengths as a resource to develop new skills. They celebrated the things that were working and didn't come down on him too hard on things he wasn't good at. This helped him build his confidence. In positive psychology, this idea is known as "strength towing," or using one strength to boost another by towing it along.

This experience taught Chris a valuable lesson—actors, like theater directors, need space for discovery. He had the space to figure out how to use what he was good at to learn what he needed to learn, and he created that same space for his actors.

One of those actors was Myles Frost, a first-time Broadway actor who played the lead role in the musical *MJ*, the next show Chris choreographed and directed. Chris knew that Myles was the right actor for the role when he first heard him sing and immediately recognized his raw talent. Despite having no acting experience, Chris saw Myles's potential and was committed to helping him develop his skills. He needed Myles to be brilliant in the show, and using his strengths was the best way to get there.

The process wasn't always smooth. At their first table read, Myles was terribly nervous–it was his first time reading a script in front of a group. Chris remained patient with Myles, just like Peter and Stuart had been with him. Since vocals were Myles's strength, Chris structured his process around that.

Two weeks later they rehearsed a full scene of the show without the script. Chris arranged the actors in a semicircle with Myles at the center. When the music took over, Myles was fully in command—he owned the stage. When he felt the confidence of the music behind him, his level of scene work increased dramatically. Chris helped Myles use his musical strength to improve his acting, much like the producers had helped Chris use his movement skills to become a better director.

MJ premiered on Broadway in 2022 and was a box office smash. The show was nominated for ten Tony Awards, including a Best Actor nomination for Myles, which he ultimately won. Chris has recently been going through his early *MJ* notes. He finds it useful to look back and see where his mind was at the beginning of a creative process. In his notes, he found a handwritten quote he had copied from the book *Creativity, Inc.* by Pixar cofounder Ed Catmull: "Only when we admit what we don't know can we ever hope to learn it." For Chris, this is a reminder to "check your ego and avoid feeling like you have to prove that you can do everything. It releases you from a state of fear and makes room for learning. That's when you can do exceptional work."

Recognizing strengths allows you to find challenges that stretch people just enough to grow, without overwhelming them. Leaders who provide this level of support are like companion plants in a garden, helping their people grow better.

THE MARIGOLD EFFECT

Meredith Glassman lives outside Boston in a charming neighborhood on a cul-de-sac. On any given Saturday in the summer, you can find her outside with her headphones on and her hands in the dirt. Meredith is a self-taught gardener who enjoys spending hours planting, pruning, and weeding her flower beds. She has planted vibrant species throughout her garden, including peonies, phlox, dianthus, salvia, wild geranium, and more. But a humble little flower, sprinkled throughout, is one of Meredith's favorites—the marigold. Meredith explains, "Marigolds are companion plants. They help stave off pests and support the growth of other plants in my garden."

Companion planting is an agricultural practice that involves growing different plants in close proximity to provide mutual benefits, such as enhancing plant growth, suppressing weeds, and repelling pests. The history of companion planting dates back centuries and can be traced to various cultures around the world. Native American tribes, for example, used the three sisters planting method, which involves planting corn, beans, and squash together. The corn provides support for the beans, the beans add nitrogen to the soil, and the squash acts as a ground cover, preventing weed growth. Together, they all grow better.

The marigold is one of the best companion plants around. Marigolds repel pests, enrich the soil, and attract pollinators. Not only do they protect plants and vegetables from pests and weeds, but they also help them grow and thrive. We can find marigolds in our workplaces too. They are the leaders and colleagues who encourage, support, and nurture us as we grow.

Meredith finds the marigold effect highly resonant as she leverages a similar supportive relationship in her product management leadership role. In a similar way to the marigold, she tries to cultivate team members by offering support, empowerment, and growth opportunities— while hopefully providing a "pop of color" while she's at it.

Leaders who provide high support for their people are like marigolds. They not only remove barriers to growth—the pests and weeds in the garden—but they also enrich the soil with opportunities for development. How can you be the marigold your team needs, providing the right opportunities and support to keep team members in the Zone of Possibility? One of the best ways we found is by having frequent and meaningful development conversations.

Development conversations are forward-looking discussions centered on growth and learning. Many organizations today have already separated these types of conversations from traditional performance evaluations. Whether through one-on-ones or check-ins, most managers connect with their teams on a regular basis to discuss progress, gain alignment, and identify potential issues. Meaning-driven leaders take it a step further. They use development conversations as an opportunity to move beyond a simple check-in and also identify growth opportunities, investigate barriers to performance goals, and give individuals a say in their career path. In the last chapter, we learned about the importance of providing an opportunity for self-directed career development. Development conversations are moments when leaders can give employees a push outside their comfort zone. By regularly engaging in open dialogue about career aspirations and development goals, these leaders tailor their guidance and support, providing resources, mentorship, and training opportunities that align with individual needs.

Deep Mahajan, the vice president of talent management at Juniper whom you met earlier, told us about a companywide development conversation process called Conversation Days. These sessions are separate from regular check-ins and provide an opportunity for managers and their teams to have meaningful discussions centered on quarterly development themes. The company provides suggested questions, but managers and their teams have flexibility to guide the conversation according to their preferences.

Conversation Days topics are generally designed around three key components, which Juniper calls "looking back, looking forward, and career development." The initial set of questions encourages individuals to reflect on their top achievements and challenges from the past quarter. Then the focus shifts to looking forward, with questions that prompt discussions around upcoming projects, tasks, and support requirements. The conversation concludes with a focus on career development, seeking insights into individuals' aspirations and how managers can support their professional growth journey in a variety of ways, ranging from structured learning options to ongoing mentoring, stretch assignments, and feedback.

Deep explained, "We intentionally take some time to look back because people want recognition. They have achievements, and we want to acknowledge and celebrate them. Then we look forward and make sure they are getting the support they need. Finally, we spend a lot of time focused on development. We want to know what actions individuals would like to take to amplify their impact within the organization."

Deep shared that during a recent Conversation Days period themed "own your career" almost a thousand new employees joined Juniper's internal career platform, signaling a heightened interest in career development within the organization. This was exactly what Deep had hoped might happen and shows that leaders at Juniper have begun embracing their roles as marigolds.

Frequent development conversations can help leaders demonstrate high support. In these conversations, the goal is to encourage open dialogue and help people take ownership of their growth journey. A leader's role is to ask questions that prompt reflection, allow employees to explore development opportunities, and figure out what support they need to get there. Then the leader can ensure employees have the support they need. We have included examples of effective development conversation questions below. Our hope is that you will customize these ideas to suit the unique dynamics of your team and organization.

- Which of your strengths could you use more in your role?
- What future role would allow you to use your strengths more often?
- What tasks or projects do you find most challenging and why?
- What new skills would you like to develop?
- What training programs or learning opportunities are you interested in exploring?
- Who would be an ideal mentor for you?

Leaders who embody the marigold effect not only remove barriers and enrich the soil with opportunities for growth, but they also infuse a pop of color and encouragement within their teams. As you assign challenging development opportunities and offer necessary support, it is crucial to acknowledge that setbacks and occasional failures are bound to happen. Like growing pains in adolescence, they are signs of rapid growth spurts. These experiences, while uncomfortable, are valuable learning opportunities. Adopting a mindset that views setbacks as stepping stones to growth empowers individuals to keep going and achieve even greater success—a perspective known as a growth mindset.

NOT THERE . . . YET

When Satya Nadella took over as CEO of Microsoft in 2014, the culture of the organization was driven by internal competition and forced rankings that pitted people against one another. In his memoir *Hit Refresh*, Satya wrote that he spent the first six months as CEO focused on listening and learning, engaging with employees at all levels to understand their perspectives, concerns, and ideas. Over the course of these conversations, Satya came to believe that the CEO's most important role is to be the curator of an organization's culture. He decided that for him, the C in CEO would stand for culture.

Tamara was fortunate to be a facilitator for the Wharton Future of Work Conference in a year when Satya shared how he led the transformation of Microsoft's culture from competition and stagnation into one of collaboration and innovation. He spoke about one of his main goals: to push people to think of themselves as students. Satya wanted to shift the culture from "know-it-all" to "learn-it-all." To do that, he borrowed from Stanford psychologist Carol Dweck's work on growth mindset.

A growth mindset is the belief that personal traits, such as intelligence and talent, can be developed with practice and effort. In a growth mindset, we view our abilities as muscles—with effort, they can grow. On the other hand, a fixed mindset is the belief that abilities are innate, unchangeable, and predetermined. In a fixed mindset, we view our abilities like our eye color—we're born with what we've got and, no matter how much we try, we can't change things. People with a fixed mindset tend to give up more quickly, since they believe their efforts won't make a difference. People with a growth mindset see challenges as opportunities for development and embrace effort as a pathway to mastery. They tend to persist in the face of setbacks.

Think about a personal or professional challenge you faced this past week. Maybe you didn't achieve a sales goal. How did you approach the setback? With a growth mindset, you might have thought, *Selling is a skill and I need more practice.* With a fixed mindset, however, your inner dialogue might have sounded more like *I am such a bad salesperson!* Most of us have both mindsets in different areas of our lives. For example, you might have a growth mindset when it comes to your work skills but more of a fixed mindset when it comes to your musical abilities.

The good news is that we can cultivate a growth mindset not only for ourselves but also for our teams and organizations, just like Satya Nadella did at Microsoft. In the summer of 2019, Microsoft rolled out a new management framework—Model, Coach, Care—aimed at instilling a growth mindset through all levels of the organization. As we explored in Chapter 3, modeling is about truly "walking the talk." Managers are expected to model Microsoft's culture and values and visibly practice a growth mindset. Coaching is about helping people become the best version of themselves. Managers are expected to coach their teams, emphasizing their potential to grow and creating a space where they learn from their mistakes. Caring is about making each person feel valued and cared for. Managers are expected to know each person's capabilities and aspirations and invest in their growth.

Satya Nadella's investment in Microsoft becoming a learn-it-all culture is paying off. Microsoft has frequently earned Great Place To Work Certification, and in 2023, *Time* magazine and Statista ranked it as the best company in the world, with a top ranking for employee satisfaction.

We recommend three strategies for you to start instilling a growth mindset in your teams:

First, normalize failure as part of growth. Research has found that it is not enough for leaders to admit they have things to learn. It is more powerful to ask for feedback and admit when you don't have all the answers or when you made a mistake. BetterUp CEO Alexi Robichaux shares his own mistakes during leadership team meetings to foster a growth mindset. Sharing his own struggles helps those who report directly to him feel more comfortable sharing theirs, which filters down to everyone. By sharing your own mistakes and failures, you create a culture where it is safe to learn.

The second practice for fostering a growth mindset is to focus your feedback—whether criticism or praise—on the process rather than the person. You'll remember that in the BEST model for positive feedback, which we described in Chapter 7, B stands for behavioral. The idea is to focus your positive feedback on what the person did rather than on the outcome they achieved. Similarly, to foster a growth mindset you want to focus your feedback on the process. For example, if one of your team members did a great job on a presentation, it is more effective to tell them, "You articulated your points clearly and kept your energy up" instead of "You are such a great presenter!" By focusing on the process, you can help your team member to replicate what they did well next time. Additionally, remember that you can reiterate your high expectations and belief in them when giving feedback.

The third strategy for fostering a growth mindset is the simplest one—leveraging "the power of yet." In her 2014 TEDx Talk, Carol Dweck emphasizes that the tiny word *yet* serves as an effective reminder that we are all learning. Imagine one of your team members, when faced with a new software system for example, stating, "I can't navigate this interface." Now, imagine the shift in perspective if you responded with, "You can't navigate this interface yet." By simply adding *yet*, you instill the belief that skills are not fixed but developable with dedication and support.

These three simple practices—sharing your own failures, focusing your feedback on process, and leveraging the power of yet—can start shifting your culture into one that not only tolerates but celebrates the journey of growth.

WHAT ELSE IS TRUE?

Most of the key practices needed to lift people into the Zone of Possibility and keep them there require little or no budget. However, many require a mindset shift. These practices involve changing the way we think about things. While crucial, changing your mindset can be demanding because it involves thinking differently rather than taking action.

If you find yourself managing someone whom you have already deemed as low potential, for example, confirmation bias makes it hard to change your mind. Confirmation bias is our tendency to favor, interpret, or recall information that confirms our preexisting beliefs. Not only do we tend to only notice information that aligns with our existing views, but we also tend to dismiss evidence that contradicts them. As you can imagine, this makes it hard to see the true potential of someone you've already mentally labeled as low potential. But, as you learned, making this shift can be a worthwhile endeavor. Countless books have been written about how to become more effective at cognitive reappraisal—the ability to reframe or reinterpret an opinion, experience, or situation. We recommend starting with Adam Grant's *Think Again*. By challenging and reconsidering our beliefs and thought processes, we can become more flexible, open-minded, and adaptable over time.

We would like to share a simple strategy to get you started, something we both do frequently. It's a small but powerful step toward shifting your mindset. Think of a question that encourages you to expand your perspective. For Tamara, this question is, "What else is true?" Wes prefers, "What is a more productive way to look at this?" The goal is to come up with a question that prompts you to consider alternative perspectives and opens your mind to different possibilities. Make this question your mantra. Whenever you catch yourself making assumptions or jumping to conclusions, pause and ask yourself the question.

By incorporating this question into your regular thought processes, you create a habit of challenging assumptions and fostering a more inclusive and optimistic approach to evaluating the potential of those you manage. The journey to recognizing and unleashing someone's potential often begins with a shift in how we think about them.

INDETERMINATE GROWTH

On November 23, 2022, Andy Hackett was fishing in Bluewater Lakes, a fishery in the Champagne region of France. Andy had made the trek from his hometown of Worcestershire, England, many times before, but this particular trip was a special one.

Bluewater Lakes is famous for providing anglers a private spot to try to catch one of its sizable fish. On this trip, Andy was on a mission to catch "The Carrot." He told the BBC, "With normal fish, you struggle to see them if they're just under the surface, but The Carrot is obviously bright orange so you can't miss it." Even though The Carrot was easy to see, it was harder to catch—no one had been able to do it for over nine months. But that fateful Wednesday was Andy's lucky day. "I knew it was a big fish when it took my bait and went off, side to side and up and down with it. Then it came to the surface 30 or 40 yards out, and I saw that it was orange." That was Andy's chance. For twenty-five minutes, he struggled with The Carrot, before finally pulling it from the lake. Moments later, he held the giant orange fish for a photo.

While anglers reel in sizable catches daily, Andy's catch stood out for a remarkable reason. The Carrot is a sixty-seven-pound goldfish.

Goldfish are what's known as indeterminate growers. This means that, given proper space and care, goldfish never stop growing. Their ability to grow is directly related to their environment. In smaller fish tanks, limited space and poor water stunt their growth. In a lake, with access to space and resources, a goldfish can end up the size of a golden retriever.

In the same way, we humans have indeterminate growth potential. Although we physically stop growing during adolescence, our ability to learn, develop, and reach our potential is limited only by our environment. When a leader believes in us, celebrates our progress, and challenges us to learn new skills, we will keep growing. Leaders who have high expectations and provide high support keep us in the Zone of Possibility. They unlock growth and increase meaning at work. Their organizations aren't tanks; they are lakes.

THE FUTURE OF MEANINGFUL WORK

The best way to predict the future is to create it.

—DENNIS GABOR

Despite seismic shifts shaping the future of work—the rise of generative AI, the shift to hybrid workplaces, and changing expectations about the role that our jobs should play in our lives—one constant remains: the human search for meaning. No matter how work evolves, our needs to experience a sense of belonging, to believe our efforts matter, and to fulfill our potential will endure.

We're in the middle of a disruptive and transformational moment in human history. Global events of recent years have forced a reckoning in our collective understanding of why we work. Maybe you've realized that the job you have isn't really the job you want. Maybe you've realized that your job is really just a way to support other things in your life that matter more to you, like time with family or creative pursuits. Maybe you've realized your career doesn't have to be the center of your world, or maybe you've realized that your new job is your life's calling.

Wherever you sit on the spectrum, chances are you will spend a significant part of your life at work. Whatever that work looks like— remote or retail, money driven or mission driven, social or solitary— that work can have meaning. To a large extent, each of us can create that meaning through our own choices, actions, and mindsets. But we can only get so far on our own.

Nearly half of meaning at work is tied to the actions and decisions of our leaders. By focusing on the Three C's, leaders can help us find and cultivate meaning in every job. Leaders, like gardeners, help create the conditions needed for us to thrive.

The idea that leaders have a responsibility to provide meaningful work can be daunting. It can feel like a leader's job has become harder and more complex in recent years. We think it's more accurate to say that the true difficulty, complexity, and promise of leadership have become more clear. The influence of leadership has always come with an opportunity and a responsibility to help bring out the best in those on your team. Great leadership goes beyond successfully managing tasks and fixing problems. We believe great leadership is measured in the meaning it provides.

As we look to the future, we don't know what the world of work will bring. It's almost certain that increased change and disruption are on the horizon. We believe that much of this disruption is the hallmark of a powerful paradigm shift—growing pains in the struggle toward a new, better model of work. There is increasing awareness of our greater potential, and a recognition that the legacy model of work won't help us achieve it. We can't predict what will happen next, but we do know that finding meaning has never been more important in the eyes of employees.

For this final chapter, we've reached out to leaders from a range of backgrounds and disciplines and asked them to share the opportunities they see when it comes to creating more meaningful work for everyone. We sought out people who are experts in their respective fields and who could provide unique insights on the critical questions that leaders face today. To their answers, we've added our own vision of what meaningful work could bring.

JOBS MUST BE ABOUT MORE THAN A PAYCHECK

A paycheck is a practical reason for work. For most of us, getting paid is critical to supporting ourselves and our families in living a decent life. In that sense, work is a transaction that benefits both the employee and the employer. In the absence of more, however, work remains just that—a transaction—and that's not enough to fulfill us or make the time we spend at work feel worthwhile. Underlying much of the paradigm shift around work is a simple question: Why?

Employees are asking themselves, and their leaders, why the tasks they do every day matter. **Adam Grant**, professor at the Wharton School at University of Pennsylvania and *New York Times* bestselling author of *Hidden Potential*, told us, "Too many people are stuck in what anthropologists call 'bullshit jobs'—they hardly matter to anyone. The greatest opportunity for making work more meaningful is to design jobs that have significant, lasting benefits to others."

Arthur Brooks, professor at the Harvard Kennedy School and Harvard Business School, and number-one *New York Times* bestselling author, voiced a similar view: "Making more money doesn't bring more meaning than earning less. Job type hardly matters either. At work, it is especially critical to believe that someone needs the service you provide. These people can't be nameless and faceless—I must know whom I am serving. Leaders have a responsibility to make this clear to employees: people need their work. Maybe that means colleagues or customers, but these people must be specific."

Even when jobs have a clear contribution, however, failure to provide basic dignity can erode the meaning that comes from it.

WORK MUST BE DECENT BEFORE IT CAN BE MEANINGFUL

Our basic needs must be met before we can satisfy higher-order desires. Without food, water, and a safe place to live, we don't have the capacity to invest in deep relationships or creative pursuits. In the same way, decent work is a prerequisite for meaningful work. Without the foundational elements of a decent job—dignity, respect, reasonable hours, and fair pay—we don't have the capacity to make meaning.

It should go without saying that all work should meet a minimum of human decency. Unfortunately, that decency is lacking in many jobs today. In millions of jobs at call centers, restaurants, nursing homes, gas stations, and retail stores, employees are paid poor wages, provided few benefits, and treated like replaceable cogs in a machine.

Even in jobs that we assume are inherently meaningful, a lack of decent working conditions and appropriate support can rob people of the meaning that comes from a purpose-driven profession. Nurses, teachers, government workers, and nonprofit employees, among others, struggle to find meaning when leaders deprive them of the foundational elements of decent work.

As we look to the future, decent work will continue to be a requirement and must be a critical focus for leaders. In recent years, we've seen countless workers in the retail, service, and hospitality sectors leave their jobs because of low pay and poor working conditions. Many haven't just left their jobs; they've left these industries altogether in search of work that better meets their basic needs. Until we recognize these needs and redesign these jobs, meaning will remain out of reach.

MIT professor **Zeynep Ton**, author of *The Case for Good Jobs*, told us, "Even the most meaningful work alone isn't sufficient for a job to be a good one. Work needs to allow people to have agency over their lives. When pay is so low or inconsistent that people are working multiple jobs, getting little sleep, stressing about putting food on the table, [and] having physical and mental health problems, as well as lower cognitive functioning, everything else can feel like a Band-Aid on a wound. The absence of sufficient pay also guarantees high employee turnover, which almost guarantees that work can't be designed for high meaning."

Even with the foundations of decent work in place, not every job needs to be a person's life calling. It would be unrealistic to expect or advocate for that. Sometimes a job is just a way to support the other things in your life that matter—and that should be OK. **Reb Rebele**, senior research fellow for the Wharton People Analytics Initiative, shared, "For some people, the most meaningful work may be having a decent job that provides the security and freedom they need for other meaningful pursuits."

Even though you may be leading someone with this kind of relationship to work, you can still give them more moments of meaning. These small moments are possible in every job, every day. When we fulfill the basic requirements of decent work and then focus on creating meaning, magic happens.

MEANING HAPPENS IN MOMENTS

Meaning comes from experiences of community, contribution, and challenge that happen in the course of our work. These can be short, but powerful, experiences of belonging, experiences of having impact, and experiences of growth. Leaders help create meaning in these moments. It is possible for these moments of meaning to happen in every job, every day with the help of a great leader.

Kelly Monahan is the director of the Upwork Research Institute. The institute studies data from Upwork, the world's largest platform for independent contractors, and other sources to provide insights on the shifts happening across work. Kelly told us, "The relationship with one's leader may hold the most significant impact on one's ability to engage in meaningful work. I think the most important thing for a leader to get right is their belief in people's ability to be generous, kind, and creative. Too many leaders do not trust their workforce to do the right thing. We've actually built entire MBA programs and training on the assumption that people do not inherently want to work. When we flip this notion on its head, the way a leader behaves changes. The behavior no longer flows from a place of distrust but rather trust. This means the leader goes from seeking compliance from their workforce to seeking the right conditions for people to flourish."

With the right leadership, we are poised to live in a world where everyone can find meaning at work and organizations can evolve to be hubs of human thriving. For us to achieve this potential, leaders must champion this change through their own actions and also through the design of the systems we use to get our work done.

AI CAN FACILITATE MEANINGFUL WORK (IF WE DESIGN IT TO)

Between the time we send this manuscript to our publisher and the time this book is released, the capabilities of AI will likely have increased by a magnitude greater than the change in computing power from World War II to the beginning of the COVID pandemic. The speed and size of this shift are hard to comprehend. It brings with it concerns that AI could replace jobs and push working people to the margins of society. We are not AI experts or futurists, but we believe that well-designed technology can provide opportunities for everyone to work at a higher level and pursue their full potential.

As technology advances, the human part of the equation becomes both more urgent and more valuable. We have to be intentional about how we design the algorithms and source the data that power AI. Artificial intelligence, if programmed and leveraged in the right way, can create more meaningful opportunities for all of us. To achieve that, AI models must be developed collaboratively. Technologists must work alongside ethicists, psychologists, sociologists, historians, and policymakers to consider and design for positive impact on society. If we can succeed at prioritizing humanity, we could automate or eliminate the bullshit jobs that Adam Grant referred to and free up space for people to engage in more meaningful tasks.

Johannes Eichstaedt, a fellow at Stanford's Institute for Human-Centered Artificial Intelligence, told us, "In general, work will move higher up the stack. Our jobs will draw more on the mixing of knowledge and skills, rather than on their mere execution. Human skills that in the past were more important for executives—such as having a sense of where the puck is going and a sense of audience—will become more critical."

Kelly Monahan of Upwork added, "The promise of GenAI is that it is able to remove much of the administration we've built into knowledge worker jobs, which often robs the meaning from work. For those who are able to learn and capture this moment in time in our modern work, I believe it offers more opportunity to craft meaningful work. I see generative AI accelerating the opportunity for contribution and challenge, while cautioning leaders it may hinder community."

That caution is an important one. In our digitally divided world, we risk turning all of our interactions into transactions. To satisfy our need for community and the meaning it brings, we must thoughtfully consider the way we design the work of the future.

BUILDING COMMUNITY WILL REQUIRE MORE INTENTIONAL DESIGN

Where and when we work continue to be hotly debated topics. Years on from the pandemic shift, we continue to struggle with hybrid design and to balance the priorities of organizations and employees. For those who have the option to work remotely, the cost of going into the office has increased.

Jennifer Deal, senior researcher at the Center for Effective Organizations at the University of Southern California, believes that the psychological burden of coming into work has shifted. "Unless you have a deep relationship with someone, the loose ties that people have with each other in organizations dissipate over time without face-to-face interaction. The problem is that the cost of those face-to-face interactions are paid by individuals, not by their employers. I have to get up and get myself to work; I have to shower and get dressed and put on makeup and get the kids where they need to be and then drive there. So there are both tangible costs, like the car and paying for the gas, but there are also opportunity costs: What could I be doing with that time if I didn't have to do those things?

Jennifer continues, "Organizations keep saying, 'But you always paid this before. What's the problem?' And the answer is that the psychological contract of work has changed. Organizations don't like it, but it has. To make work more meaningful by investing in community, the organization needs to take on those costs."

Taking on the costs of face-to-face interactions means that organizations must invest in new resources and capabilities. The design of the office must shift to meet a new set of needs, and leaders must develop programming that makes the effort to come into the office worthwhile.

"There's a greater need for leaders to create more engagement around meaning and authenticity in the office in a way that really resonates with their values," said **Diane Hoskins**, the global cochair of the design firm Gensler. Diane works with clients like NVIDIA, Marriott, and Adobe to rethink how people come together to work and design workspaces that are optimized for the future workforce. "It's not about asking what other companies are doing, but rather thinking about what's right for their organization, their people, and their culture. This needs to be married with places that provide a heightened level of experience and a sense of choice that supports the ways teams and individuals want to work. It's an exciting opportunity to rethink the future of place and the spaces that we choose to be in. I'm a believer in the power of being together because it increases organizational performance and individual growth at the same time. It's a win for people and companies."

Being together allows us to best take advantage of the range of perspectives spanning generations, genders, races, and backgrounds. Bringing those perspectives together effectively will be critical to successfully navigating the future of work.

NEW APPROACHES FOR A NEW WORKFORCE

The psychological contract hasn't just shifted around where we work. It has shifted, and continues to shift, around the entire relationship between organizations and employees. That shift in expectations feels most dramatic when we look at Gen Z, the latest entrants to the workforce.

More than 40 percent of Gen Z employees have refused a work assignment because of ethical concerns. Nearly four in ten have turned down a job with a company that doesn't align with their values. In the workplace, they are driving the conversation around social justice, mental health, and work-life balance. More than 90 percent of workers say they've been influenced by Gen Z on issues of meaning at work, and more than six in ten say Gen Z has made them more likely to speak up when they don't approve of something at work.

Some of the generational differences we're experiencing are just career stage differences. While the Three C's are important for everyone, different people will value different sources of meaning more highly. In particular, those newer to the workforce tend to prioritize opportunities to learn and grow. Jennifer Deal, who has studied generational changes at work for many years, said, "When people talk about generations, what they do is they think about lumps of people cohorts that were born at a particular time, and that doesn't really have as much of an effect in the workplace as does life stage, career stage, and level in the organization. Young people want to be challenged. While you should focus on all Three C's for everybody, you might want to put more weight on challenge for people who are new to the workforce and weigh things differently for people who are middle or later career."

Other generational differences, however, represent a shift in employees' expectations of organizations and their leaders. **Arthur Brooks** shared, "Every year I teach Harvard MBA students about happiness and its unique relationship to leadership. These students are almost all destined for tremendous success as measured in worldly terms: money, prestige, and power. To most people in our society, this seems like a dream come true and the secret to happiness. Yet each year, when I speak to my MBA students—both in class and in private office hours—many are concerned. Are they truly on the path to happiness because of their near-certain success? They talk to alumni who complain about workaholism, broken relationships, and trouble finding passion. This provokes a lot of anxiety about *meaning*."

In our consulting work, we're frequently called in to help leaders navigate the divide between younger and older employees. We commonly hear things like, "These kids just don't want to work." We find it more accurate to say, "These kids don't want to work the way you did." While younger employees of course have a lot to learn, we believe this generation also has some things to teach. As we move toward a new, better model of work, this rising cohort is challenging many long-held ideals and broken structures. They aren't encumbered by the old system because they haven't invested in it.

Kahlil Shepard, the Gen Z worker from A–B, whom you met earlier, said, "I want to do things that matter. I want to feel like I'm constantly evolving. I want to work at a place where leaders are facilitating not just my growth broadly but also my ability to live out my values in the world."

Leaders can, and should, challenge this cohort to temper their ideals with practical realities. At the same time, leaders have an opportunity to take their aspirations of a better model and help bring it to life. This requires leaders to unlearn some of the meaning-killing behaviors that are a part of the old model and adopt better ways of working.

The future holds the promise of better work for all of us. We all want meaningful work—work that builds community, that contributes to others, and that challenges us to grow. As a leader, you have far more influence than you think in creating this meaning for others. Throughout this book, we've given you tools to create moments of meaning across each of the Three C's. These small moments can create ripples that reach our families, friends, and neighbors. The impact of these moments can extend far into the future.

We believe that now and into the future every job can, and should, be meaningful with the help of a great leader. And we believe that leader is you.

WHAT IF ALL JOBS WERE MEANINGFUL?

Imagine a world where every job is designed to be sustainable and fulfilling. Where jobs offer not just a paycheck but also a sense of contribution. Imagine work environments that prioritize relationships and connections over mere transactions. What if every employee was valued not as a temporary fix or a number on a balance sheet but as a crucial, long-term contributor to the organization's success? Imagine a world where earning a living did not come at the cost of living a meaningful life. How would this shift in work impact our organizations, our society, and our personal well-being?

Over the course of this book, we've looked at dozens of stories of high-performing organizations and the leaders committed to creating this world—a world where people experience meaning at work. We heard from presidents and hairstylists, tech leaders and consultants, NFL players and world-class choreographers. Each of these leaders faced different challenges, but their organizations thrived in the same way—through a commitment to making work meaningful for everyone.

Making work meaningful is not an item to check off your to-do list. It is the critical lens through which you must view every decision, interaction, and task. Meaning is created—or destroyed—in daily moments. Every conversation in which you truly listen, every piece of positive feedback you give, and every project you assign that encourages learning and growth don't just add up—they multiply.

We began this book by stating that leaders who wanted to build a more meaningful workplace lacked a road map. Now, as we come to the end, we hope this book has been the map you needed. When work builds *community*, gives us a sense of *contribution* to something bigger, and *challenges* us to learn and grow, both individuals and organizations thrive. With the Three C's framework, you now have a set of tools and strategies to make every job more meaningful.

If this new set of strategies feels like a lot to take in, remember that starting small can lead to big changes. Here's one question for each C to help you get started. Use these questions for personal reflection or to spark deeper engagement with your team:

- **Community:** Did I connect with someone today?
- **Contribution:** Is anything better in the world because of what I did today?
- **Challenge:** Did I learn something new today?

Start with a simple action to plant the seeds of meaning in everyday work. With the right nurturing, these seeds can grow into a flourishing garden where everyone thrives.

ACKNOWLEDGMENTS

Nearly five years ago, when we gave ourselves six months to research and write this book, we considered this auspicious project through the lens of the Three C's. We had the great fortune to be a part of a wonderful community of positive psychology practitioners and leadership experts who had encouraged and supported our efforts. We primarily saw this project as an opportunity to contribute to the well-being of others—by providing a playbook that leaders could use to create more meaning at work for their teams, we thought we could scale our impact to help more people find better work and, in turn, live better lives.

In our naivete, we didn't truly consider the challenge we were taking on. To say this project stretched our capabilities is an understatement. There were many moments when we doubted our work and our abilities. Moments when we questioned whether it was worth it. Moments when we faltered.

But through the process of research and writing and rewriting, we also experienced some of the most meaningful moments of our careers. Those moments overwhelmingly came from connecting with brilliant people; from the knowledge, guidance, and counsel they provided; and from the relationships, new and old, that sustained us.

So many people contributed to our efforts as we developed our framework, conducted research, and iterated on versions of each chapter. To the following people who made this book possible, we offer our deepest and most heartfelt appreciation.

ACKNOWLEDGMENTS

Many inspiring, meaning-driven leaders participated in our research, and many more shared stories that inform this book. Even though we weren't able to include all of the incredible stories in the book itself, the great privilege of learning from each of you is not lost on us. Thank you to Matt Fishman, Tom Rath, Kristin Deokisingh, Rushmie Nofsinger, Debbie Marriott Harrison, Katie Burke, Devon Still, Christine Deputy, Rob Waldron, Kenneth Cole, Jed Berger, Ingrid Yan, Andre Banks, Kahlil Shepard, Claudia Saran, Deep Mahajan, Chad Thomas, Erica Elan, Mark DiMassimo, Augusto Giacoman, Michelle Lozzi, Jeff Gibson, Theresita Richard, Dee Ann Turner, Christa Foley, Kelcy Scolnik, Emily Santos, Pete Berridge, Tunde Oyneyin, Lisa Richardson, Tom Cortese, Eimear Marrinan, Courtney Bigony, Jeff Smith, Susan Hwang, Carla McIntosh, Terri Jordan, Tina Mylon, Sonali Sapathy, Kyle Bodt, Hamish Cook, Michael Biggs, Brianne Goguen, Kaitlin Desselle, Chris Hurn, Chris Gabaldon, Amanda Joiner, Lindsey Tomaszewski, Christopher Wheeldon, Spencer Durden, Meredith Glassman, Matt Eversmann, Marty LaSalle, Nisha Patel, Andrew Kromelow, Shondrea McCargo, Jeremy Heimans, and Kathryn Mathews. We are deeply grateful that you were willing to offer your time, energy, and expertise to this project. Thank you for showing us how you create meaningful work and, in turn, for inspiring us to see what is possible.

We offer immense gratitude to our amazing literary agent, Sylvie Carr, for believing in us and pushing us to become better writers. Thank you for always asking the right questions, for challenging us, for offering your expertise, and for your commitment to our vision.

Thank you to the team at PublicAffairs and Hachette who made this book a reality, especially Colleen Lawrie, our editor, for seeing possibility and potential in us and in this project. We are so grateful for your advice, feedback, and wisdom. Thank you to Kate Mueller and Michelle Welsh-Horst for your attention to detail and for ensuring that all the t's were crossed and all the i's were dotted. Thank you to Jessica Breen, Liz Wetzel, and Jenny Lee for guiding us with your keen marketing and PR expertise.

ACKNOWLEDGMENTS

Thank you to the team at Cave-Henricks Communications, Barbara Henricks, Melissa Connors, and Pam Peterson, for helping us spread the message of meaningful work to more people than we could ever reach on our own. We truly value your expertise and sage guidance throughout the many years that it took to make this book a reality.

Thank you to the team at Target Marketing for helping us refine our brand and market our message. The creativity and expertise of Kenneth Gillette, Ruth Shelling, Nonnie Noffke, Charlie Foley, Lindsay Carter, Amy Duncan, Argjent Haradinaj, Gonzaga Gómez-Cortázar Romero, Krasimir Galabov, Megan Kramer, Melanie Holmes, and Miguel Trindade helped make the idea of meaningful work a part of the popular zeitgeist.

Thank you to our research partners Zach Mercurio and Jer Clifton for your intellectual rigor and for inspiring us with your extraordinary brilliance. Your keen insights and unwavering dedication have profoundly enriched our work and have been instrumental in shaping the ideas that form the core of this book. We look forward to many more collaborations.

Many scholars were kind enough to mentor us, offer advice, answer our questions, and point us to relevant research. We are eternally grateful to Marty Seligman, Kim Cameron, Angela Duckworth, Jane Dutton, Scott Barry Kaufman, Michelle McQuaid, Meredith Myers, Mike Steger, Bob Quinn, Judy Saltzberg, Karen Reivich, and Amy Wrzesniewski. Thank you for being so generous with your time and your expertise.

Several thought leaders that we deeply admire surprised us with their unexpected generosity by contributing their thinking to our final chapter. We are deeply grateful to Adam Grant, Arthur Brooks, Zeynep Ton, Reb Rebele, Kelly Monahan, Johannes Eichstaedt, Jennifer Deal, Diane Hoskins, and Carter Jernigan for your invaluable insights and perspectives. Your contributions have enriched our perspectives and inspired us to think more deeply about the future of meaningful work.

Thank you to Jan Stanley, Jack Benecke, Rachel Peterson, Raf Lopez, Arthur Villa, Madison Romney, Jodi Wellman, Emily Esfahani

Smith, Lisa Sansom, Stephanie Armistead, Haley Barrows, Cindy Chou, Liz Corcoran, Margaret Greenberg, Liz Meissner, Patrick Menasco, Caroline Miller, Cory Muscara, Shannon Polly, Adam Reiber, Orlan Boston, and Aviya Slutzky, for your unwavering support, your sage advice, and introductions to trailblazers who shaped our thinking.

Many friends and family members helped improve earlier drafts. For their invaluable insights, we thank Ted Myles, Meredith Glassman, Tina Mylon, Andrew Soren, Jennifer Beatty, Ross Rayburn, and Claudia Patton.

Thank you to our clients for trusting us to guide you through your leadership journey and for allowing us to be a part of your meaningful work. You make work meaningful for the two of us.

To the immense community of colleagues and friends that we did not mention individually, please know that we are incredibly grateful.

GRATITUDE FROM TAMARA

Wes, I am so grateful that we got to partner up in this adventure. It has been a profoundly meaningful experience—filled with awe, struggle, fun, and growth—and I cannot imagine doing it without you!

To my friends, I could not have done this without your love and support. Thank you for asking about how the writing was going, for listening when I needed to vent, for introducing me to leaders whose stories illustrate this book, and for consistently showing up to book club every month so we can share our love of books. Thank you for being my village. To Caroline Miller, Jan Stanley, and Erin Dullea, thank you for your continued support—our mastermind meetings are a constant source of inspiration, guidance, and motivation.

To my extended family—my aunts and uncles, cousins, in-laws, nieces and nephews—thank you for your unwavering love and support and enrichment of my life. To my brother-in-law Brian, thank you for your support and for connecting me to the right legal team. To my sister-in-law Rachel, a world-class fashion designer, thank you for helping me look stylish and feel confident on every occasion. To Emily and Ted, thank you for being so encouraging, for helping with the kids and puppies, for our daily catch-ups, for being proud of me, for always listening. To my brother-in-law Jayson, thank you for always being willing to be our on-call physician and for taking such great care of us.

To Daniela, my sister and best friend, thank you for your support and encouragement, for our daily talks and menu planning, for always being there for me. To Eduardo, my brother, and Aninha, my sister-in-law, thank you for your unwavering pride in my work and for always making us feel so welcome. To my grandmother, Vovó Morena, thank you for embodying joy and positivity. Thank you for teaching your six children, fourteen grandchildren, and twelve great-grandchildren (so far!) that happiness is a choice. I love you so much and am so grateful for your presence in my life.

To my dad, Sergio, thank you for your endless love, for teaching me the value of hard work, and for your constant encouragement and support. To my mom, Adelina, thank you for always believing in me and for infusing my life with the teachings of positive psychology before I ever knew it was a field of study, for teaching me that "my experience is what I agree to attend to" and for filling my life with optimism and hope.

To Ted, my true partner in every sense: I'm in awe of this beautiful life we have together. Thank you for being proud of me, for letting me babble on about my research and insights, for reading along with countless positive psychology books. Thank you for infusing humor in my life at all the right moments and for making me laugh every day. You are a true meaning-driven leader. I love you and am so lucky to call you mine.

To Bella, Eddie, and Vivi, my forever babies, you are the definition of "what makes life worth living." Thank you for your support, for being my positive psychology research subjects through countless experiments, for always having a hug and a snuggle available when I needed it. There are no words that adequately describe the depth of my love for you. You fill my life with meaning.

ACKNOWLEDGMENTS

GRATITUDE FROM WES

Tamara, you inspire me every day with your curiosity, persistence, integrity, and love. As a coauthor, a partner, and a friend, you have challenged me to be better in countless ways. I could not have hoped for anyone better with whom to ride this roller coaster. I'm grateful for every moment of this adventure and can't wait for our next chapter.

To Mom, you helped till the soil for this work from the moment we met. Your love, guidance, and unconditional support have shown me the true meaning of life. You have always pushed me to learn, guided me to help others, and championed every one of my endeavors. For that I am eternally grateful. I love you.

To Claudia and Rex, my life is much brighter for all the meaningful moments you've given me. Your encouragement, support, and love mean the world to me. It's been such a gift to be on this journey with you.

To Courtney, Andy, Josh, and Clara, thank you for showing me the meaning of family and for giving me the opportunity to be a loving uncle.

To my grandparents, Janet Elliott Daugherty and Alfred Clark Daugherty, I realize more each year how you shaped my life in so many amazing ways. My gratitude for you continues to grow and I miss you every day.

Without the resilience network of Amanda Rivera, Hamish Cook, Joe Simenic, Charles O'Byrne, David Blumenfeld, Meghan Shakar, Jake Vettoretti, James Bruni, Genève Stewart, Cindy Chou, Ani Ajeminan, Dan Wright, Delfo Trombetta, Orlan Boston, and Justin Trop, I would have quit many times over. Your encouragement and support help me see what I'm not always able to for myself. I'm fortunate to have you in my life.

To my amazing collaborators Matt Fishman, Dustin Mullis, Preston James, Kath Clemons, Bryce Raynor, Carice Anderson, Lauren Cohen, Martijn Boomsma, Lauren Heavern, Eric Carlson, Nadra Hunter, Guido Pellegrino, Tracy Moravek, Henry Donahue, Neil Yeager, and

ACKNOWLEDGMENTS

Tony Daloisio, I'm so grateful for the opportunities you've given me to put this work into practice. Thank you for trusting me with your teams and for being meaning-driven leaders. You are the people who create my meaningful work.

To Teresa Hargrave, CJ Pippen, and Tristan McAllister, your partnership over the years in shaping and refining my thinking, my language, and my communication contributed so much to the final version of this book.

To my therapist, Emily Joslin-Roher, and my coaches, Jenny Peterson and Dan MacCombie, thank you for helping me successfully navigate the ups and downs of this project, and life, with values alignment.

To the MAPP community, I could take up dozens of pages listing all the ways you've inspired, challenged, and supported me through this process. I'm awed by each of you and so grateful to have found my tribe.

APPENDIX

THE MEANING-DRIVEN LEADERSHIP SELF-ASSESSMENT

We invite you to take five minutes to complete the Meaning-Driven Leadership Self-Assessment. The self-assessment will help you identify which meaning-building leadership practices you are already using and where there is room for growth. It is meant to be a starting place for your journey and to help guide you through the rest of this book.

Take the assessment for free on our website using this link: www.makeworkmeaningful.com. After answering all the questions, you will receive a score for each of the Three C's—community, contribution, and challenge—as well as an overall score.

You can also take and score the assessment yourself on the following pages.

AREA	STATEMENT	Strongly Disagree (0)	Disagree (1)	Slightly Disagree (2)	Slightly Agree (3)	Agree (4)	Strongly Agree (5)	
Alignment	I set a good example for how others in my organization should behave							
Alignment	I act in line with my organization's values							
Alignment	I model behaviors that are valued in my organization							
Alignment	I make it clear that I expect others to speak up if I see someone acting in a way that is not aligned with the organization's values							
TOTAL								
Community	I ask about a candidate's alignment with my organization's values in the interview process							
Community	During the hiring process, I ask candidates about their personal values							
Community	During the hiring process, I have conversations with candidates about the organization's purpose							

AREA	STATEMENT	Strongly Disagree (0)	Disagree (1)	Slightly Disagree (2)	Slightly Agree (3)	Agree (4)	Strongly Agree (5)	
Community	During onboarding, I share stories to communicate my organization's core values and expected behaviors							
Community	I create opportunities for my team to do fun things together like volunteering or playing games							
Community	I demonstrate that I care about what's happening with my team outside of work							
Community	I make time for my team to get to know one another							
Community	I create spaces for my team to connect with others around shared interests							
TOTAL								
Contribution	I talk about the impact of my organization's work on society							
Contribution	I encourage my team to think about and discuss our organization's values							

AREA	STATEMENT	Strongly Disagree (0)	Disagree (1)	Slightly Disagree (2)	Slightly Agree (3)	Agree (4)	Strongly Agree (5)	
Contribution	I talk about the "why" of our work when discussing the organization's long-term goals							
Contribution	I often share stories about the impact our organization has on customers and clients							
Contribution	I regularly thank my team for their work							
Contribution	I give my team positive feedback when they've done something well							
Contribution	I create opportunities for my team to recognize each other when things go well							
Contribution	I publicly celebrate the big accomplishments of my team							
TOTAL								
Challenge	I help my team determine where they can grow and develop							
Challenge	I connect my team with opportunities to develop skills that interest them							

AREA	STATEMENT	Strongly Disagree (0)	Disagree (1)	Slightly Disagree (2)	Slightly Agree (3)	Agree (4)	Strongly Agree (5)	
Challenge	I give my team challenging assignments to help them grow							
Challenge	I encourage my team to use their unique strengths							
Challenge	I give my team the freedom to make decisions about how to do their work if they follow my organization's values							
Challenge	I give my team a lot of say in how they get their work done according to the organization's values							
Challenge	I give my team the freedom to work as they see fit as long as they adhere to the organization's values							
Challenge	I trust my team to make decisions on their own if they stay true to our values							
TOTAL								
OVERALL TOTAL								

SCORING INSTRUCTIONS

Answer each item and score it 0–5 in the column on the left. For each section, add up your total score and write it in the total box.

For Alignment

15–20: You're in good shape! Keep up the good work.

10–15: This area needs some work and could be getting in the way.

0–10: A lack of alignment is holding you back. Focus on improving your scores here first.

For Community, Contribution, and Challenge

35–40: This is a strong score. Keep investing in this area and exploring new ways of reinforcing your existing practices.

30–35: Solid work here. Read through the appropriate section of the book to learn how to take your efforts to the next level.

25–30: This could be an area of concern for you. Read through the section carefully and make a plan to use the tools provided.

0–25: This area could be a meaning-killer for your team. Use the tools and guidance in the appropriate section to create a plan to invest significantly in this area.

LIST OF ORIGINAL RESEARCH PARTICIPANTS

COMPANY	PARTICIPANT NAME AND TITLE
15Five	Courtney Bigony, Director, People Science and Jeff Smith, Director, Best Self Academy
BetterUp	Susan Hwang, Director, Special Projects (Office of the CEO)
Chick-fil-A	Dee Ann Turner, former Vice President, Talent and Sustainability
Curriculum Associates	Rob Waldron, Chief Executive Officer
Google	Carla H. McIntosh, Head, Talent Acquisition and Senior Staff Solutions Consultant
HubSpot	Katie Burke, Chief People Officer
KPMG	Claudia Saran, Vice Chair of Culture
Marriott	Debbie Marriott Harrison, Global Officer, Marriott Culture and Business Councils
Microsoft	Terri Jordan, General Manager, Global Data Center Operations
Nutanix	Deep Mahajan, Senior Director and Head of People Development and Culture

BIBLIOGRAPHY

INTRODUCTION

Reece, Andrew, Gabriella Kellerman, and Alexi Robichaux. *Meaning and Purpose at Work.* BetterUp, 2018. https://f.hubspotusercontent40.net/hubfs/9253440 /Asset%20PDFs/Promotions_Assets_Whitepapers/BetterUp-Meaning &Purpose.pdf.

Weeks, Kelly Pledger, and Caitlin Schaffert. "Generational Differences in Definitions of Meaningful Work: A Mixed Methods Study." *Journal of Business Ethics* 156, no. 4 (June 1, 2019): 1045–1061. https://doi.org/10.1007/s10551-017 -3621-4.

CHAPTER 1: THE POWER OF MEANINGFUL WORK

De Smet, Aaron, Bonnie Dowling, Marino Mugayar-Baldocchi, and Bill Schaninger. "'Great Attrition' or 'Great Attraction'? The Choice Is Yours." McKinsey & Company, September 8, 2021. https://www.mckinsey.com/capabilities /people-and-organizational-performance/our-insights/great-attrition-or -great-attraction-the-choice-is-yours.

Gallup. "Employee Wellbeing Starts at Work." Gallup, July 20, 2022. https://www .gallup.com/workplace/394871/employee-wellbeing-starts-work.aspx.

Glassdoor. "Marriott International: A Company That Cares—Sales Coordinator Marriott International Employee Review." May 31, 2023. https://www .glassdoor.com/Reviews/Employee-Review-Marriott-International -RVW76959478.htm.

Grant, Adam M., Elizabeth M. Campbell, Grace Chen, Keenan Cottone, David Lapedis, and Karen Lee. "Impact and the Art of Motivation Maintenance: The Effects of Contact with Beneficiaries on Persistence Behavior." *Organizational Behavior and Human Decision Process* 103, no. 1 (May 2007): 53–67. https: //www.sciencedirect.com/science/article/abs/pii/S0749597806000641.

Hurst, Aaron, Cammie Erickson, Scott Parish, Lauren Vesy, Allison Schnidman, Meg Garlinghouse, and Andrea Pavela. *2016 Workforce Purpose Index: Purpose at Work.* Imperative, 2016. https://40823263.fs1.hubspotusercontent-na1

.net/hubfs/40823263/Content%20Downloads/2016%20Workforce
%20Purpose%20Index.pdf.

Office of the US Surgeon General. *Workplace Mental Health & Well-Being*. US
Department of Health and Human Services, May 23, 2024. https://www.hhs
.gov/surgeongeneral/priorities/workplace-well-being/index.html.

Reece, Andrew, Gabriella Kellerman, and Alexi Robichaux. *Meaning and Purpose
at Work*. BetterUp, 2018.

Workhuman. *The Future of Work Is Human*. Workhuman Analytics & Research
Institute, 2019.

Wrzesniewski, Amy, and Jane E. Dutton. "Crafting a Job: Revisioning Employees
as Active Crafters of Their Work." *Academy of Management Review* 26, no. 2
(April 2001): 179–201. https://doi.org/10.5465/amr.2001.4378011.

CHAPTER 2: HOW LEADERS MAKE WORK MEANINGFUL

Deep Tech Insights. "HubSpot Stock: Undervalued and Growing Rapidly."
Seeking Alpha, October 4, 2022. https://seekingalpha.com/article/4544508
-hubspot-undervalued-and-growing-rapidly.

Diener, Ed, Sarah D. Pressman, John Hunter, and Desiree Delgadillo-Chase.
"If, Why, and When Subjective Well-Being Influences Health, and Future
Needed Research." *Applied Psychology: Health and Well-Being* 9, no. 2 (July
2017): 133–167. https://doi.org/10.1111/aphw.12090.

Gallup. *Empowering Workplace Culture Through Recognition*. Gallup, 2023. https:
//www.gallup.com/analytics/472658/workplace-recognition-research.aspx.

Heath, Dan. *Upstream: The Quest to Solve Problems Before They Happen*. New York:
Avid Reader Press, 2020.

"HubSpot Retention Score." Comparably, updated daily. https://www.comparably
.com/companies/hubspot/retention.

Lukianoff, Greg, and Jonathan Haidt. *The Coddling of the American Mind: How
Good Intentions and Bad Ideas Are Setting Up a Generation for Failure*. New
York: Penguin Books, 2018.

Maddux, James E. "Self-Efficacy: The Power of Believing You Can." In *Oxford
Handbook of Positive Psychology*, edited by S. J. Lopez and C. R. Snyder, 333–
345. 2nd ed. New York: Oxford University Press, 2009.

Mercurio, Zach. "How to Create Mattering at Work." *Zach's Blog*, November 15,
2022. https://www.zachmercurio.com/2022/11/mattering-at-work/.

Ryan, Richard M., Veronika Huta, and Edward L. Deci. "Living Well: A Self-
Determination Theory Perspective on Eudaimonia." *Journal of Happiness
Studies: An Interdisciplinary Forum on Subjective Well-Being* 9, no. 1 (2008):
139–170. https://doi.org/10.1007/s10902-006-9023-4.

CHAPTER 3: ALIGNMENT

Avual, Kavita, Lisa McKay, and Sébastien Galland. *Amnesty International: Staff Wellbeing Review.* The Konterra Group, January 2019. https://www.amnesty .org/en/documents/org60/9763/2019/en/.

Bandura, Albert. *Social Learning Theory.* Oxford, UK: Prentice-Hall, 1977.

Barry-Wehmiller. "Our History." https://www.barrywehmiller.com/story /history.

———. "Three Lessons on Leading Through Crisis from Barry Wehmiller." Conscious Capitalism. https://www.consciouscapitalism.org/story/three -lessons-on-leading-through-crisis-from-barry-wehmiller.

BBC staff. "Amnesty Loses Five Bosses After Report on 'Toxic Workplace.'" BBC, May 28, 2019. https://www.bbc.com/news/uk-48431652.

Cardador, M. T., and Deborah Rupp. "Organizational Culture, Multiple Needs, and the Meaningfulness of Work." In *The Handbook of Organizational Culture and Climate*, edited by N. M. Ashkanasy, C. P. Wilderom, and M. F. Peterson, 158–180. Thousand Oaks, CA: Sage, 2011. https://doi.org /10.4135/9781483307961.n10.

Chapman, Bob. "CEO's of the Future Must Not Be Penny-Wise and People-Foolish." Dave Alexander Center for Social Capital, February 15, 2024. https: //centerforsocialcapital.com/ceos-of-the-future-must-not-be-penny-wise -and-people-foolish/.

———. "How a Family Shared a Burden." Barry-Wehmiller, April 24, 2024. https://www.barrywehmiller.com/post/blog/2020/03/05/how-a-family -shared-a-burden.

Deci, Edward L., Anja H. Olafsen, and Richard M. Ryan. "Self-Determination Theory in Work Organizations: The State of a Science." *Annual Review of Organizational Psychology and Organizational Behavior* 4 (2017): 19–43. https://doi.org/10.1146/annurev-orgpsych-032516-113108.

Edelman. *2023 Edelman Trust Barometer: Special Report; Trust at Work.* Edelman, 2023. https://www.edelman.com/trust/2023/trust-barometer/special-report -trust-at-work.

Gneezy, Uri. *Mixed Signals: How Incentives Really Work.* New Haven, CT: Yale University Press, 2023.

Manz, Charles C., and Henry P. Sims Jr. "Vicarious Learning: The Influence of Modeling on Organization Behavior." *Academy of Management Review* 6, no. 1 (1981): 105–113. https://www.proquest.com/docview/230010724?source type=Scholarly%20Journals.

Peterson, Christopher. *A Primer in Positive Psychology.* New York: Oxford University Press, 2006.

Pinterest Careers. "Life at Pinterest." Our Life. https://www.pinterestcareers.com /our-life/.

Pratt, Michael G., and Blake E. Ashforth. "Fostering Meaningfulness in Working and at Work." In *Positive Organizational Scholarship: Foundations of A New Discipline*, edited by Kim Cameron, Jane E. Dutton, and Robert E. Quinn, 309–327. Oakland, CA: Berrett-Koehler, 2003.

Teller, Astro. "The Unexpected Benefit of Celebrating Failure." TED Talk, 2016. YouTube video, 15:32. https://www.youtube.com/watch?v=2t13Rq4oc7A.

Van Dam, Nick, and Eileen M. Rogers. "People, Purpose and Performance at Barry-Wehmiller: Business as a Powerful Force for Good." IE Business Publishing, January 2020. https://docs.ie.edu/center-for-corporate-learning-innovation /Business-as-a-Powerful-Force-for-Good.pdf.

X Development. "Life at X." X, the moonshot factory. https://x.company/life -at-x/.

PART II: CREATING MEANING THROUGH COMMUNITY

Putnam, Robert. *Bowling Alone: The Collapse and Revival of American Community*. New York: Simon & Schuster, 2000.

Waldinger, Robert, and Marc Schulz. "What the Longest Study on Human Happiness Found Is the Key to a Good Life." *Atlantic*, January 24, 2023. https: //www.theatlantic.com/ideas/archive/2023/01/harvard-happiness-study -relationships/672753/.

CHAPTER 4: CULTIVATE CONNECTION

Becker, Jennifer A. H., Amy Johnson, Elizabeth A. Craig, Eileen Gilchrist, and Michel M. Haigh. "Friendships Are Flexible, Not Fragile: Turning Points in Geographically-Close and Long-Distance Friendships." *Journal of Social and Personal Relationships* 26 (December 2, 2009): 347–369. https://doi.org /10.1177/0265407509344310.

BetterUp. "The Connection Crisis: Why Community Matters in the New World of Work." BetterUp, 2022. https://grow.betterup.com/resources/build-a -culture-of-connection-report.

Bombas. *The Bombas 2022 Impact Report*. https://beebetter.bombas.com/impact.

Bowers, Anne, Joshua Wu, Stuart Lustig, and Douglas Nemecek. "Loneliness Influences Avoidable Absenteeism and Turnover Intention Reported by Adult Workers in the United States." *Journal of Organizational Effectiveness: People and Performance* 9, no. 2 (January 1, 2022): 312–335. https://doi.org /10.1108/JOEPP-03-2021-0076.

Cigna and Edelman. *Loneliness and the Workplace: 2020 U.S. Report*. Ipsos, 2019. https://legacy.cigna.com/static/www-cigna-com/docs/about-us/newsroom

/studies-and-reports/combatting-loneliness/cigna-2020-loneliness-report.pdf.

Cohen, Geoffrey L. *Belonging: The Science of Creating Connection and Bridging Divides.* New York: W. W. Norton, 2022.

Dropbox Team. "What We've Learned Our First Year as a Virtual First Company." *Work in Progress*, June 16, 2022. https://blog.dropbox.com/topics/company /what-weve-learned-our-first-year-as-a-virtual-first-company.

Dutton, Jane E. *Energize Your Workplace: How to Create and Sustain High-Quality Connections at Work*, 1st edition. San Francisco: Jossey-Bass, 2003.

Fisher, Jennifer D. "4 Strategies to Create Connections in a Hybrid Workplace." *Wall Street Journal*, September 30, 2022. https://deloitte.wsj.com/cmo/4 -strategies-to-create-connections-in-a-hybrid-workplace-01664555195.

Fredrickson, Barbara L. "Positive Emotions Broaden and Build." In *Advances in Experimental Social Psychology*, vol. 47, edited by Patricia Devine and Ashby Plant, 1–53. Cambridge, MA: Academic Press, 2013. https://doi.org/10.1016 /B978-0-12-407236-7.00001-2.

Holt-Lunstad, Julianne, Timothy B. Smith, Mark Baker, Tyler Harris, and David Stephenson. "Loneliness and Social Isolation as Risk Factors for Mortality: A Meta-Analytic Review." *Perspectives on Psychological Science: A Journal of the Association for Psychological Science* 10, no. 2 (March 2015): 227–237. https: //doi.org/10.1177/1745691614568352.

Jabr, Ferris. "The Social Life of Forests." *New York Times Magazine*, December 3, 2020. https://www.nytimes.com/interactive/2020/12/02/magazine/tree -communication-mycorrhiza.html.

Kitterman, Ted. "World's Best Workplaces Make Strong Case for Building Trust with Workers." *Insights* (blog), Great Place To Work, November 16, 2023. https://www.greatplacetowork.com/resources/blog/worlds-best-workplaces -make-strong-case-for-building-trust-with-workers.

MacLellan, Lila. "What Happened When I Forced My American Colleagues to Take Coffee Breaks." Quartz, June 13, 2018. https://qz.com/work/1300 469/can-swedish-fika-breaks-improve-productivity-for-american-work aholics.

Mayer, Roger C., James H. Davis, and F. David Schoorman. "An Integrative Model of Organizational Trust." *Academy of Management Review* 20, no. 3 (1995): 709–734, https://doi.org/10.2307/258792.

Murthy, Vivek. *Together: The Healing Power of Human Connection in a Sometimes Lonely World.* New York: Harper, 2020.

———. "We Don't Have to Fight Loneliness Alone." Interview by Adam Grant. *WorkLife with Adam Grant* (podcast), TED Audio Collective, April 2022. https://www.ted.com/talks/worklife_with_adam_grant_we_don_t_have_to _fight_loneliness_alone/transcript?subtitle=en.

Ozcelik, Hakan, and Sigal G. Barsade. "No Employee an Island: Workplace Loneliness and Job Performance." *Academy of Management Journal* 61, no. 6 (2018): 2343–2366. https://doi.org/10.5465/amj.2015.1066.

Perry, Elizabeth. "Here's How to Build a Sense of Belonging in the Workplace." BetterUp, May 11, 2021. https://www.betterup.com/blog/belonging.

Rath, Tom, and Jim Harter. "Your Friends and Your Social Well-Being." Gallup, August 19, 2010. https://news.gallup.com/businessjournal/127043/Friends -Social-Wellbeing.aspx.

Reichheld, Ashley, and Amelia Dunlop. "How to Build a High-Trust Workplace." *MIT Sloan Management Review*, January 24, 2023. https://sloanreview.mit .edu/article/how-to-build-a-high-trust-workplace/.

Rodell, Jessica. "Volunteer Programs That Employees Can Get Excited About." *Harvard Business Review*, January 1, 2021. https://hbr.org/2021/01/volunteer -programs-that-employees-can-get-excited-about.

Simard, Suzanne. *Finding the Mother Tree: Discovering the Wisdom of the Forest*. New York: Knopf, 2021.

———. "Suzanne Simard," *Canada Files*. Interviewed by Valerie Pringle. PBS, May 21, 2023. https://www.pbs.org/video/canada-files-suzanne-simard -ufgnol/.

Tay, Louis, and James O. Pawelski, eds. *The Oxford Handbook of the Positive Humanities*. New York: Oxford University Press, 2022.

Waber, Benjamin N., Daniel Olguin Olguin, Taemie Kim, and Alex Pentland. "Productivity Through Coffee Breaks: Changing Social Networks by Changing Break Structure." *SSRN Electronic Journal*, January 11, 2010. https://doi .org/10.2139/ssrn.1586375.

Williams, Sue, and Bonnie Braun. "Loneliness and Social Isolation—a Private Problem, a Public Issue." *Journal of Family & Consumer Sciences*, February 2019. https://www.researchgate.net/publication/331677412_Loneliness_and _Social_Isolation-A_Private_Problem_A_Public_Issue.

Zak, Paul J. "The Neuroscience of Trust." *Harvard Business Review*, January 1, 2017. https://hbr.org/2017/01/the-neuroscience-of-trust.

CHAPTER 5: EMBRACE AUTHENTICITY

Baumeister, Roy F., and Mark R. Leary. "The Need to Belong: Desire for Interpersonal Attachments as a Fundamental Human Motivation." *Psychological Bulletin* 117, no. 3 (1995): 497–529. https://doi.org/10.1037/0033-2909.117.3.497.

Bradley, Bret H., B. E. Postlethwaite, A. C. Klotz, M. R. Hamdani, and K. G. Brown. "Reaping the Benefits of Task Conflict in Teams: The Critical Role of Team Psychological Safety Climate." *Journal of Applied Psychology* 97, no. 1 (2012): 151–158. https://doi.org/10.1037/a0024200.

Bresman, Henrik, and Amy C. Edmondson. "Research: To Excel, Diverse Teams Need Psychological Safety." *Harvard Business Review*, March 17, 2022. https://hbr.org/2022/03/research-to-excel-diverse-teams-need-psychological-safety.

Brown, Brené. *Dare to Lead: Brave Work. Tough Conversations. Whole Hearts.* New York: Random House, 2018.

De Smet, Aaron, Kim Rubenstein, Gunnar Schrah, Mike Vierow, and Amy Edmondson. "Psychological Safety and the Critical Role of Leadership Development." McKinsey & Company, February 11, 2021. https://www.mckinsey.com/capabilities/people-and-organizational-performance/our-insights/psychological-safety-and-the-critical-role-of-leadership-development.

Deloitte. *Uncovering Culture: A Call to Action for Leaders.* Meltzer Center for Diversity, Inclusion, and Belonging, NYU School of Law, 2023. https://www2.deloitte.com/us/en/pages/about-deloitte/articles/uncovering-culture.html.

Duhigg, Charles. "What Google Learned from Its Quest to Build the Perfect Team." *New York Times Magazine*, February 25, 2016. https://www.nytimes.com/2016/02/28/magazine/what-google-learned-from-its-quest-to-build-the-perfect-team.html.

Edmondson, Amy C. *The Fearless Organization: Creating Psychological Safety in the Workplace for Learning, Innovation, and Growth.* Hoboken, NJ: Wiley, 2018.

Elliott, Gregory, Suzanne Kao, and Ann-Marie Grant. "Mattering: Empirical Validation of a Social-Psychological Concept." *Self and Identity* 3, no. 4 (2004): 339–354. https://doi.org/10.1080/13576500444000119.

Fredrickson, Barbara L. "What Good Are Positive Emotions?" *Review of General Psychology* 2, no. 3 (September 1998): 243–246. https://journals.sagepub.com/doi/10.1037/1089-2680.2.3.300.

Gable, Shelly L., Gian C. Gonzaga, and Amy Strachman. "Will You Be There for Me When Things Go Right? Supportive Responses to Positive Event Disclosures." *Journal of Personality and Social Psychology* 91, no. 5 (2006): 904–917. https://doi.org/10.1037/0022-3514.91.5.904.

Gable, Shelly L., and Jonathan Haidt. "What (and Why) Is Positive Psychology?" *Review of General Psychology* 9, no. 2 (June 2005): 99–102. https://journals.sagepub.com/doi/10.1037/1089-2680.9.2.103.

Kegan, Robert, and Lisa Laskow Lahey. *An Everyone Culture: Becoming a Deliberately Developmental Organization.* Cambridge, MA: Harvard Business Review Press, 2016.

McGregor, Jena. "This Former Surgeon General Says There's a 'Loneliness Epidemic' and Work Is Partly to Blame." *Washington Post*, December 5, 2021. https://www.washingtonpost.com/news/on-leadership/wp/2017/10/04/this-former-surgeon-general-says-theres-a-loneliness-epidemic-and-work-is-partly-to-blame/.

Peterson, Chris. *Pursuing the Good Life: 100 Reflections on Positive Psychology.* Oxford, UK: Oxford University Press, 2013.

Shafik, Minouche. "Minouche Shafik." Alain Elkann Interviews, April 1, 2018. https://www.alainelkanninterviews.com/minouche-shafik/.

Smith, Emily Esfahani. *The Power of Meaning: Crafting a Life That Matters.* New York: Crown, 2017.

Winfrey, Oprah. "Winfrey's Commencement Address." *Harvard Gazette,* May 31, 2013. https://news.harvard.edu/gazette/story/2013/05/winfreys -commencement-address/.

CHAPTER 6: BEGINNINGS MATTER

Bamboo HR. *The Definitive Guide to Onboarding for 2024.* https://www .bamboohr.com/resources/ebooks/the-definitive-guide-to-onboarding.

———. "First Impressions Are Everything: 44 Days to Make or Break a New Hire." https://www.bamboohr.com/resources/guides/onboarding-statistics -2023.

Cable, Dan, Francesca Gino, and Bradley R. Staats. "The Powerful Way Onboarding Can Encourage Authenticity." *Harvard Business Review,* November 26, 2015. https://hbr.org/2015/11/the-powerful-way-onboarding-can-encourage -authenticity.

De Smet, Aaron, Bonnie Dowling, Marino Mugayar-Baldocchi, and Bill Schaninger. "'Great Attrition' or 'Great Attraction'? The Choice Is Yours." McKinsey & Company, September 8, 2021.

Dixon-Fyle, Sundiatu, Kevin Dolan, and Sara Prince. *Diversity Wins: How Inclusion Matters.* McKinsey & Company, May 2020.

Fyock, Catherine D. "Managing the Employee Onboarding and Assimilation Process." Society for Human Resource Management, February 27, 2012.

Groysberg, Boris, Ashish Nanda, and Nitin Nohria. "The Risky Business of Hiring Stars." *Harvard Business Review,* May 1, 2004. https://hbr.org/2004/05/the -risky-business-of-hiring-stars.

Harter, Jim. "5 Questions Every Onboarding Program Must Answer." Gallup, March 13, 2019. https://www.gallup.com/workplace/247598/questions-every -onboarding-program-answer.aspx.

Heath, Dan, Emily Dia, and Hubert Joly. "How to Change Your Workplace." Interview by Adam Grant. *WorkLife with Adam Grant* (podcast), TED Audio Collective, June 27, 2022. https://www.ted.com/podcasts/worklife/how-to -change-your-workplace-transcript.

Hsieh, Tony. "Tony Hsieh: Bad Hires Have Cost Zappos Over $100 Million." Interview by Henry Blodget. *Inspiring Performers Making the Right Hires,*

Business Insider. YouTube, 2:22, November 11, 2010. https://www.youtube.com/watch?v=9C36EYM-mWQ.

———. "Zappos Only Hires People Who Are Weird and Lucky in Life." Interview by Henry Blodget. *Inspiring Performers Making the Right Hires*, Business Insider. YouTube, 4:33, November 11, 2010. https://www.youtube.com/watch?v=_BpWz-vw35M.

Jin, Jing, and James Rounds. "Stability and Change in Work Values: A Meta-Analysis of Longitudinal Studies." *Journal of Vocational Behavior* 80, no. 2 (April 1, 2012): 326–339. https://doi.org/10.1016/j.jvb.2011.10.007.

Johnson, Dave. "Opening a Chick-Fil-A Franchise Costs Just $10,000—Here's How to Do It." Business Insider, 2019. https://www.businessinsider.com/chick-fil-a-franchise-cost-opening-2019-7.

Klinghoffer, Dawn, Candice Young, and Dave Haspas. "Every New Employee Needs an Onboarding 'Buddy.'" *Harvard Business Review*, June 6, 2019. https://hbr.org/2019/06/every-new-employee-needs-an-onboarding-buddy.

Maze, Jonathan. "Chick-Fil-A Had Another Strong Year in 2022." Restaurant Business, April 5, 2023. https://restaurantbusinessonline.com/financing/chick-fil-had-another-strong-year-2022.

Patagonia. "What We Do Video Series." Patagonia, November 8, 2023. https://www.patagonia.com/stories/what-we-do-video-series/story-144483.html.

Razzetti, Gustavo. "Why You Need Team Rituals (and When to Use Them)." Fearless Culture, July 31, 2020. https://fearlessculture.design/blog-posts/why-you-need-team-rituals-and-when-to-use-them.

Schmall, Emily. "The Cult of Chick-Fil-A." *Forbes*, July 16, 2012. https://www.forbes.com/forbes/2007/0723/080.html.

Vonnegut, Mary, and George B. Bradt. *Onboarding: How to Get Your New Employees up to Speed in Half the Time*. Hoboken, NJ: Wiley, 2009.

Wrzesniewski, Amy, Jane E. Dutton, and Gelaye Debebe. "Interpersonal Sensemaking and the Meaning of Work." In *Research in Organizational Behavior: An Annual Series of Analytical Essays and Critical Reviews,* vol. 25, edited by Roderick M. Kramer and Barry Staw, 93–135. Oxford, UK: Elsevier Science, 2003.

PART III: CREATING MEANING THROUGH CONTRIBUTION

Carton, Andrew M. "'I'm Not Mopping the Floors, I'm Putting a Man on the Moon': How NASA Leaders Enhanced the Meaningfulness of Work by Changing the Meaning of Work." *Administrative Science Quarterly* 63, no. 2 (June 7, 2017). https://journals.sagepub.com/doi/abs/10.1177/0001839217713748.

CHAPTER 7: THE POWER OF POSITIVE FEEDBACK

Allan, Blake, Ryan Duffy, and Brian Collisson. "Helping Others Increases Meaningful Work: Evidence from Three Experiments." *Journal of Counseling Psychology* 65 (May 11, 2017). https://doi.org/10.1037/cou0000228.

Ariely, Dan. "What Makes Us Feel Good About Our Work?" TED Talk, 20:12, October 2012. https://www.ted.com/talks/dan_ariely_what_makes_us_feel_good_about_our_work.

Bright, David S., Kim S. Cameron, and Arran Caza. "The Amplifying and Buffering Effects of Virtuousness in Downsized Organizations." *Journal of Business Ethics* 64, no. 3 (March 1, 2006): 249–269. https://doi.org/10.1007/s10551-005-5904-4.

Buckingham, Marcus, and Ashley Goodall. "The Feedback Fallacy." *Harvard Business Review*, March–April 2019. https://hbr.org/2019/03/the-feedback-fallacy.

Chowdhury, Madhuleena Roy. "The Neuroscience of Gratitude and Effects on the Brain." *Positive Psychology*, April 9, 2019. https://positivepsychology.com/neuroscience-of-gratitude/#neuroscience.

Eskreis-Winkler, Lauren, and Ayelet Fishbach. "Not Learning from Failure—the Greatest Failure of All." *Psychological Science* 30 (November 8, 2019): 095679761988113. https://doi.org/10.1177/0956797619881133.

Fehr, Ryan, Ashley Fulmer, and Jared A. Miller. "The Grateful Workplace: A Multilevel Model of Gratitude in Organizations." *Academy of Management Review* 42, no. 2 (April 2017): 361–381. https://doi.org/10.5465/amr.2014.0374.

Gallup and Workhuman. *Transforming Workplaces Through Recognition*. Gallup, 2022.

Gittell, Jody Hoffer, Kim Cameron, Sany Lim, and Victor Rivas. "Relationships, Layoffs, and Organizational Resilience: Airline Industry Responses to September 11." *Journal of Applied Behavioral Science* 42 (May 7, 2005).

Grant, Adam M., and Francesca Gino. "A Little Thanks Goes a Long Way: Explaining Why Gratitude Expressions Motivate Prosocial Behavior." *Journal of Personality and Social Psychology* 98, no. 6 (2010): 946–955. https://doi.org/10.1037/a0017935.

Gross, Jessica. "What Motivates Us at Work? More Than Money." Business, Ideas .Ted.Com, May 21, 2015. https://ideas.ted.com/what-motivates-us-at-work-7-fascinating-studies-that-give-insights/.

Harter, Jim. "A Great Manager's Most Important Habit." Gallup, May 30, 2023. https://www.gallup.com/workplace/505370/great-manager-important-habit.aspx.

Kluger, Avraham N., and Angelo DeNisi. "The Effects of Feedback Interventions on Performance: A Historical Review, a Meta-Analysis, and a Preliminary Feedback Intervention Theory." *Psychological Bulletin* 119, no. 2 (1996): 254–284. https://doi.org/10.1037/0033-2909.119.2.254.

Kumar, Amit, and Nicholas Epley. "Undervaluing Gratitude: Expressers Misunderstand the Consequences of Showing Appreciation." *Psychological Science* 29, no. 9 (September 1, 2018): 1423–1435. https://doi.org/10.1177/0956797618772506.

Locke, Edwin A., and Gary P. Latham. "The Development of Goal Setting Theory: A Half Century Retrospective." *Motivation Science* 5, no. 2 (2019): 93–105. https://doi.org/10.1037/mot0000127.

O.C. Tanner Institute. *Shift: 2024 Global Culture Report*. O.C. Tanner, 2023. https://www.octanner.com/global-culture-report.

Richardson, Lisa R. "Peloton as a Facilitator of Hope: Pathways to Initiate and Sustain Behaviors That Enhance Well-Being." Dissertation, University of Pennsylvania, August 1, 2020. https://repository.upenn.edu/handle/20.500.14332/38824.

Smith, Jeremy Adam. "Five Ways to Cultivate Gratitude at Work." *Greater Good Magazine*, May 16, 2013. https://greatergood.berkeley.edu/article/item/five_ways_to_cultivate_gratitude_at_work.

VIA Institute on Character. "Bring Out the Best in Yourself and Others with Strengths-Spotting." VIA Institute. https://www.viacharacter.org/topics/articles/bring-out-the-best-in-yourself-and-others-with-strengths-spotting.

Walsh, Lisa, Annie Regan, and Sonja Lyubomirsky. "The Role of Actors, Targets, and Witnesses: Examining Gratitude Exchanges in a Social Context." *Journal of Positive Psychology* 17 (January 5, 2022): 1–17. https://doi.org/10.1080/17439760.2021.1991449.

Workhuman. "Empowering Workplace Culture Through Recognition." Workhuman, September 27, 2023. https://www.workhuman.com/resources/reports-guides/empowering-workplace-culture-through-recognition-gallup-report/.

———. "From Appreciation to Equity: How Recognition Reinforces DEI in the Workplace." Workhuman, June 7, 2023. https://www.workhuman.com/resources/reports-guides/from-appreciation-to-equity-gallup-report/.

———. "From Praise to Profits: The Business Case for Recognition at Work." Workhuman, March 29, 2023. https://www.workhuman.com/resources/reports-guides/from-praise-to-profits-workhuman-gallup-report/.

———. "From 'Thank You' to Thriving: A Deeper Look at How Recognition Amplifies Wellbeing." Workhuman, May 18, 2023. https://www.workhuman.com/resources/reports-guides/from-thank-you-to-thriving-workhuman-gallup-report/.

CHAPTER 8: COMMUNICATE BIGGER IMPACT

Allan, Blake A., Cassondra Batz-Barbarich, Haley M. Sterling, and Louis Tay. "Outcomes of Meaningful Work: A Meta-Analysis." *Journal of Management Studies* 56, no. 3 (May 2019): 500–528. https://doi.org/10.1111/joms.12406.

Atlanta Ventures. "Tope Awotona: Impatiently Scheduling Our Calendars, One Meeting at a Time." Atlanta Ventures in Profiles, May 31, 2018. https://www.atlantaventures.com/stories/tope-awotona.

Dong, Chengcheng, and Nahida Nisa. *The Total Economic Impact of Calendly.* Forrester Consulting, August 2023. https://pages.calendly.com/rs/482-NMZ-854/images/Ebook_2023_Forrester_TEI_Study.pdf.

Embroker Team. "Checklist: How to Become a Unicorn Startup in 2024." Embroker, January 4, 2024. https://www.embroker.com/blog/unicorn-startup-checklist/.

Feldman, Amy. "Nigeria-Born Tope Awotona Poured His Life Savings into Calendly. Now He's One of America's Wealthiest Immigrants." *Forbes*, April 6, 2022. https://www.forbes.com/sites/amyfeldman/2022/04/06/nigeria-born-tope-awotona-poured-his-life-savings-into-calendly-now-hes-one-of-americas-wealthiest-immigrants/.

Fowler, James H., and Nicholas A. Christakis. "Dynamic Spread of Happiness in a Large Social Network: Longitudinal Analysis over 20 Years in the Framingham Heart Study." *British Medical Journal (Clinical Research Ed.)* 337 (December 4, 2008): a2338. https://doi.org/10.1136/bmj.a2338.

Grant, Adam M. "Relational Job Design and the Motivation to Make a Prosocial Difference." *Academy of Management Review* 32, no. 2 (2007): 393–417. https://doi.org/10.2307/20159308.

Grant, Adam M., and Marissa S. Shandell. "Social Motivation at Work: The Organizational Psychology of Effort for, Against, and with Others." *Annual Review of Psychology* 73 (2022): 301–326. https://doi.org/10.1146/annurev-psych-060321-033406.

Radiological Society of North America. "Patient Photos Spur Radiologist Empathy and Eye for Detail." ScienceDaily, December 14, 2008. www.sciencedaily.com/releases/2008/12/081202080809.htm.

PART IV: CREATING MEANING THROUGH CHALLENGE

Frankl, V. E. *Man's Search for Meaning: An Introduction to Logotherapy.* Washington Square Press, 1963.

CHAPTER 9: BALANCED AUTONOMY

Allan, Blake A., Kelsey L. Autin, and Ryan D. Duffy. "Self-Determination and Meaningful Work: Exploring Socioeconomic Constraints." *Frontiers in*

Psychology 7 (February 2, 2016). https://doi.org/10.3389/fpsyg.2016.00071.

Alrabai, Fakieh. "The Influence of Autonomy-Supportive Teaching on EFL Students' Classroom Autonomy: An Experimental Intervention." *Frontiers in Psychology* 12 (September 8, 2021). https://doi.org/10.3389/fpsyg.2021.728657.

Ambrose, Maureen L., and Carol T. Kulik. "Old Friends, New Faces: Motivation Research in the 1990s." *Journal of Management* 25, no. 3 (June 1999): 231–292. https://journals.sagepub.com/doi/10.1177/014920639902500302.

Berg, Justin M., Jane E. Dutton, and Amy Wrzesniewski. "Job Crafting and Meaningful Work." In *Purpose and Meaning in the Workplace*, edited by Bryan J. Dik, Zinta S. Byrne, and Michael F. Steger, 81–104. Washington, DC: American Psychological Association, 2013. https://doi.org/10.1037/14183-005.

Deci, Edward L., Anja H. Olafsen, and Richard M. Ryan. "Self-Determination Theory in Work Organizations: The State of a Science." *Annual Review of Organizational Psychology and Organizational Behavior* 4 (2017): 19–43. https://doi.org/10.1146/annurev-orgpsych-032516-113108.

Goetz, Kaomi. "How 3M Gave Everyone Days Off and Created an Innovation Dynamo." *Fast Company*, February 1, 2011. https://www.fastcompany.com/1663137/how-3m-gave-everyone-days-off-and-created-an-innovation-dynamo.

Grolnick, Wendy S., and Richard M. Ryan. "Autonomy in Children's Learning: An Experimental and Individual Difference Investigation." *Journal of Personality and Social Psychology* 52, no. 5 (1987): 890–898. https://doi.org/10.1037/0022-3514.52.5.890.

Hackman, J. Richard, and Greg R. Oldham. "Motivation Through the Design of Work: Test of a Theory." *Organizational Behavior and Human Performance* 16, no. 2 (August 1, 1976): 250–279. https://doi.org/10.1016/0030-5073(76)90016-7.

Hurn, Chris. "Stuffed Giraffe Shows What Customer Service Is All About." *The Blog*, HuffPost, May 17, 2012. Updated December 6, 2017. https://www.huffpost.com/entry/stuffed-giraffe-shows-wha_b_1524038.

Kotler, Steven. "Why a Free Afternoon Each Week Can Boost Employees' Sense of Autonomy." *Fast Company*, January 20, 2021. https://www.fastcompany.com/90595295/why-a-free-afternoon-each-week-can-boost-employees-sense-of-autonomy/.

Lund, Susan, Anu Madgavkar, James Manhika, and Sven Smit. *What's Next for Remote Work: An Analysis of 2,000 Tasks, 800 Jobs, and Nine Countries.* McKinsey Global Institute, November 2020. https://thebusinessleadership.academy/wp-content/uploads/2021/01/MGI-Whats-next-for-remote-work-v3.pdf.

Pendell, Ryan. "Frontline Workers Want Flexibility Too." Gallup, December

4, 2023. https://www.gallup.com/workplace/544775/front-line-workers -flexibility.aspx.

Pinterest Careers. "Makeathon: Behind the Scenes." Pinterest Careers, August 7, 2023, https://www.pinterestcareers.com/life-at-pinterest-blog/pinterest-life /makeathon-behind-the-scenes/.

Razzetti, Gustavo. "5 Ways to Create a Strong Virtual Culture." Fearless Culture, October 12, 2020. https://fearlessculture.design/blog-posts/5-ways-to-create -a-strong-virtual-culture.

Rock, David. "Managing with the Brain in Mind." Strategy+Business, August 27, 2009. https://www.strategy-business.com/article/09306.

Wrzesniewski, Amy, and Jane E. Dutton. "Crafting a Job: Revisioning Employees as Active Crafters of Their Work." *Academy of Management Review* 26, no. 2 (April 2001): 179–201. https://doi.org/10.5465/amr.2001.4378011.

CHAPTER 10: THE ZONE OF POSSIBILITY

Abubakar, A. Mohammed, Elaheh Behravesh, Hame Rezapouraghdam, and Huda A. Megeirhi. "Burnout or Boreout: A Meta-Analytic Review and Synthesis of Burnout and Boreout Literature in Hospitality and Tourism." *Journal of Hospitality Marketing & Management* 31, no. 4 (May 19, 2022): 458–503. https://doi.org/10.1080/19368623.2022.1996304.

BBC staff. "Kidderminster Man Catches Giant Goldfish." BBC, November 22, 2022. https://www.bbc.com/news/uk-england-hereford-worcester-63707394.

Bent, Steve. "Study Finds That 74% of Millennial and Gen Z Employees Are Likely to Quit Within the Next Year Due to a Lack of Skills Development Opportunities." International Association of Workforce Professionals, November 14, 2022. https://iawponline.org/study-finds-that-74-of-millennial-and-gen -z-employees-are-likely-to-quit-within-the-next-year-due-to-a-lack-of-skills -development-opportunities/.

Bersin, Josh. "The Definitive Guide to Learning: Growth in the Flow of Work." Josh Bersin, 2022. https://joshbersin.com/definitive-guide-to-learning/.

Bretherton, Roger, and Ryan M. Niemiec. "Character Strengths as Critique: The Power of Positive Psychology to Humanise the Workplace." In *The Routledge International Handbook of Critical Positive Psychology*, edited by Nicholas J. L. Brown, Tim Lomas, and Francisco Jose Eiroa-Orosa. London: Routledge, 2018.

Coutifaris, C. G., and A. M. Grant. "Taking Your Team Behind the Curtain: The Effects of Leader Feedback-sharing and Feedback-seeking on Team Psychological Safety." *Organization Science* 33, no. 4 (2022): 1574–1598.

De Smet, Aaron, Bonnie Dowling, Marino Mugayar-Baldocchi, and Bill Schaninger. "'Great Attrition' or 'Great Attraction'? The Choice Is Yours."

McKinsey & Company, September 8, 2021.

Dweck, Carol S. *Mindset: The New Psychology of Success*, 1st ed. New York: Random House, 2006.

———. "The Power of Yet." TEDxNorrköping, 2014. YouTube video, 11:18. https://www.youtube.com/watch?v=J-swZaKN2Ic.

Eden, Dov. "Leadership and Expectations: Pygmalion Effects and Other Self-Fulfilling Prophecies in Organizations." *Leadership Quarterly* 3, no. 4 (December 1, 1992): 271–305. https://doi.org/10.1016/1048-9843(92) 90018-B.

Fox, Dale. "British Man Catches One of World's Biggest Goldfish—67lbs 4oz." *Daily Mail* (London), November 21, 2022. https://www.dailymail.co.uk /news/article-11452587/British-angler-catches-one-worlds-biggest-goldfish -weighing-whopping-67lbs-4oz.html.

Gonzalez, Jennifer. "Find Your Marigold: The One Essential Rule for New Teachers." Cult of Pedagogy, August 29, 2013. https://www.cultofpedagogy .com/marigolds/.

Hone, Lucy Clare, Aaron Jarden, Grant M. Schofield, and Scott Duncan. "Measuring Flourishing: The Impact of Operational Definitions on the Prevalence of High Levels of Wellbeing," *International Journal of Wellbeing* 4, no. 1 (May 14, 2014). https://internationaljournalofwellbeing.org/index.php/ijow /article/view/286.

Isa, Aerni, Hazril Izwar Ibrahim, Hira Khan, Amar Hisham Jaafar, Zulkefli Muhamad Hanapiyah, and Ghaith Abdulraheem Ali Alsheikh. "The Relationship Between Talent Management Practices and Perceived Organizational Support: Evidence from Government Linked Companies." *Journal of Positive Psychology & Wellbeing* 5, no. 4 (December 15, 2021): 1519–1528.

Kegan, Robert, and Lisa Laskow Lahey. *An Everyone Culture: Becoming a Deliberately Developmental Organization*. Cambridge, MA: Harvard Business Review Press, 2016.

Lavy, Shiri, and Hadassah Littman-Ovadia. "My Better Self: Using Strengths at Work and Work Productivity, Organizational Citizenship Behavior, and Satisfaction." *Journal of Career Development* 44, no. 2 (February 25, 2016). https: //doi.org/10.1177/0894845316634056.

Mickle, Tripp, and Karen Weise. "Microsoft Tops Apple to Become Most Valuable Public Company." *New York Times*, Technology section, January 12, 2024. https://www.nytimes.com/2024/01/12/technology/microsoft-apple-most -valuable-company.html.

Moeller, Julia, Zorana Icevic Pringle, Arielle White, Jochen Menges, and Marc A. Brackett. "Highly Engaged but Burned Out: Intra-Individual Profiles in the US Workforce." *Career Development International* 23, no. 1 (2018): 86–105.

https://doi.org/10.31219/osf.io/h6qnf.

Nadella, Satya, and Adam Grant. "Windows into the Future: Why Managers Matter as Much as Tech." Future of Work Conference, 2022. YouTube video, 29:09. https://www.youtube.com/watch?v=G0E8eUQ5KXg.

Nadella, Satya, Greg Shaw, and Jill Tracie Nichols. *Hit Refresh*. New York: Harper Business, 2017.

Nicioli, Taylor. "Fisherman Catches 67-Pound Goldfish." CNN, November 23, 2022. https://www.cnn.com/travel/article/fisherman-catches-giant-goldfish -carrot-scn/index.html.

Rosenthal, Robert, and Kermit L. Fode. "The Effect of Experimenter Bias on the Performance of the Albino Rat." *Behavioral Science* 8, no. 3 (1963): 183–189. https://doi.org/10.1002/bs.3830080302.

Rosenthal, Robert, and Lenore Jacobson. "Pygmalion in the Classroom." *Urban Review* 3, no. 1 (September 1, 1968): 16–20. https://doi.org/10.1007 /BF02322211.

Saks, Alan M., and Jamie A. Gruman. "What Do We Really Know About Employee Engagement?" *Human Resource Development Quarterly* 25, no. 2 (2014): 155– 182. https://doi.org/10.1002/hrdq.21187.

Semuels, Alana. "World's Best Companies of 2023." *Time* and Statista 2023. https://time.com/collection/worlds-best-companies-2023/.

Shibu, Sherin, and Shana Lebowitz. "Microsoft Is Rolling Out a New Management Framework to Its Leaders. It Centers Around a Psychological Insight Called Growth Mindset." *Business Insider*, November 11, 2019. https://www .businessinsider.com/microsoft-is-using-growth-mindset-to-power -management-strategy-2019-11.

Spiegel, Alix, and Lulu Miller, hosts. "How to Become Batman, Pt. 1." *Invisibilia* (podcast), NPR, January 22, 2015. YouTube video, 3:11. https://www .youtube.com/watch?v=hbhwlRRW_3o.

Stock, Ruth Maria. "Is Boreout a Threat to Frontline Employees' Innovative Work Behavior?" *Journal of Product Innovation Management* 32, no. 4 (October 8, 2014): 574–592. https://onlinelibrary.wiley.com/doi/abs/10.1111 /jpim.12239.

Yeager, David Scott, Julio Garcia, Patti Brzustoski, William T. Hessert, Valerie Purdie-Vaughns, Nancy Apfel, Allison Master, Matthew E. Williams, and Geoffrey L. Cohen. "Breaking the Cycle of Mistrust: Wise Interventions to Provide Critical Feedback Across the Racial Divide." *Journal of Experimental Psychology: General* 143, no. 2 (2014): 804–824.

Zenger, Jack, and Joseph Folkman. "Companies Are Bad at Identifying High-Potential Employees." *Harvard Business Review*, February 20, 2017. https://hbr.org/2017/02/companies-are-bad-at-identifying-high-potential -employees.

EPILOGUE: THE FUTURE OF MEANINGFUL WORK

Deloitte. *2024 Gen Z and Millennial Survey.* Deloitte Touche Tohmatsu, 2024. https://www.deloitte.com/global/en/issues/work/content/genz -millennialsurvey.html.

Edelman. *2023 Edelman Trust Barometer: Special Report; Trust at Work.* 2023. https://www.edelman.com/trust/2023/trust-barometer/special-report-trust -at-work.

INDEX

INDEX

INDEX

INDEX

Wes Adams is founder and CEO of SV Consulting Group, where he works with high-performing companies to develop leadership excellence, build organizational resilience, and deepen employee engagement through a meaningful work lens. He has more than two decades of experience as a successful entrepreneur and strategic partner for clients including Microsoft, KPMG, BlackRock, Google, and the United Nations, along with a range of high-growth organizations. Wes has been featured at South by Southwest Interactive and the Nobel Peace Prize Forum, and his work has been covered by the *New York Times*, BBC News, *Forbes*, and *Business Insider*. His teams have won multiple Webby Awards and been recognized as one of *Fast Company*'s Most Innovative Brands. His early career was spent launching and managing high-profile hospitality businesses, for which he was nominated twice for a coveted James Beard Award. He is a graduate of Vanderbilt University and holds a master's degree from the University of Pennsylvania in Applied Positive Psychology.

Tamara Myles is an accomplished consultant, author, and international speaker with over two decades of experience helping leaders improve business performance. She is the author of *The Secret to Peak Productivity*, which introduced her proprietary Peak Productivity Pyramid framework. Tamara's insights have been featured in leading publications such as *Forbes, Fast Company, USA Today,* and *Business Insider.* She has worked with clients such as Microsoft, KPMG, MassMutual, and Google. Tamara has a master's degree in Applied Positive Psychology from the University of Pennsylvania, where she also serves as an instructor in the master's program and a trainer for the world-renowned Penn Resilience Program. She is a professor in the Master of Science in Leadership program at Boston College, where she integrates cutting-edge research into practical applications for leadership and organizational success.

PublicAffairs is a publishing house founded in 1997. It is a tribute to the standards, values, and flair of three persons who have served as mentors to countless reporters, writers, editors, and book people of all kinds, including me.

I. F. Stone, proprietor of *I. F. Stone's Weekly*, combined a commitment to the First Amendment with entrepreneurial zeal and reporting skill and became one of the great independent journalists in American history. At the age of eighty, Izzy published *The Trial of Socrates*, which was a national bestseller. He wrote the book after he taught himself ancient Greek.

Benjamin C. Bradlee was for nearly thirty years the charismatic editorial leader of *The Washington Post*. It was Ben who gave the *Post* the range and courage to pursue such historic issues as Watergate. He supported his reporters with a tenacity that made them fearless and it is no accident that so many became authors of influential, best-selling books.

Robert L. Bernstein, the chief executive of Random House for more than a quarter century, guided one of the nation's premier publishing houses. Bob was personally responsible for many books of political dissent and argument that challenged tyranny around the globe. He is also the founder and longtime chair of Human Rights Watch, one of the most respected human rights organizations in the world.

•   •   •

For fifty years, the banner of Public Affairs Press was carried by its owner Morris B. Schnapper, who published Gandhi, Nasser, Toynbee, Truman, and about 1,500 other authors. In 1983, Schnapper was described by *The Washington Post* as "a redoubtable gadfly." His legacy will endure in the books to come.

Peter Osnos, *Founder*